PENGUIN BOOKS

WOMEN'S BURNOUT

Herbert J. Freudenberger, Ph.D., has practiced psychoanalysis for the past thirty years, and frequently conducts seminars on Women's Burnout. In 1983, he was given the Distinguished Psychologist of the Year Award, Division of Psychotherapy, American Psychological Association.

Gail North is a New York–based journalist and writer. She is the co-author of *Situational Anxiety*.

Women's Burnout

How to Spot It, How to Reverse It, and How to Prevent It

Dr. Herbert J. Freudenberger and Gail North

PENGUIN BOOKS

PENGUIN BOOKS
Viking Penguin Inc., 40 West 23rd Street,
New York, New York 10010, U.S.A.
Penguin Books Ltd, Harmondsworth,
Middlesex, England
Penguin Books Australia Ltd, Ringwood,
Victoria, Australia
Penguin Books Canada Limited, 2801 John Street,
Markham, Ontario, Canada L3R 1B4
Penguin Books (N.Z.) Ltd, 182–190 Wairau Road,
Auckland 10, New Zealand

First published in the United States of America by
Doubleday and Company, Inc., 1985
Published in Penguin Books 1986

LIBRARY OF CONGRESS CATALOGING IN PUBLICATION DATA
Freudenberger, Herbert J.
    Women's burnout.
    Reprint.   Originally published: Garden City, N.Y.:
Doubleday, 1985.
    Bibliography: p.
    Includes index.
    1. Women—Mental health.   2. Burn out (Psychology)
I. North, Gail, 1939–   .   II. Title.
[RC451.4.W6F74   1986]   155.6'33   86-5087
ISBN 0 14 00.9414 8

Printed in the United States of America by
R. R. Donnelley & Sons Company, Harrisonburg, Virginia
Set in Electra

To a special person, Arlene, whose decency, kindness, insight, caring, love, and understanding have made so many dreams become a reality.

H.F.

To Jeanne, Bibsie, Veronica, and Belle—my mother, sister, grandmother, and aunt . . . the women of my life. And to Harvey . . . my father.

G.N.

ACKNOWLEDGMENTS

This book would not have been possible without the thoughts, feelings, and life experiences of the many women who graciously gave us of their valued time. Further thanks go to the many women clients, members of workshops and seminars who, over these many years, have helped to raise questions that needed to be answered. Their concerns, struggles, joys, tribulations, and eventual successes are the inspirations shared in this book.

A very deep and special thanks goes out to Rosaire Appel, Laura Wachtel, Jill Gallen, Joanmarie Kalter, Pam Black, Liz Weiner, Rochelle Lefkowitz, Barbara Presley Noble, Marian Goodrich, Maya Travaglia, Jessie Shestack, Marie Brown, Louise Bernikow, and Kathy Ryan. Their generous insights, candor, trust, and support greatly contributed to the substance of this book.

We also owe a debt of gratitude to our agent, Carol Mann, to our editor, Loretta Barrett, to Elizabeth St. John, Marilyn Ducksworth, Cynthia Barrett, Amy Herring, and to the other good people at Doubleday who are always supportive and encouraging.

CONTENTS

INTRODUCTION

If the subject of this book has captured your interest and your imagination, chances are you either feel burned out, think you might be burning out, or are concerned about a friend or loved one who seems to be burning out. As you begin to read, it would be to your advantage to understand that you've already begun to take charge of that condition. Self-awareness is the first and most critical step you can take in battling burnout. Since you've elected to seek some information concerning the burnout condition, that self-awareness is undoubtedly already expanding, and you're most assuredly on a direct path to reversing, resolving, and preventing burnout, perhaps for the rest of your life.

Women's Burnout has been written in response to the scores of women who are seeking treatment for burnout symptoms. Many of you may not as yet be aware that what you're experiencing is defined as burnout. You may be confused by the symptoms. You may believe you're in a chronic depression, or that you've lost control of your life, or that you've slipped into a never-ending cycle of agitation and exhaustion for which there is no cure. While it's often more convenient to explain yourself away in terms of depression or agitation, it would be more accurate and far more prudent to investigate the factors which led to your recent symptoms and begin to take some simple steps to reverse what quite frequently turns out to be a solid case of burnout.

If you are experiencing symptoms that suspiciously point to burnout, one question quite commonly prevails: "How do I know they're linked to burnout?" You may not be able to immediately identify your distressing symptoms with the concept of burnout. However, it is certain that if your life has become a series of internal and external pressures, and if you're experiencing your personality, spirit, attitudes, and functioning as negatively different from what they were six months ago, last year, or even in the past five years, the burnout issue may be a solid base from which to begin exploring your malaise.

Women's burnout has come to be a most prevalent condition in our modern culture. The daily stresses and pressures placed on women are often blatantly obvious but, just as often, they are subtly misperceived. For many, the notion of burnout has come to be associated with those women who are high achievers in the business or professional world. While these women do make up a high percentage of those who fall prey to burnout symptoms, others—homemakers, mothers, widows, the single, the married, and the divorced—are just as easily pulled into the wake of emotional freneticness, which then squires them into burnout. The ways in which women burn out often differ, but there is one typical common denominator. When the insidious symptoms begin to affect your life, the most common response is to dig in deeper, hold on tighter, and respond to those symptoms as adversaries which must be beaten down. Most women approach burnout with the idea of triumphing over its hold by bettering themselves, and end up perpetuating the condition.

There are many variations on the burnout theme for women. One woman may feel she can handle and cope with her multiple tasks and roles by the sheer force of her will; another may feel she can lick what she perceives as her failure to keep up with the others by mimicking someone else whose rhythms are totally different from hers; and yet another woman will pretend she's immune to the demands on her life, yet find herself becoming brittle and edgy with her friends, colleagues, and lovers and experiencing unexplained crying jags. No matter what the mode, a woman suffering from burnout typically feels that by *denying* the messages her body and mind are sending out, she will overcome the stresses and pressures of her life.

The confusion over how to handle burnout symptoms often drives women deeper into the burnout stages. Many women admittedly believe that if they could just work harder, if they could just toughen themselves up, or, if they could just get through this next week, month, or year, they'll pull it all together. Their emotional exhaustion, their physical fatigue, their vulnerabilities and exasperations will magically take a turn and they'll bounce back to "normal." Unfortunately, when you're coping with burnout, the symptoms are cumulative; with little understanding of your own personal limits, the value of pacing yourself, or the danger of isolation, that goal may remain a constantly elusive vision.

It's imperative for you to understand at the outset, however, that this notion can be reversed. Since self-awareness is a major antidote to burnout, the prognosis for women is most positive. In the majority of cases, women are quick to catch on to the idea of burnout. And once that identity has been established, with the help of a few critical guidelines, the insights begin to increase and the condition becomes distinguishable. Once you know what you're dealing with, you're in a good position to alter patterns of thinking, living, and caring for yourself. Energies are regained, spirits are renewed, and burnout symptoms are diminished, reversed, and then cured.

Women's Burnout offers many suggestions for identifying the core of the problem and many solutions for preventing burnout acceleration. Once you've grasped the dynamics of your burnout—how the momentum is triggered, how the movement is accelerated, and how the exhaustion manifests in your body and mind—reevaluating your wants and your needs and then altering some of your more destructive thought patterns becomes a controllable proposition. Women who have already confronted their burnout proclivities and have taken control of their wants and their needs have found that their intellectual, emotional, and physical potentials have been not only renewed but strengthened.

It's equally important to understand that burnout is no respecter of age. The condition does not discriminate between the young and the old. All too often, young women construe their vitality and youthfulness as a free ticket for assuming functions and roles beyond their natural capacities and wonder why they become disillusioned so early in life. As one young woman stated: "If I keep on with this pace for another two years, I'm going to be haggard and old by the time I'm twenty-seven."

In your twenties, you may be pressing yourself and excessively stretching your energies in order to gain a foothold in the business or professional world—a niche you may feel can only be achieved by overextending your time, energy, nurturing proclivities, and natural limits to prove you're the right stuff for future considerations. In your thirties, you may feel the

ongoing desire to legitimize yourself in the "Men's Club," by performing
impeccably and without complaint. Many women in their late twenties to
mid-thirties experience an underlying pressure to juggle business and domestic roles with equal excellence and high standards. Interestingly, while
demonstrating their ability to "have it all," to balance work, love, children, friends, and families, they rarely blame others for refusing to acknowledge their burdens but instead indict themselves for not living up to
an imagined standard of excellence. Women who are approaching their
mid-thirties have the additional burden of facing their biological time
clocks and often quietly absorb the strain while attending to a score of
other tasks. Women in their forties and older are frequently internally and
externally exhausted by years of concerted efforts to raise families, excel in
their work, and gain recognition for their years of service. They often
address themselves to an inner fatigue that colors their worldview as well
as their assumptions about themselves—their potential and their value. All
of these age groups are candidates for burnout; yet, again, each individual
woman must understand that there are solutions and there are cures for
her particular set of pressures.

In speaking with women who are burning out, the most vivid perception one has is that of a woman who is somewhat ashamed of her inability
to juggle the myriad aspects of her life. Women who come into therapy
for burnout exhaustion are rarely looking to heal themselves. Instead,
they're looking for a method with which to regain energy in order to
return to the same arenas with renewed vigor. And, again, quite frequently
a woman will begin defining her malaise by asking, "How can I better
myself?" When, through treatment, she begins to understand that there is
nothing wrong with her, but perhaps with the expectations surrounding
her, she's then in a position to begin learning how to pace herself, how to
back off, how to detach without isolating herself, and how to alter her
patterns of intensity that are proving to be insurmountable. At that point,
she's usually delighted at having obtained outside permission to relax, to
experience pleasure, to take care of her intimate needs, and to reclaim her
own life. The slow accumulation of troubling symptoms that have been
threatening to erode the contours of her life are gradually diminished and
she's able to see with new eyes again.

This book has been written to alert you to the often indistinguishable
but frequently insidious stress-producers and stress-extenders within your
life. It addresses itself to the questions women most frequently ask, and

the methods by which they can successfully treat their own burnout symptoms. While burnout is not mysterious, it is quite often overlooked as the prime cause for a number of distressing feelings and attitudes. While you may have experienced burnout, or while you may currently be struggling with its effects, you may also want to use the information in this book to help someone else identify her confusing and troubling symptoms. The hope here is that burnout will eventually be demystified and viewed as a first cause instead of a last idea. In this way, self-awareness will become the standard by which women will judge their own capacities and limitations. The burden of pressures will be measured against what each individual woman knows about herself, and not the expectations of others.

As you will see, the first half of *Women's Burnout* is devoted to "The Basics of Women's Burnout":

Chapter I, "If You Think You're Burning Out," will help you to shed light on the causes of burnout depression and to distinguish between chronic depression and burnout. Additionally, you'll learn to identify long-term and short-term burnout, and be provided with some tools for recognizing the many ways in which you may be denying your burnout condition.

Chapter II, "Why Women Burn Out," addresses the four major themes underlying women's burnout patterns: overnurturing, loneliness and aloneness, powerlessness, and the controversy surrounding authentic autonomy and authentic dependency.

Chapter III, "Some Family Dynamics of Women's Burnout," details the conditioning many women experienced in childhood which promotes burnout in their adult lives.

Chapter IV, "The Symptoms of Women's Burnout," delineates in detail the twelve stages and corresponding symptoms on the burnout cycle. This chapter will hopefully not only provide you with insight into your own burnout proclivities, but help you to identify the symptoms in friends, family members, colleagues, and lovers.

The second half of the book is devoted to "Women's Burnout in Action":

Chapter V, "Business Burnout," discusses the problems of perfectionism and legitimacy which arise in the professional and business arenas. It offers preventive steps and solutions for the stress-producers and stress-extenders women in business experience on a daily basis.

Chapter VI, "So Little Time, So Little Love," details the conflicts that emerge when important aspects of personal lives are suppressed and neglected. You'll also find some important information concerning the use of alcohol and cocaine, as well as the stress and pressure women experience who are searching for a mate.

Chapter VII, "Relationship Burnout," focuses on the causes behind what often appears to be a dying relationship. It offers many solutions and preventive steps for assuaging burnout conflicts between partners.

Chapter VIII, "How to Handle a Burned-out Person," provides you with a number of methods for appropriately responding to those in your personal or professional constellations whom you suspect may be burning out.

In the Conclusion, "A Twelve-Point Checklist for Burnout Prevention and Recovery," you'll find a quick-study list of signals to alert you to an incipient burnout condition.

The information in this book has been compiled in the main from the many women who have been and currently are in treatment for burnout, as well as personal interviews with over a hundred women who graciously and generously offered their time to speak candidly of their personal, professional, and private lives. The identities of all participants have been altered . . . the words are their own.

If you think you may be burning out—read on. You may have begun to completely alter a course you previously believed to be intractable, and you may find yourself completely reclaiming your life.

Herbert J. Freudenberger and Gail North
New York City, 1985

WOMEN'S BURNOUT

WOMEN'S BURNOUT (wiḿ inz bûrń out) *n.* 1. the point at which you exhaust your energies by overextending yourself: *Burnout depleted her spirit and sense of joy.* 2. the result of your excessive intensity and conscientiousness to other people and situations: *Continually nurturing others promoted her burnout.* 3. the consequence of denying yourself attention— pleasure, affiliation, intimacy: *Emotional deprivation prompted her burnout.* —*v.t.* burned out; 4. when motivation is lost due to overabundant responsiveness to your husband, lover, or job: *She had burned out her emotions and had little left to give.* —*v.i.* burning out; 5. waning enthusiasm, irritability, and feelings of disengagement caused by stress, pressure, and exhaustion: *When she was burning out, she perceived herself as pushing too hard, but didn't know how to change it.*

Part I

THE BASICS
OF WOMEN'S BURNOUT

CHAPTER I

If You Think
You're Burning Out . . .

"... my whole life had been a series of seven-minute-mile races and that's why I felt so burned out."

Myrna T.

"The first time I ran a seven-minute mile it became exceedingly important that I match that time on every run. I'd eat a lot of carbohydrates to give myself that extra push, then I'd just run like hell. I'd push myself incredibly—way beyond my natural limits. The pressure was enormous . . . I wouldn't remember who I was or why I was racing . . . all I knew was that I had a tremendous amount of convoluted energy which was focused on making that time. My whole identity was wrapped up in it. I shot past myself, lost all sense of time and, more important, all sense of myself as a total organism. As I began to tire and to hurt, my frustration increased, and I'd push harder to compensate for those weaknesses. At the end of the race I'd be depleted, sick, and . . . burned out.

"One day I decided to pace myself and consciously hold back. I felt I was moving too slowly, that everyone was passing me, that I was failing, that I wasn't good enough. But, at the end of the mile, I realized there was only a half-minute difference in my time. Instead of a seven-minute mile, I ran a seven-and-a-half-minute mile. I understood then that my whole life had been a series of seven-minute races, and that's why I always felt burned out.

"I think it's fair to say that when you're on the edge, when you think burnout is a possibility, you should go with the fatigue . . . go with what your body is telling you. When your identity and whole sense of self gets wrapped up in the image of achieving that goal, you lose all perspective on what the race is really about. When you *want* to achieve something that badly, you forget what you *need*. It's a terrific conflict. Succeeding becomes more important than being alive."

Do you think you may be burning out? Are there situations in your life in which you're tired, hurting, but "push harder to compensate for those weaknesses"? If you're toying with those thoughts, then you, like Myrna, are probably confronting some critical conflicts between what you want in your life, and what you need to balance your efforts. You may desperately want to succeed in your work, with your friends, and in love; you may need to loosen your hold in order to gain some perspective. You may passionately want to keep on pushing; you may need to back off and rebalance yourself with some critical emotional supplies. You probably alternate between feeling pressured and drained, panicked and driven—those feelings often coexist. There's a quarrel going on between what you want to attain and what you need to attain it. Somewhere along the line, your needs have gotten short shrift; there may not seem to be any accessible resolution. And so, you're often irritable, harassed, and anxious—some mornings you just don't want to get out of bed.

"I'm exhausted but can't stop to deal with that right now . . ." is one of your recurring mental refrains. You're beginning to feel used up and sometimes worry that you've lost the ability for genuine relaxation or fun. You may spend a lot of time figuring out how to become stronger, more resilient, better—anything that will help keep your momentum going. At times you probably long to "lean on someone else," but either don't know how to ask for help, are uncomfortable receiving help, or feel that the need for help demeans you. You may have the desire to slow down and back off for a while to rethink your life but are convinced you cannot—"Not now, anyway, I'm too busy . . . I just don't have the time." Today you may feel your services are irreplaceable—but tomorrow you may feel they're expendable. Either way, your inclination is to deny the conflict and to dig in deeper.

Think about it for a moment. Are you often agitated from constantly anticipating the spoken and unspoken demands from those considered important? Tired from acting as the resident nurturer at home, at work, and with friends? Frustrated from jumping from role to role and finding yourself even further behind? Does it occur to you from time to time that your job may be your only lover? Do you feel scarred by the notion that no matter how much you do, you're still "not good enough"? And, at times, do you find yourself staring into space wondering, "Is this all there is?" then feel guilty over losing time? If you're nodding in agreement, you probably also press yourself harder, persistently adhering to that old familiar refrain: "I can't be bothered by that now . . . I'm just too busy."

Why do women burn out? The answers are as varied as the personalities of the women themselves. Yet there are some significant common denominators which highlight the conflicts women face in our contemporary life. Here's a sample of burnout styles from five women who were interviewed for this book:

—At 28, Nancy sometimes likes to reminisce about "that young idealist who used to be me—the one filled with invincibility and purpose," who plunged into marriage, motherhood, and a solid career. She found she definitely could "have it all," but only by giving her all. "I'm juggling way too many demands," she said, "and I'm beginning to feel used up. Between the dual-career issues which haven't been resolved or even temporarily reconciled in my house, the baby's needs, the pressures of my job, my parents, friends—I'm constantly feeling guilty or harassed, or both. I'm racing from role to role to role and feel emotionally split into fragments . . ."

—Paula is 33 and thundering along in her career, yet wonders why she's not "putting roasts in the oven at four, preparing a family dinner," why she eats alone in front of the television, "too many nights to count." She's always been the group nurturer, overextending herself to friends, family, and men. She brought those caregiving qualities with her to her job, and now extends them to her bosses and colleagues. "I've been conditioned to take care of everyone else," she said, "but I don't feel I'm getting much of it back." In spite of her involvement with everyone else, Paula's personal life is "barren," and her evening fatigue is exacerbated by the "dread of being alone for the rest of my life." Paula gets frequent colds and has been smoking more this past year "than any time in my life."

—Elaine is 36 and holding off having a child until she's promoted to upper management. She worries she may be "too haggard and tired when that time comes to handle a baby . . . I'm afraid if I get pregnant now, I'll lose the ground I've gained at work. I've spent too much time legitimizing myself to be replaced by someone who's available while I'm on maternity leave." Convinced that the promised promotion will settle this issue, Elaine drives herself, hoping the announcement will be made before her biological time clock runs out. She complains of stomach ailments, and recently she's seen several doctors for the cysts which are breaking out on her face and chest.

—Janet is a 30-year-old homemaker with two young children. Lately she's noticed a suspicious obsessiveness about her house: she cleans and recleans but can't seem to get her home clean enough to satisfy her anxieties. "I'm in constant motion," she said. "I'm racing around with no real motive, compelled to keep things spotless and orderly, to make a perfect home for my family. I know this is nuts, but I feel driven . . ." Janet is also on a strenuous diet, suffers from lower-back pain, and experiences "frequent crying jags."

—Susan, a 44-year-old single parent, said: "I wish I didn't feel so guilt-ridden and resentful—a lot of women are in my position." She's volleying a job, a home, a child, financial problems, friends, and what she calls "a nowhere sex life." She works as an executive secretary, "a dead-end job in my company." Her job is ungratifying, leaves her enervated, irritable, and "I end up taking it out on my kid. I'm either too critical or too overprotective. Sometimes I'd like to dump him at his father's and run away . . ." Susan suffers from severe insomnia, takes Valium during the day, and has "a couple of scotches before I go to bed . . ."

Despite the individual differences in the lives and personality styles of these five women, each spoke of feeling driven, irritated, depleted, sometimes unseen, at other times weary and alone. All of them are conscientious, reliable, and industrious, yet each is missing something vital and sustaining in her life. What they want and what they need have fallen out of balance. They all believe if they don't either slow down, back off, or alter the quality of their lives, they're going to be severely burned out within the year.

If any of these situations rings a familiar bell, you've probably thought about burnout and spent some time seeking guidelines for preventing it. Some of you may not understand what you're experiencing, yet perceive something unpleasant and debilitating happening to you which must be changed. Potential burnouts are an enterprising group, not usually satisfied with simple security or the status quo. If that were the case, women would be nodding passively, still yielding to an unnatural lassitude, and the important transformations in our society would never have occurred. To the contrary, women suffering from burnout are personal strivers and achievers with high expectations of themselves and the world around them. They're not content to quit and "pack it in"; they have an ideal in mind and are usually rife with determination, intelligence, and resourcefulness. Yet, it's that very resourcefulness that sometimes goes askew. In the absence of guidelines or models, it becomes confused with raw endurance. That's when the burnout process gets a firm toehold in your life.

So, if you're feeling exhausted, frustrated, or guilt-ridden by what your life's situation is yielding, don't be discouraged. It doesn't have to be a series of seven-minute-mile races, and it doesn't have to be confronted alone. Somewhere between raw endurance and total resignation there are preventive steps which can be taken to circumvent the burnout experience. There's not only hope, there are solutions.

WOMEN'S BURNOUT: A DEFINITION

Burnout is a condition which evolves slowly over a period of prolonged stress and expenditure of energies. In order to fully understand why so many women suffer from burnout, it might be wise to consider a definition of the term:

BURNOUT IS A WEARING DOWN AND WEARING OUT OF ENERGY. IT IS AN EXHAUSTION BORN OF EXCESSIVE DEMANDS WHICH MAY BE SELF-IMPOSED OR EXTERNALLY IMPOSED BY FAMILIES, JOBS, FRIENDS, LOVERS, VALUE SYSTEMS, OR SOCIETY, WHICH DEPLETE ONE'S ENERGY, COPING MECHANISMS, AND INTERNAL

RESOURCES. IT IS A FEELING STATE WHICH IS ACCOM-
PANIED BY AN OVERLOAD OF STRESS, AND WHICH
EVENTUALLY IMPACTS ON ONE'S MOTIVATION, ATTI-
TUDES, AND BEHAVIOR.

In light of women's unique position in our society, the definition takes
on some unexpected colorations. Many women have become so inured to
the stress and pressure endemic to their lives and roles, the feeling state of
exhaustion is construed as normal living. Complaints of fatigue, lost motivation, and waning enthusiasm are tossed off as though they come with
the female territory—not to be taken too seriously. And yet those complaints can act as crucial indicators of a burnout condition.

WOMEN'S BURNOUT AND DENIAL

Denial is a prime feature of burnout. It is a mechanism that allows one
to avoid looking at reality and to defend against a multitude of unpleasant
feelings, perceptions, and experiences. If you think you're burning out,
you can be certain you've assumed the posture of denial in critical areas of
your life. Your troublesome situations, events, or relationships are not being perceived for what they authentically are, or for what they actually
mean. The physical and emotional strains on yourself are probably being
shunted aside by your insistence that "they're just not happening to me."
If you are consistently denying your frustrations, threats to your position,
confusions, burdens, stress, aloneness, or anger, you can be sure you're well
on the road to burnout. If you further abuse yourself by denying your need
for immersions in pleasure—laughter, affiliation, intimacy, closeness,
touch, or simply the space to think—you're guaranteeing severe burnout
exhaustion.

Listen carefully to your own language. If you think you're burning out, a
bell should go off each time you hear yourself use the language of denial:

—"What happened to Jane can't happen to me."
—"In time this will get better and go away."
—"I know he's untrustworthy, but this is different."
—"What you're telling me about my health just isn't true."
—"I don't have any negative feelings."

—"I never get sick, I thrive on pressure . . ."
—"I just need a few days off—a vacation—and I'll be fine . . ."

When your conversations and, more important, your inner thoughts are seasoned with impromptu justifications of this kind, there are some seriously draining situations in your life which you may want to maintain but need to confront realistically.

DENIAL TECHNIQUES

Denial is a process. In terms of burnout, it frequently begins with a desire to shut out a specific thought or feeling regarding the excessive overextension of physical, mental, or emotional energy. When initially confronted with something unpleasant, a big "NO" resounds in your mind which acts as a barrier between you and the reality of the situation at hand. Over time, the repetition of "NO" has a cumulative effect and is transformed into a habitual reaction to uncomfortable or unpleasant facts. But that's just the beginning phase, the more primitive underbelly of denial. The feeling of "NO" is quickly transformed into more sophisticated trappings, and, in time, subtler, more acceptable techniques for denying reality are born.

—*Suppression* is a prime denial technique that is commonly employed. When you consciously deny information, when a truth or insight is perceived and noted, then restrained and stuffed away, you are concealing or suppressing what you know from yourself, as well as from others.

—*Displacement,* on the other hand, is an unconscious denial technique. Your unpleasant feelings are transferred onto a less meaningful object, person, or situation. For instance, it's easier to be angry with a child or a colleague than to admit that your marriage may be failing, or that the job in which you've invested so much time and energy is becoming a dead end. And, it's easier to "lose" yourself in work than to acknowledge loneliness, or to "fuse" yourself up with a loved one when your work is ungratifying.

—*Humor* is another denial technique which is a bit more slippery. It's frequently used to cover and deny a serious condition or situation. By making a joke out of your fatigue, loneliness, or anger, you then diminish

your own anxiety and, along the way, throw concerned friends off the
track. It's all a good laugh.

—*Projection* is another technique sometimes used to circumvent diffi-
culties. By focusing blame on someone else ("If he was more dependable,
I wouldn't have to do the work of two . . . !") you continue to deny the
drain on your own energies and take no responsibility for changing the
situation.

—*Fantasy* and *daydreaming* are even subtler denial techniques. They
allow you to postpone confrontations with authentic reality through the
invention of a reality you would prefer.

—*Selective memory* is a frequent manifestation of denial. In this case,
your memory is conveniently intruded upon, and you are able to deny how
tired you've been in the past. You tend to forget what you experienced
yesterday, last week, last year, and if you should recall those depleted
feelings, you may resort to lying as your form of denial.

—*Lying* is a conscious method of denying and serves a twofold purpose.
It gets concerned friends and family members, perhaps even colleagues,
off your back, and it allows you to momentarily fool yourself into thinking
you're indomitable and totally in control.

—*Self-labeling* is a denial technique which acts to explain and excuse
your exhaustion or irritability. "Well, that's me," you might remark with
an attitude of casual indifference, "I'm neurotic, a workaholic, a perfectionist, a sicko, a nut, a mess . . ." anything to continue on with your
selected burnout path uninterrupted. Along with self-labeling, you may
cope with symptoms by making them ego-syntonic, which means you
often tie your symptoms in with your character, personality, or life-style by
telling others, "I'm the tense type," "I've always been quick to anger," "I
unerringly get headaches in the summer," "I'm just a real loner . . ."

—*Selective incomprehension* is a technique that allows you to deny
what others are telling you by refusing to "understand": "I don't understand what you mean when you say I'm not myself"; "You'll have to
explain. I don't get it"; "What do you mean, I need 'closeness'?" By
stubbornly clinging to a lack of comprehension, you're able to continue to
deny the self-destructive and self-defeating burnout activity.

THE HABIT OF DENIAL

When these denial techniques become habitual, they can lead to some rather serious consequences. Denial has a purpose: it allows you to persistently work harder and longer; to stay in a sinking relationship; to continue seeing the married man; to take on more professional responsibilities; to volunteer your services at your child's school when you're already depleted; to continue smoking; to continue drinking; to camouflage fatigue with cocaine or amphetamines; to obliterate anxiety and stress with tranquilizers; to put off pleasure; and, often, to live without love. In the process, the ever-expanding habit may lead to a denial of the existence of dangerous circumstances. The usual anxiety which signals the threat of danger may be suppressed. You may be responding to anxiety-laden situations with counterphobic "reactive courage," pretending a fearlessness that does not exist to deny your fears and your mortality.

Increasingly, through denial you begin to accept the notion that you're stronger than others, more resilient, more resistant to stress-related illness, or more capable of enduring isolation. At the same time, a denial of age is usually percolating. By denying years, you concomitantly deny the limitations of your body and place unrealistic burdens on its capacity to function. You may worry excessively over the external signs of aging—lines around the mouth and eyes, the slight sag at the jawline, the slack in your muscle tone—but not the internal changes. Frequently, that same denial of age also obliterates the perception of passing time. You may continue to remain in an unrewarding job, postpone your plans for having a child, put off the desire for finding a mate, or habitually deny your growing concern for financial security. When you're locked into critical patterns of denial, your concerns are usually focused on the present—the future is too threatening to think about and therefore denied its importance.

THE FEELING OF DENIAL

At the outset you may choose to deny, as a means of coping with disappointments, loneliness, or feelings of impotence. It follows that physical, emotional, and mental exhaustion will also be denied, which sets you up as a perfect candidate for burnout. When you begin to deprive yourself of nourishment—replenishment or repair—your sense of self is subtly undermined. Very soon you begin to experience a distortion of your values and an estrangement from yourself. In time, the denial is heightened and you may perceive yourself as disengaged from your work, your friends, or your mate. Disengagement from your external connections fosters feelings of depersonalization—a snapped connection from your own inner world. You may begin to feel more like a commodity than a person, yet continue to cover your disoriented moorings by promising to "think about it tomorrow." Of course, that Scarlett O'Hara syndrome is delusive: it informs of firm but very fleeting intentions. With no replenishment of physical or emotional supplies, a sense of emptiness pervades, and life seems sapped of meaning. Feelings of depression may emerge, but because denial is now habitual, you may push yourself further toward total burnout exhaustion.

The feeling of denial is a nagging sense of "something off." That "something" may be alternately acknowledged and dismissed, in spite of the fact that you could become ill or are abusing yourself emotionally. There is a "missed" connection between your ability to perceive the symptoms—"I know I have headaches, recurring coughs, sudden crying jags, a sleep disorder, an irritated colon"—and the feeling of the symptom itself. You may have an unconscious wish, or a conscious willingness, to "miss" that critical connection and to deny the link between the two. If you admit to the connectedness, then a drastic change in life-style may be necessary, and those changes are usually heavy with uncertainty.

In essence, denial is the handmaiden of burnout, and therefore it's easy to understand why you may devalue, if not consciously suppress, your conflicts and exhaustion. A woman with a life-style of denying unpleasant feelings—from annoyance to loneliness to outrage—is a prime candidate for denying and perhaps disguising the stress she habitually experiences in her life. That stress acts as a threat to ambition and accomplishment. When you're committed to a goal and that goal has attained a high priority in your life, fatigue becomes the enemy. It's easier to deny the fatigue than to detach from the passion for the goal.

Quite typically, a woman under months of pressure will report: "I know I'm exhausted, but this is a temporary situation. All I need is a good night's sleep and I'll be fine." Exhaustion that can be extinguished by "a good night's sleep" is not a symptom of burnout, but of a situational overload which can be quickly remedied. Therefore, it's critical to bear in mind that not every woman who claims exhaustion is burning out. However, it's equally critical to understand that when that "temporary situation" lingers for weeks, months, or years, denial is at work and the exhaustion deserves serious attention.

Often, the only surefire method for heading off denial is a breakdown in physical functioning. You may continue to deny you're under the burnout gun until you become physically impaired. When the body breaks down, all plans are postponed and activity is stopped. The hope here is that if you think you're burning out, you'll catch that denial and its subsequent momentum long before it reaches that critical stage.

STRESS AND WOMEN'S BURNOUT

Daily stress is a major aspect of women's burnout. Over a short period of time, an "overload of stress" produces a cranky, irritable person. Over a long period of time, that same daily stress places a demand on one's energy sources and produces a burned-out person. "Motivation, attitudes, and behavior" are all affected by the loss of energy. In fact, when one is enervated, the very meaning of life can be diminished to inconsequential.

However, since stress is also a positive feature in our lives, sparking as it does the incentive to grow, to learn, to produce, and to connect, distinguishing between "good" and "bad" stress is essential. "Bad" or negative stress can only be recognized when one begins to feel worn down and worn out by its "excessive demands." When negative stress becomes a life-style, it hides in the guise of regularity. Like the old cliché, "You can't see the forest for the trees," ongoing stress camouflages itself by its own consuming momentum. "But I thought this was the way I was supposed to feel," one woman in treatment for burnout has repeatedly declared. "I thought this was the natural state of things—this is the way I've always lived." Only when it was pointed out to her that her coping mechanisms were rubbed raw by the excessive demands on her external and internal life and how little nourishment she received for herself was she able to fathom the degree and extent of her inner exhaustion.

STRESS-PRODUCERS AND STRESS-EXTENDERS

We all know there are certain situations that are unqualified stress-producers in life and cannot be avoided: a heavy burden of daily responsibilities; financial crises; a sick child at home; the declining health of a parent; the loss of a home; the severing from a loved friend, husband, or lover. Stress is also the product of a threatened job or an accost on the street by a menacing stranger. The experience here may be unusual, but the accompanying wallop of stress on your nervous system is neither unexpected nor alien. The "fight or flight" response is activated, which propels you to "fight" for your job or take "flight" from danger. These are ancient survival mechanisms. The body tries to make accommodations for these stress-producers by adapting itself and making the necessary internal adjustments.

Yet there are other stress factors not as clearly delineated or revealed which aid burnout strain. These are called *stress-extenders*. Any powerful emotion which is consistently denied or neglected works to extend the day-to-day stress of "normal" living.

—*Backed-up anger is a critical stress-extender.* From childhood, women are taught that displays of anger are prohibited. If you should express it, you do so surreptitiously, rarely confronting the appropriate person directly. The anger is stored and frequently threatens to erupt, placing an additional strain on personal and professional relationships.

—*Denied hostility is a deadly stress-extender.* One example relates to women who have never dealt successfully with authoritative fathers or mothers, and who have the additional burden of coping with repressed and unexpressed enmity. The hostility is denied, then displaced onto someone or something else, or sublimated in excessive expressions of self-sacrifice, orderliness, or perfectionism.

—*Neglected needs are important stress-extenders.* Traditionally, a young girl is trained to be nurturing, to be "nice," and to put her needs last. This translates itself in your adult life into becoming a reliable source of attention and service for others but leaves you in a position of neglect. When there is no reciprocity from husbands, lovers, colleagues, family members, or even employers, your own dependency needs go unrecognized and unmet. The experience is one of loneliness, and that feeling further enlarges your stress index.

—*Guilt is a significant stress-extender.* If you are married and in a dual-career family, or if you are a divorced single parent, you may feel guilty over leaving your children for the job. To mollify the old inner attitude toward what a "good" mother is or isn't, you may work full-time and continue to assume all of the household chores and tasks. Guilt may goad you into extending yourself beyond your normal endurance and prevent you from asking for help from either your husband or your children.

—*Low self-esteem is an insidious stress-extender.* Your personal family dynamics from the past can illustrate how low self-esteem extends stress. Your parents may have been overly critical and judgmental, causing you to suffer from a poor self-image in your adult life. The sense of not being "good enough" pressures you into an unrealistic striving for excellence, recognition, and approval and places an additional burden of stress on your life.

These hidden stress-extenders are often overlooked, but they are as crucial to understanding women's burnout as the more easily identified stress-producers of day-to-day living. If you think you're burning out, it's important for you to begin to explore the degree of hidden stress you experience that has previously gone unacknowledged.

STRESS-RELATED ILLNESS AND "FALSE CURES"

Not surprisingly, the number of women suffering from stress-related diseases has been on the upswing in the past two decades. Stress-producers and stress-extenders can affect the immune system and lower resistance to illness. Women who have neutralized their feelings and continue to deny and neglect their aggregate of specific needs are wide open to physical ailments which can manifest in a variety of symptoms and diseases.

Tension and migraine headaches are common complaints, as are stomach and backaches. The frequently recurring cold, the cough that won't abate, constipation or diarrhea, an irritable colon, skin eruptions, dizziness, insomnia or narcoleptic napping, ulcers, sometimes colitis, and even coronaries are all typical examples of the ailments to which women (and men) under unrelieved stress are prone.

Paradoxically, in an attempt to diminish the anxiety high stress creates, you may find yourself turning to "false cures" to keep the burnout momentum going: alcohol, smoking, tranquilizers and amphetamines, cocaine, the coffee-caffeine "high," overeating, or not eating at all. When you're overstressed, overtired, or just plain exhausted, perceptions and judgments become distorted. Feelings of paranoia or worthlessness may emerge; confusion over time; anxiety over identity; masochistic slights against yourself may be acted out. You may turn to a "false cure" to change your inner environment, to make it livable and to temporarily mask the symptoms. You're then able to return to your burnout path with renewed vigor, unaware that the "false cure" has camouflaged and exacerbated your underlying condition. By going along with the "false cure" solutions, you may be blinding yourself to the fact that you're propelling yourself deeper into the Burnout Cycle and becoming further alienated from that which is really needed.

THE BURNOUT SYMPTOM CYCLE AND BURNOUT STAGES

Women burn out when they become seriously overstressed and deny their exhaustion. You may legitimately ask, as many women have, "Just when does burnout begin?" or "How can I tell if burnout is what I'm experiencing? After all, everyone I know feels pressured and overstressed."

There is, of course, no unfailing method for recognizing the exact moment the process begins. Unfortunately, a burnout rarely admits that she's having trouble with the pressures in her life, much less that she's feeling overwhelmed. Since most women burnouts pride themselves on their endurance and ability to volley and cope with their many roles, they rarely own up to inner exhaustion until they become physically ill. Once again, the exhaustion is denied. It's only when the feeling state of burnout becomes a perceptible certainty that women usually will seek assistance, guidance, or real solutions. It must be remembered that not every woman who is fatigued is suffering from burnout. As was discussed above, if a good night's sleep can replenish your energies and restore you to a healthy frame of mind, you may be troubled by a situational overload. There are, however, twelve recognizable stages within the Burnout Symptom Cycle which reflect the feeling state of burnout, and which will help you to distinguish between a temporary fatigue and an incipient burnout condition.

The stages on the Burnout Symptom Cycle are loosely as follows:

1. The Compulsion to Prove
2. Intensity
3. Subtle Deprivations
4. Dismissal of Conflict and Needs
5. Distortion of Values
6. Heightened Denial
7. Disengagement
8. Observable Behavior Changes
9. Depersonalization
10. Emptiness
11. Depression
12. Total Burnout Exhaustion

If you're suffering from burnout, you may be experiencing symptoms in one or several of these stages at the same time. The progression of burnout is not neatly plotted. Stages often blend into one another. You may be fixed in one stage, or you may be jumping from one to another. The effects of one stage may elude you while the intensity of another may appear to be intractable. The duration and intensity of these stages depend upon your individual situation, your personality, your inclinations, previous history, and your ability to cope with stress.

For a more detailed discussion of the various stages, you might want to turn to Chapter IV, "The Symptoms of Women's Burnout." Each stage on the cycle is delineated with accompanying examples to assist you in identifying your own symptoms. What's important here is to understand that if your symptoms go unchecked, if they are denied or masked by "false cures," they will escalate in severity. For this reason, it's critical to avoid becoming bogged down in what one woman accurately called "that ever-revolving wheel of denial."

IS IT BURNOUT OR DEPRESSION?

Many women deep into the Burnout Symptom Cycle initially describe themselves as "depressed." As you can see from the list of stages, Stage 11 is described as Depression. However, depression born of burnout and a chronic depression are quite dissimilar. Much confusion prevails over this issue, and too many women complaining of low energy, a feeling of detachment from the world, and an invasion of cynicism are treated for depression instead of burnout exhaustion. *This is a critical diagnostic mistake.*

Quite simply, chronic depression and burnout depression manifest themselves in similar feeling states; however, the causes and treatment are quite different. Burnout is caused by an excess of stress and fatigue and is characterized by a subsequent erosion of your energy and attitudes. Over a period of time, the unrelenting pressures and the inability to control your environment or cope with demands and inner expectations create a change in your feelings and perceptions. Depression is caused by the onset of an event or series of events triggered by a loss and is characterized by sadness, enervation, a feeling of mourning. The death of a spouse or a parent, a divorce or severing from a mate, a move to a new city, being fired from a job, a traumatic accident or injury, or any other number of sudden and harsh events can catapult you into a depression.

If you're burning out, you may be turned off, deflated or disenchanted, at work or at home, but not, perhaps, in a social situation. Or, you may be burning out on the job, but revive when surrounded by a few good friends. The combinations are various. A depression affects your feelings and mood across the board. There is little or no joy in any function or role. Feelings of worthlessness, ennui, or grief infiltrate and often flood every aspect of your life. Nothing alters those feelings of loss. Often the condition may require medical attention and medication for relief.

In short, a depressed person tends to give up. This is not the case with burnout. A person burning out may look to drugs or alcohol to regain the energy she has lost. She may turn to the false cures to reclaim an inner fire, her original excitement, her motivation. A depressed woman seeks out drugs or alcohol to deny the painful feelings of depression. She's looking for respite—not for a reclamation of enthusiasm.

The tricky part in deciphering the differences between the two emerges when a woman on the Burnout Cycle slips into Stage 11—Depression. When this occurs, it must be remembered that the depression is a symptom of the burnout condition—a result of prolonged stress—and not an event unto itself. Burnout exhaustion is often misdiagnosed as chronic depression because the symptoms superficially resemble each other. However, if you're attempting to distinguish between the two, you might begin by investigating your own history.

If you're suffering from chronic depression, there are specific debilitating or demoralizing events which have touched your life. They may have initially shocked your system with their suddenness and you may now feel as though in continual mourning. You may find it difficult to work or eat as you can neither concentrate, express yourself, nor respond without great effort. You may feel as though you are wasting away and helpless to end the inner grief that has overcome you.

If you're suffering from burnout exhaustion and are experiencing the depression as one aspect of burnout, you may have been striving for too long to achieve a set of goals or rewards which are either not forthcoming or not commensurate with your expectations. Or, you may have deprived yourself of intimate connections for too long and have lost a closeness with yourself. Over a period of time, you've probably undergone a series of personality changes. Your behavior may have changed from calm and centered to angry and irritable; your attitudes from trusting to cynical; your perception of the world from safe to dangerous; your judgment patterns from rational to skewed. The progression to depression is based on diminishing energy and returns.

Depression caused by burnout exhaustion can and should be addressed and treated as one of the symptoms (albeit, one serious symptom) on the entire Burnout Symptom Cycle. Using these distinctions as guidelines, hopefully you should be able to identify the cause of the depression and direct your attention toward some burnout prevention methods and solutions for recovery.

If your doubts persist and you remain unclear in determining your condition, it might be appropriate for you to seek out a professional—a psychiatrist, psychoanalyst, psychologist, or social worker.

LONG-TERM AND SHORT-TERM WOMEN'S BURNOUT

"I feel as if I've been burning out all my life."

"I think I have a burnout personality."

"Burnout is a way of life for me . . ."

Do any of these statements sound familiar? If they do, you may be suffering from long-term burnout. These statements reflect a life-style characterized by anxiety and exhaustion. Women who describe themselves in this fashion may have recently begun to understand that much of their emotional and physical lives, perhaps spanning years, has been spent battling burnout symptoms.

"I feel as if I've been running on fumes most of my life," one woman stated. "I'm never completely relaxed. My mind is always racing, my wheels spinning, and even when I think I'm relaxed, I'm not. I'm making mental lists, worrying, trying to perfect my looks, my personality, my skills, my friendships . . . I mean, it's crazy! Every event or situation becomes a reason for more frenetic activity . . . I exhaust myself. There doesn't seem to be any way out. Sometimes I think I'm burned out on life . . ."

Long-term burnouts are constantly seeking solutions for "a way out" of their exhaustive inner life. Their coping mechanisms tend to become increasingly ineffective; they often speak of feeling "wiped out" or "drained." Intermittently, their energy totally wears out and they're thrown into the more serious stages of the Burnout Cycle. This process has a repetitive pattern.

If you suspect you're in a long-term burnout pattern, you may consciously and unconsciously select new coping mechanisms with which to mollify the hurts and disappointments you experience, but your choices rarely address themselves to what you authentically need. Because of your incessant mental activity, you may experience extreme shifts in your attitudes. One week you'll direct your disenchantment outwardly—deny your emotional responses ("I'm not angry!"), blame your external situation ("It's this apartment that's getting to me—I need to move to another . . ."), criticize others ("It's those incompetents who are causing this . . ."), and generally suffer from paranoid feelings ("You can't trust anyone here . . ."). The next week, you'll turn on yourself, engaging in long bouts of self-doubt, self-recrimination, and self-abuse. You may unconsciously move in and out of these two modes, never fully grasping the fact that you're racing past yourself and are not receiving any needed emotional supplies with which to sustain your life.

Most long-term women burnouts have a history of acting as part- or full-time nurturers and have devoted much of their energy giving out care, attention, and affection to others. Often that nurturing comes from an unconscious "giving to get" syndrome, but just as often it was encouraged by your early training and now acts as a learned response to what you intuit as other's needs. Frequently, women are not comfortable receiving the nurturing they need for themselves. You may feel you'll lose the people you care about if you ask, or believe that if you were completely autonomous, you wouldn't need outside nurturing. To compensate, you may fill up on the symbols of pleasure—alcohol, cocaine, junk food treats, a shopping spree you cannot afford, a party when you're overtired, or a lot of casual sex—but still feel empty and disconnected from yourself. Consequently, your burnout exhaustion intensifies and the vicious cycle of burnout symptoms is stepped up.

Real or imagined expectations and judgments are the main culprits in long-term burnout. Mental activity is forever churning. When there are no actual situations or people demanding of you, the demands are self-sculpted, then self-imposed. The compulsion to prove or achieve and to do it perfectly becomes undifferentiated and indiscriminate. You feel you must excel in every area of your life. When you are defeated by exhaustion, personal limits, time, or skill, that defeat acts as a defining principle of your totality. Life, indeed, becomes a "series of seven-minute-mile races."

Long-term burnout is a consequence of old personal family dynamics and the subsequent inattention to both physical and emotional needs. Most women with long-term burnout spend a great deal of time worrying over whether they're "making the grade," anticipating the needs and whims of those around them, always pushing themselves further. Caught in the grip of stress-extenders—guilt, anger, hostility, low self-esteem, or neglected needs—they carry a lot of old, obsolete psychological baggage around with them. Not surprisingly, however, when outside exigencies do emerge, no matter what her energy level may be, a long-term burnout woman will rise to the occasion with conscientious reliability and efficiency. Later she will reexperience the depths of her anxiety and fatigue. This pattern repeats itself frequently.

Short-term burnout is *not* an ongoing pattern in a woman's life, but a condition which arises out of one or many situations which are either elected or have been thrust upon her. A job, relationship, financial burdens, children, family, illness, or any number of events experienced singly or en masse can throw you into short-term burnout. You may meet the challenge with high ideals and expectations, but over a period of time your energies become increasingly exhausted and your spirit for the tasks eroded. In one instance, your job may take on a compulsive focus which obliterates your need for a social life. In another, your home life may become so all-consuming it eclipses your need for alone time. Again, what is wanted and what is needed become jumbled and confused, and your real values ultimately become blurred and indistinct. During the short-term, you'll find yourself attending to all of the external emergencies, but none of your critical internal needs.

Unlike the long-termer, the short-term woman burnout is not personally familiar with the symptoms of burnout. Her life has not been a series of races. You may have heard something about burnout and understand it has to do with fatigue, but the repeated flatness of feelings and attitudes has not been in your experience. As a short-term woman in treatment for her burnout stated: "I've never felt like this before in my life . . . I keep giving out and giving out, and feel nothing anymore. I've never been so out of control . . . I just want to be left alone. I've lost my concentration, feel like screaming at everyone, my husband and I are constantly bickering or not talking at all, and I've lost all my enthusiasm for my job. I feel like a zombie . . . This just isn't *me* . . ."

Short-term burnouts aren't familiar with feeling overwhelmed, nor are they used to seeking solutions like the long-termer; they haven't been faced with the same disorientation in their lives. They feel they can "lick this thing" and dig in deeper, convinced the pressures will let up, be resolved, or just disappear, and they'll bounce back. However, like her long-term burnout counterpart, the short-term burnout usually doesn't understand that she desperately needs emotional support and attention from outside sources.

Both short- and long-term burnouts suffer from real and imagined expectations and judgments, but the short-term woman doesn't usually suffer from the same stress-extenders. You may not be struggling as severely with psychological family wars from the past. And, until you're thrust into the critical stages of the Burnout Symptom Cycle, your defeats are not usually construed as a definition of yourself.

However, some short-termers will experience repetitions of the short-term burnout experience at another time in their lives, typically emanating from another source. A short-term woman facing burnout for the second time put it this way: "Last year I burned out on my relationship . . . I put everything into it and lost myself. He was my whole focus . . . and it ended because of the intensity. Neither of us could take it. I swore I'd never commit myself to anyone or anything as intensely again. Well, this year I'm burning out at my job. When I think about it, the symptoms are precisely the same, only I'm catching it earlier this time . . ."

You might want to consider for a moment whether your inclinations are pointed toward long-term or short-term burnout. How does each feel when applied to your life? Try to remember that neither is insurmountable and that both are reversible. You'll be reading a number of methods for reestablishing a union between what you want and what you need which should ease your mind about finding solutions which are right for you, including "How to 'Unlearn' Denial."

But first, now that you know some basics, you may want to know what causes the condition and just why women burn out.

CHAPTER II

Why Women Burn Out

"Basically, I think we're all in a conflict between the way we were raised and the reality out there . . . For women, there are always two standards—what's expected of you, and who you really are."

Cynthia L.

ON NURTURING

"My mother used to tell me that 'warmth attracts warmth,' and if I wanted to be well liked I should set a good example for others. She taught me to be polite, warm, and to take care of people . . . Sometimes I wish she hadn't—I wear myself out anticipating what others need. I have a lot of guilt when I say 'no' or when I have to give negative criticism to anyone— that includes my husband and friends. But I've got to change all that, especially professionally. The first time I was called on to fire someone was horrendous for me. She showed up the next day for work. I supported her so much during the firing, she never got the message."

Jenny—28

ON ALONENESS

"When you've been working very hard and feeling job burnout, it's difficult not to have someone to be with at home. It gets worse and worse over time . . . you begin to long for warmth and closeness. I spent years running around, dating, partying, sleeping with a lot of men . . . and then I ran out of steam. I was exhausted from planning and initiating a social life—giving dinner parties, finding dates, and doing it all alone. Now I'm spending too many evenings alone and I'm scared that this is how I'm destined to spend the rest of my life. When I was growing up, the idea of being alone as an adult woman was nonexistent. No one ever talked about it . . . it just wasn't what any of us had in mind . . ."

Dorothy—35

ON POWERLESSNESS

"I'm certainly not helpless—but I'm beginning to feel a sense of powerlessness at work. I was always told if you did a good job, if you were cooperative and talented, you'd be rewarded—you'd be asked to join the club. But I'm dealing with a 'Men's Club' and no matter what I do, I'm still blackballed from membership. It's all very subtle . . . you think you're all on the same team and then you discover they won't let you catch. The team captain talks to you on the bench, but before you know it, he's helping you out of the game. I'm just not in my own environment and the exclusion is wearing me down . . ."

Katherine—41

ON AUTONOMY VS. DEPENDENCY

"It's difficult being autonomous, self-reliant, in control . . . I feel very dependent at times and that panics me. It's as if the mud on my boots is showing—if I don't wipe it off I'll blow my cover and turn people off. I put a lot of energy into not looking like I need . . . I work at being assertive and confronting people appropriately. But I feel as though it's all make-believe autonomy. Something's happening to me that I

don't like . . . I don't laugh like I used to anymore. I just run
from role to role, changing identities and keeping everything
intact. Basically, I think we're all in a conflict between the way
we were raised and the reality out there . . . For women,
there are always two standards—what's expected of you, and
who you really are."

Cynthia—26

Jenny, Dorothy, Katherine, and Cynthia are all suffering from
burnout symptoms and each is grappling with the reasons behind why
women burn out. The issues they raise have a basic area of agreement.
They each pose an uncertain question: How can I meet the new cultural
demands and still be me?

As a female, you were raised with certain expectations which, allowing
for differences in family dynamics, personality, and inclination, reveal
themselves in the quality of your lives. You didn't simply arrive in your
present situations; you were groomed by a family, the culture, politics, the
media. What puzzles most women struggling with burnout echoes those
statements; they want to know how to juggle their old conditioning with
their new consciousness. This is very specific to women.

Married or single, divorced or widowed, with or without children,
women at any stage of the Burnout Cycle basically perceive themselves as
lacking. There's something you need that you're not getting. There's an
element of mystery in your lives that needs to be decoded. Usually, your
first line of defense is to locate the "trouble area" within yourself, then try
to fix it. The "trouble area" often points to the conflict between old,
deeply embedded attitudes and the new shifts in cultural consciousness
concerning roles. Since it's somewhat easier to change external behavior
than it is to alter an internal attitude, many women focus their energies on
behavior makeovers. "I need to become more assertive," one woman says,
"I'm way too tentative with people." "I need to become more objective,
less emotional," says another. A third woman reports that she's "trying to
think faster and say less, to gain some control over my life," while someone else states: "I think I've become too assertive—I've got to tone myself
down. I'm turning people off."

These women are struggling with conflicting ideas regarding the roles
they should or should not be playing and what behavior to choose. Most of
you have been trained in your homes to project a certain passivity—to

behave with a degree of deference; to accept a *pro forma* powerlessness. But the culture pressures you to be assertive, to stand up for rights and beliefs, to "say what you need to say." For many, this role conflict, with its issues of attitude and behavior alterations, serves as an ongoing stress-producer which wears down your energies. "I'm trying to be everything at once," a young woman in sales stated. "I'm trying to keep my humanity and be caring; I'm trying to earn a reputation through merit; I'm trying to be autonomous and professional in my behavior; and I'm trying to still have a private life which brings me some pleasure. I'm not making it . . . I'm wired too tightly and am about to snap."

These are serious pressures which many women are attempting to shake off. Too many intersecting dilemmas and conflicts are bound to cause disenchantment with life. The conflicts between old and new values can, however, be taken apart and explored with an eye toward a satisfactory resolution. Do you feel you're often taken for granted as the "resident" nurturer? Has the shock of aloneness and perhaps loneliness found its way into your life? Has a sense of powerlessness infiltrated your professional and/or private life? And, have the notions of autonomy and dependency become frustrating emotional confusions? The main question here, however, is this: How do these four issues deplete your inner resources and goad you on to burnout?

BURNOUT AND THE NURTURER

Are you grappling with the need to give and receive nurturing, and, perhaps, even the right to those feelings? If you are, the habit of giving may be so firmly entrenched in your behavioral style, you cannot easily separate your "services" from your definition of yourself. If you are a nurturer, you were most likely trained to act as a nurturing figure to men, children, and a host of secondary figures, and you may assume that you'll lose what you perceive as your real value if you withdraw those attentions. Some women feel shaky and vulnerable when they begin to transfer their attentions to jobs or careers. Others feel disoriented when the job is the only arena they have in which to offer their nurturance. Those who go into the job market after starting a family often assuage their guilt by redoubling their nurturing efforts at home while intensifying their professional output at the office. In effect, they plug into a rigged defeat. In the struggle for self-realization, they tend to give up their own nurturance needs—perhaps deny that they have any at all—and, by assuming emotional distance, begin to feel stress, fatigue, and the first stages of burnout.

The problem becomes more convoluted when you do not know how to take. One woman may feel her only true position in life is being threatened, that the nurturing prerogative is being usurped. Another may feel that her nurturing attentions are barter material, that she can openly trade because she has some marketable emotional goods. Someone else may be extremely uncomfortable in the taking position—it's not compatible with her image of herself—or that she'll end up obligated in some way and experience a loss of control. More often than not, however, a nurturer doesn't know how to ask, and isn't even sure if what she's asking for is possible or politically correct. And so she continues to give, conscious that even though the behavior and orchestration feel right to her, she's experiencing an inner void.

That nurturing, however, is not always nourishing. It is sometimes experienced by others as "stuffing." Jenny, a 28-year-old woman who previously spoke of her conflict in firing a staff member, talked about her mother's nurturing patterns:

> "(She) was never satisfied with what you took from her or what she gave. There had to be more. At mealtimes, with company, she wasn't satisfied until the guests had three helpings . . . She'd insist you were still hungry and tyrannize our guests. 'If you don't have more I won't think you liked it,' she'd say, humiliating someone into yet another helping. It was very controlling, but it seemed to satisfy some deep need in her . . ."

In this case, the nurturing or feeding is a way of seeking mastery over one area in an otherwise subordinate life. This was Jenny's mother's only outlet for dominance. Other women gain significance, consequence, or a presence through the nurturing. When it becomes excessive, there is a franticness in the giving. A woman can lose perspective and her intuitive judgment. She only feels alive if she's putting out, for when she stops, she's confronted with the horror over how little is coming in.

Those are the negative sides to the nurturing issue. Most women have been endowed with an early nurturing training that is consciously or unconsciously grafted onto their lives. The training "takes," but later, as adults, they may find it difficult to have their own nurturance needs answered.

Let's look at a broad model of how a nurturer is trained.

A. *The Anatomy of a Nurturer*

The role of "giver" is not new to nurturing women. One of the first lessons a female child often learns, either on a conscious level or as an unconscious message, is how to anticipate. This lesson is then carried with her piggyback throughout her life. The model of the anticipator is usually acquired through her mother, the first person to attend to the child's world of needs—the first to provide against hunger, illness, and emotional deprivation. Even though mothers have a full complement of their own needs which are sometimes unmet, she understands that one of her functions is to care for her child and offer the support her daughter will need to become fully realized in her image. After all, mothers were once daughters and trained similarly.

Infants of both sexes first perceive themselves as being cared for, but you, as a female child, probably perceived that later you would in turn care for others. Watching your mother, you learned how to predict what was needed and by whom. You intuited who was angry, who needed attention, when to be quiet, when to be charming. And, you probably learned something about entertainment as well. Entertainment is a subplot of anticipation. Female children, taking cues from their mothers, understand that good entertainers are pleasant, amiable, cheerful, interesting, often flirtatious, and sometimes funny. Operating to a great extent upon senses and feelings, you, as a young female nurturer, learn to negotiate and often to manipulate the world of emotions, sometimes more successfully than your brothers. You're being trained to listen.

As a budding anticipator, you acquire an acute sensitivity to the needs of others, yet do not necessarily feel you're in charge of or able to mold your own environment. You may have understood that you were unable to shape your place and identity through pure logic, but that you could make yourself substantially known through the use of what you may have perceived as "feminine characteristics." Daughters frequently learn that girlish helplessness can have impact, that seductiveness works sometimes, but that being "good" is the key. "Goodness" means stuffing down any trace of anger or meanness of spirit. It connotes generosity, thoughtfulness, softness, gentleness, and putting others before yourself. Further, while you may have received the attention you craved when you were ingenuous, you could also receive punishment for audaciousness. In many families, a fine line is drawn between the two. You may at times be pleasingly impertinent, but you must be careful not to present yourself as an intelligent nuisance. When these behaviors are applauded, they are indelibly stamped on your consciousness as workable methods for holding your own—sometimes for your very survival.

Female children conditioned to be nurturers understand that to obtain the rewards of a good girl they must accurately anticipate the moods of the principals in their families. They must develop a profound sensitivity to facial expressions, body language, modes of dress, vocal sounds, and all other visual and aural symbols. One woman interviewed described her childhood this way:

> "I knew by my father's tie whether it was a bad night or a good one. If the knot was still in place when he came home, I could run up and kiss him. If it was undone or just loosened, I ran to my room and waited . . . And I could tell how my mother might act by the clatter of dishes in the kitchen. I knew there'd be a fight if the plates resounded a decibel higher when she placed them on the stove . . ."

This then is the essence of anticipation: interpreting signals—the whims and desires of those around you—before deciding upon the appropriate response to their presence. It is one of the first requirements of a nurturer. Yet, *in no way does this lesson take into account the daughter's need for nurturing, her skill in asking for it, or her ability to accept it when given.*

As a young nurturer grows older, she adds more nuances to her repertoire as care-giver. She incorporates the subtle colorations and textures of people into her perceptions and becomes fairly expert at predicting their emotional responses to situations and events. Since her powers of anticipation all but obscure what her own needs are, she offers herself and her services to others and develops a fine choreography of giving which mimics itself throughout her life. "I'm fine, thank you" becomes a standard phrase, followed closely by "Don't worry about me" and "Can I get you something to eat?" She may climb trees and play baseball outside of the house, but inside, she contains her fantasies of expansion, finding expression through reading books and observing others. If she's angry, she swallows the emotion, understanding all too well that, given the dynamic in her particular family, if she expresses it, she could lose the psychic support of her mother, her father, or older siblings. When hurt, she doesn't usually lash out—lashing out impulsively could lead to dire consequences. Instead, she takes the hurt back upon herself and, while trying to hold back tears, wonders what she did wrong.

Does this childhood experience have a familiar ring to you? If you identify with those feelings from the past, you may also remember understanding that you were completely dependent on your parents for your psychic safety and stability and may have gradually learned to stuff down the look of need, training yourself to control your emotions. You might have perceived that you could not win affection if you were a burden. Unless he was depressed himself, your father probably didn't respond well to a needy daughter, and your mother could have become edgy and clipped if confronted with yet another demand for her attention. As a result, you may have become surreptitious in the way you expressed yourself. You may have leaked your discontents through sarcasm or subtle putdowns. But those forms of expression are mild acts of self-assertion which may not have counted too much with the family, especially if they were not interpreted accurately. Too often, your caustic rejoinders were probably fluffed off with a curt one-liner—"She's going through her adolescent changes" or "They know everything at that age." If you remember those responses, you probably felt that they tended to diminish your individuality and demonstrated the lack of understanding you hoped you would defeat in your life as an adult.

Being a keen observer, you may have noted that special intimacy among women—between your mother and your mother's friends. The women were probably fairly open and expressive when discussing their private lives, but you may not easily have known how to incorporate their set of values and experiences into your life. What you heard could have been more complaint than activism, more standard values of their generation than radical expression of your own. And, while listening, you may secretly have felt that you were out of sync with their views, or that you were in some way damaged—that your own desires were in much larger proportion to what they said was available in life. Even though you maintained the fantasy of building your own Eden in your own way, you were probably frightened that you might not have the talent, skill, energy, or even the intelligence to create it.

Jenny also spoke about the fantasies she created when she was 14:

> "When I felt hurt or betrayed, or unseen, I'd sit in the bathtub and plan my future. I'd have a useful, appreciated, and somewhat glamorous job—maybe even be a movie star . . . but more important, I'd be with a man who put me first. I wasn't going to live out my mother's life—I was going to be recognized, loved for my specialness. I was going to be *understood,* you know, have a husband who would respect and adore me, and then I would go out and conquer the world. I remember feeling I could take care of everyone and everything, and that because *I* was so understanding, other people would *be there* for me. I'd never feel unseen again . . . You know, living in the future was my escape hatch. I had no idea how to make people understand me in the present . . . I didn't think I was smart enough, maybe pretty enough . . . I don't know. Whatever it was, I didn't have it."

Somewhere along the line, for many daughters, the nurturing they received as children vanishes and is replaced by approval. We all know that approval is coveted and that it helps build self-esteem. Yet, approval is often not enough to provide the measure of warmth and love commensurate with the neediness inside. Therefore, you may have reasoned that since you were so often longing for something else, something must be wrong with you—you must be lacking. Even though you learned to sometimes capture the approval of others, it didn't seem to heal the heart of neglect. You might have figured you weren't trying hard enough. Outwardly, no one else seemed to feel what you were feeling, so you may have suspected you were being selfish to expect to be touched in that raw, needing place. To conceal your unspecified flaw, you may have worked harder at caring for and giving to others, sometimes wondering how you could toughen yourself up even more. Perhaps, you reasoned, you should find a way to choke off your own needs and focus more intently on your intellectual and mental capabilities. In this way, you might blunt those intrusive yearnings which you already interpreted as "wrong." Aspects of this idea might have become fixed in your mind as an attitude to take on when coping with others.

At this point, you may have been fully tuned to the reactions of others, but ill-equipped to listen to your own needs. Like Jenny, you may have fantasized about fulfilling your needs but could hardly articulate them. They seemed to elude the language at your command. However, you could expertly hear and read the needing language of others, and probably applied your learned care-giving choreography to their needs instead.

B. *The Nurturer and Work*

As a young adult, determined to mold your own place, you may have moved into a career which has potential and interest, yet still find yourself yearning for something you can't accurately express. The skills you've acquired as a nurturer are no longer testable certainties here. In fact, you may find that to excel as a nurturer is not always advantageous or even desirable. With high expectations of yourself (and, consequently, of others), you work hard to prove yourself worthy and to inspire trust. But this expectation level, you swiftly discover, may be easier to achieve with friends than with colleagues.

At the office, you now anticipate what your colleagues need, what your boss needs, what the clients need. Intent on quelling your growing anxieties, you double up on your efforts and possibly become driven in the need to legitimize yourself. You may take on more work than you can handle, work overtime and weekends, help others with their workloads— but quickly discover that your efforts are not being rewarded, that you're gradually becoming something of a fixture, an unknowing colluder with the power structure. You're no longer thanked, you're expected. And the feelings generated by this situation are suspiciously familiar with those which you felt as a young girl.

Audrey, a marketing assistant for a clothing manufacturer, described that experience:

"I worked very hard to become competent and well liked at my job; I did it so well, I can do everyone else's work as well as mine. So, everyone depends on me. When push comes to shove, all the other assistants know that if they're not around, I'll do their work. Sometimes they sneak out of work because they know I'm there . . . and that I'm kind of a pushover. Sometimes I'm asked to take on a project which isn't mine because that person knows I'll do it better than his or her assistant. For a while this made me feel very special,

> but now I just feel used—taken for granted . . . I don't know how
> to change their attitude toward me . . . I'm really getting tired of
> it all . . ."

If you're in this situation, like Audrey, you may for a while calculate
that it's better to be expected and wanted than not, and that sooner or
later you'll reap the recognition and benefits of your goodwill. But the
benefits are not always forthcoming. This is especially frustrating when
someone who is not the good girl steps over your head and takes the
position you deserve.

The need to excel usually enlarges at this point and may compel you to
dig in deeper. You may also begin to realize that you don't know when or
how to back off—you haven't learned the fine line between attachment
and detachment. It's becoming clear that too much attachment is dangerous: it promotes dependency on others and then self-denial. Yet, too much
detachment may be frightening: it connotes a definition of yourself as
cold, remote, and aloof. Bouncing back and forth between the two extremes becomes fatiguing—you cannot seem to find the appropriate balance. Since you may not as yet have gained mastery over your professional
skills, and since the nurturing techniques you were taught at home have
little impact here, you may begin to feel ineffective and uncomfortably
powerless. Weariness eventually replaces eagerness. Understanding that
something is wrong, you may increasingly lack the energy to continue in
the same way and begin to complain of burnout.

Single women aren't the only ones targeted for the nurturer's dynamic
of conflict and stress at the office. As a married woman you may extend
your sense of family responsibility out toward others on your job. If you
feel emotionally neglected at home—if there is strife and distance within
your marriage—you may offer your nurturance to the "office family"
which becomes a compensatory relationship through which you may try to
fulfill your needs. And if you're returning to the job market after an
extended leave, or after a long-term marriage abruptly ends, you may look
to that same "office family" as the only outlet you have for feeling needed.
If you are a nurturer, your job can become the defining principle for your
self-worth. As such, you will probably find your endurance level diminishing, experience an annoying overtone of fatigue, and feel the emergence
of some physical symptoms which suspiciously point to burnout.

C. *The Nurturer and Lovers*

The recognition a nurturer seeks may be found in her personal life. Perhaps you meet a man or woman and for the first six weeks together you live in bliss. This is the Eden you've been waiting for. Someone is relating directly to you—to your needs, thoughts, actions, and your love. You both swear to be open and honest, to fight out the problem areas, to "be there" for each other, and never go to bed angry. Your nurturing impulses weren't "off" after all—your new mate basks in your attention and returns it in kind. But then you find your lover's attentiveness to you waning. Startled by this turn of events and overcome by a fresh wave of anxiety, you probably, once again, double your nurturing efforts—anticipating their moods, whims, and desires—hoping, by example, what you want will be understood. Soon, however, you might discover that here, too, you're not appreciated anymore—you're expected. When you try to articulate what it is you need, your lover may become distant and defensive. Your assertiveness techniques send them into a panic. What you basically feared is coming true: you have something lacking in you. Why else would you be so incapable of making yourself known? Why else would your demands be mistaken for criticism? Focusing on the terror of losing the relationship (even though it isn't making you the least bit happy), you may become obsessed with "fixing" it—but more to the point, fixing yourself. Exhausted by the continual battle against a losing proposition, you may tell a friend, "I think I'm burning out."

D. *The Nurturer and Women Friends*

As a single woman, you may have a friend or roommate with a similar nurturance struggle. Although you both may view your living arrangement as temporary, nonetheless, you build a small, intimate world together on which you both depend. But then your friend meets a lover, and, quite suddenly, you're alone again on Saturday night, astounded by the angry, hurt feelings welling inside of you. You may be mortified over these feelings of betrayal—after all, you're only friends and you've often spoken about how much you both want to find a lover. You're supposed to feel goodwill, but instead you feel abandoned. Now you're steeped in guilt as well as betrayal, and your sense of shame may drive you deeper into secrecy. You either distance yourself from your friend, or, in a counterphobic response, throw yourself into the storybook version of "good friend," "good person," "good girl," denying your feelings of envy and loss. To reveal these feelings would demonstrate that old meanness of spirit which, as nurturers know all too well, is taboo. Your denial and your nurturing impulses now grow in equal proportions. In short order, you begin to think of yourself as a "small" person, and realize you're burning out.

E. *The Nurturer as Single Parent*

As a single parent, your nurturing role is better etched, yet even more convoluted. Although this wasn't what you had in mind for yourself (you never imagined you'd be raising your children alone), you may be driven to overcome your considerable anguish by devoting yourself to your children's needs. Soon, however, your need for a personal life intrudes upon your devotion, and as you begin to go out with other men and form new alliances with women, your guilt augments. Frustrated by the little time you have for yourself, by your lack of privacy for intimate sexual relationships, by demanding the promised monthly child-support check which may or may not arrive on time, by working, shopping, locating baby-sitters and day-care centers, you may, once again, experience that dreaded meanness of spirit. Occasionally you may flare up, but afterward be stricken by contrition. To make up for these "lapses," you might intensify your good mothering and again begin to deny your needs. In speaking with your women friends, you may state with certainty, "I'm afraid I'm burning out."

F. *The Nurturer and the Dual Career*

As a woman in a dual-career marriage, especially if there is a child, you may find yourself in a head-on collision with your mother's values. The "good nurturer" role, so thoroughly absorbed from your training, is now challenged by aspirations outside the home. As you pursue your career, you may experience yourself as abandoning your family and be beset with guilt. Your own ambitions may be at war with your mother's imprint and metamorphose into anger at your mother. The guilt/anger syndrome perpetuates a psychic drain on you. Each time you ask your husband to attend to a household task, and each time your child says, "Mommy, do you have to go . . ." your "wrongness" is reinforced. To compensate for what you view as your inability to handle all of your elective roles and to satisfy your child, your husband, and your mother's voice, you become supermom and wife. You try to keep your complaints to a minimum (to voice dissatisfaction would be admitting defeat), to reflect an earnestness of will, and to make it all right for everyone but yourself. The continual denial of yourself promotes ever more anxiety and keeps you psychically hopping. In time, you too will begin to experience a disenchantment with aspects of your life and realize you're burning out.

Of course, these are only a few examples of the dynamics the nurturer brings to bear upon her life. There are an infinite number of tasks your servicing functions direct you to do. You may also feel compelled to be a good listener, to be available for every emotional emergency, to lend money and clothes, to bring two dishes to the party when everyone else was elected for one, to be on call for help, support, advice—as well as insightful perceptions—and to create a warm intimacy between people in your constellation. Again, not surprisingly, as a nurturing woman, you may frequently not believe you have the right to say "no," or to ask for anything for yourself—even in return. When and if the nurturing is returned, however, you're probably at sea for what to do with it. You may be overwhelmed with self-consciousness, gratitude, or guilt over not being stronger and more autonomous than you actually are.

In essence, nurturers have a proclivity for long-term burnout. Sometimes there is an expectation of returns on their nurturing investment, but, as was stated above, just as often they have incorporated that role as standard practice. It's not too difficult to understand why the care-giving nurturer is a marked candidate for burnout.

BURNOUT: ALONENESS AND LONELINESS

Scores of women who put out enormous expenditures of energy and concentration have nothing or no main person to nurture them in return. If illness doesn't land on them, fatigue, a sense of despair, aloneness, or loneliness often does. When a woman has been actively nurturing, pleasing, servicing, and catering to everyone but herself, the emotional deprivation transforms into feelings of aloneness, and from aloneness into alienation—an experience which is palpably painful and draining.

If you are single, widowed, divorced, or separated, you may just be beginning to understand that you may have sole responsibility for your financial, social, and domestic lives, perhaps for the rest of your life. This notion takes a hard emotional toll, especially on a woman who has always envisioned a future of a shared life with a mate.

How can you do it all alone when you were groomed for something unequivocably different? The fear of such a life is twofold. First is loneliness, which indicates an absence of intimacy with others; the second is aloneness, which is experienced as a lack of closeness with yourself. The loneliness and aloneness factors are startling and often trigger panic. When the perception or the reality of sole responsibility strikes, it can have the force of an electric charge, shocking the woman into an immediate reevaluation of her priorities and options.

Lisa, a research assistant at a pharmaceutical lab, described that shocking moment this way:

> "I had just turned 35, and had broken up with a man I'd been living with for some time. I figured I'd probably meet someone else fairly soon, but as time went by I realized it wasn't happening, and there didn't seem to be many eligible men around. I saw that I had no intimate relationships in my life, and then it hit me. 'Good God,' I thought, 'I'm responsible for my own life and probably always will be! My job doesn't pay me very much and there's the very real possibility that I never will get married.' I knew I had to support myself . . . I had to get my life together, fast! Then I really became frantic and scared."

Hard-hit by the possibility that there may never be a mate with whom to connect as a friend, to share financial and domestic responsibilities, to share the bed, or to love, women who are burnout prone often hurl themselves into a mental anguish which accelerates their anxiety and promotes a fear of the future. The shopping bag lady may become a symbol of all that could go wrong. She summons up visions of desolation, homelessness, lovelessness, and utter abandonment. Many, many women readily identify themselves with her. The perception creates a deep dread.

To offset this nagging perception, you may surround yourself with a collection of friends upon whom you can shower your nurturance and, as a result, begin to feel valued and safe. An abundance of activity masks the feelings of incipient isolation. Frequently though, you may overextend and exhaust yourself with ceaseless caring for each and every friend. Dorothy, a 35-year-old publicist, knows this experience well:

> "I spent a lot of time racing around, filling up spaces, and making sure I'd never be alone. I had dozens of friends and my phone rang incessantly. Sometimes I'd have fifteen calls on my phone machine at night . . . that made me feel esteemed and safe. If there were only one or two calls, I'd panic. I was constantly disbursing advice and comfort—I knew what everyone was up to and what plans were being made. I was also very busy arranging meetings, parties, dinners . . . I couldn't stand being alone. As long as I was in demand, I didn't have to deal with that issue . . . I was too busy. I was also a wreck . . . Then I backed off—I stopped a lot of the nurturing . . . I was beginning to feel burned out on friends. But I backed off too far and spent too much time alone. I'm not reconciled with this panic or loneliness . . . with my empty bed. I just don't like it. What if I don't meet someone . . . ?"

Dorothy's conflict is very real. Somewhere between the "racing around, filling up spaces" and placing herself in quarantine is a balance she's trying to find. Some of what she wants is already there—a career, friends she can call on, a semblance of financial security—but she doesn't have what she needs, warmth and closeness, that special intimate connection with a man. Her sense of the future is continually being jarred by the absence of that mate.

The fear of sole responsibility is intensified when, as Lisa earlier suggested, a significant relationship is broken off and a woman finds herself without the primary person she was taught she eventually would have. She's not only lost the tangible sharing of her life, she's lost her source of nurturance—her intimate support has been lopped off. Her life immediately becomes characterized by exigencies of awesome proportions. Decisions are now laden with a sense of emergency. Carving out a safe place for herself—and doing it swiftly—becomes imperative. She must earn enough money, settle career issues, opt for an immediate promotion or change jobs, safeguard children, provide herself with a satisfactory social life, and, most crucial, learn to live with what could be a very realistic but nonetheless brutal revamping of future plans.

The perception of aloneness or loneliness in the future can also be quite insidious. As often as it strikes with sudden clarity, it can just as often evolve slowly, without fanfare. For women who have built a denial structure around their lives, the holidays often trigger a profound vulnerability to the aloneness and loneliness in their lives. Glenda, a 42-year-old woman, divorced for six years, had this experience:

> "When I was growing up, over the holidays our house was the center of activity. My mother and I cooked for an army . . . We invited friends and other people my mother called 'strays.' Those were the people who had nowhere to go and didn't have any family. I was always especially nice to the 'strays'; I couldn't understand how they managed to be so alone. When I was married, my house was again the center of activity, and I 'became my mother' on the holidays. I repeated the whole event, invited close friends and all the 'strays' I knew. After my divorce, the holidays became a nightmare. My second Christmas alone, I was invited to the home of friends—a married couple. I knew then that I, too, had become a 'stray,' and the insight was brutal . . ."

Other women are pressured into reassessing their lives and their futures as their childbearing years approach and fade. Still others suddenly realize that their job setting doesn't provide them with the community needed to offset the loneliness they feel in other crucial areas of their lives. Some are alerted to the possibility of aloneness and loneliness by the absence of lovers and the shortage of prospects "out there." "I don't know where to meet men and I'm tired of looking" is a common lament of many single women. Lisa told this story:

> "After my breakup, everyone told me I had to 'put myself out there.' That's just what I did . . . I went to every function, party, lecture . . . museums on weekends, as my friends suggested—'You never know where you'll meet someone, Lisa' . . . I learned how to ask for telephone numbers at parties, and even made calls and went out a few times. But I just don't like doing it that way. I think of myself as liberated, but I guess I'm really traditional inside. I'm uncomfortable switching roles . . . It's not the way I was raised. I'm forcing an issue on myself . . . I'm pressuring myself into be-

havior that doesn't feel right . . . I think I've got mate-search burnout."

Lisa's plight is repeated over and over by many women. Caught between old conditioning and a newer, fledgling code of behavior, these women often speak of feeling drained and depleted by the struggle. Yet, the other extreme—waiting to be asked, waiting to be chosen, waiting to be called—is often described as "morally debilitating." Few women are content to revert to those old waiting patterns and are justifiably rebelling against that passive stance. But they're caught in a cultural bind. "We're very focused on keeping busy," Lisa added.

"At my office the telephone conversations are a clue to the restlessness women feel. On Monday and Tuesday you can hear people saying, 'What did you do over the weekend?' On Wednesday there's a lull. On Thursday you hear 'What are you going to do on the weekend?' and by Friday it's pandemonium—'What shall we do tonight?' 'Where should we go?' 'Can I come along with you—I just don't want to spend the night alone . . .' A lot of energy is consumed by weekend panic."

Loneliness is a psychic, emotional longing for closeness—a need to be part of someone or something. When your nurturance needs are unfulfilled, you might place all of your vital energies in a relationship that is essentially unproductive—perhaps even destructive. You may choose a man or woman who is dependent and needy in the extreme—an alcoholic or drug abuser—someone whom you can "help," "support," or "straighten out." Some women speak of burning out on loneliness in their marriages or with their live-in mates. The fear of "ending up alone" perpetuates denial in these relationships—you may cling to the illusion of intimacy on which you can lean to avoid an uncertain future. And often, if a male or female mate is not available, then, out of loneliness, you may funnel all of your energies into a job or profession. This, then, becomes the nurtured object which serves to diminish feelings of isolation.

Any one of these aloneness or loneliness factors or "cures" can provoke the type of obsessive mental and physical activity which feeds burnout. Since most women were not trained or impressed with the possibility of living alone, and since our culture up to this point has not made affirmative accommodations for the woman alone, viable options for closeness

rs must be rethought. If the habit of denying loneliness continued ..o long, it can propel you into the serious stages of the Burnout
Cycle.

BURNOUT AND POWERLESSNESS

It follows that the reasons behind women's burnout are closely bound to
the issues women bring into psychotherapy and counseling offices. Many
of those reasons are related to societal expectations—positions and definitions culturally assigned to women—and, more often than not, find their
genesis in the lack of nurturance—the relinquishing of dependency needs
—aloneness, loneliness, and the loss of power in their lives. It's in these
areas that the conflict you may experience between your authentic inner
content (feelings and needs) and your assumed external style (behavior
and image) can become aggravated. Typically, through your socialization
you learned that, along with being a care-giver, if you do your job with
excellence and perfection you can then expect approval rewards for merit.
And yet, experience isn't necessarily in sync with the messages you've
absorbed. Often you may find that authenticity and dedication are not
freely rewarded and, more frequently, that those in power positions (particularly on the job, but just as often in the home) reject behavior which
does not preserve their rank and status.

Women are often locked out of power constellations and must do fierce
battle to gain entrance and visibility. Or, if you are let in, you feel you
must perform not only impeccably but twice as well as your male counterparts to prove you've earned the right to remain.

Katherine, a woman who has been engaged in such a corporate battle
for many years, offered this perception:

> "I think women really do buy the American dream: if you're really
> very good at what you do, you're going to be rewarded and accepted
> eventually. I'm not so sure that happens. The power structure's been
> fortified against interlopers and an enormous number of career
> women are now having to deal with it . . . It's just very exhausting
> . . ."

Repressing resentments and frustrations while performing optimally
and faultlessly is an imprisoning stress. You may feel you're, once again,

caught in a tangled web of attempts to better yourself. When and if you falter, you may dig in with even greater tenacity. You may fuse up with the notion of perfectionism, which hopefully will provide you with approval, of course, but, more important, with recognition and its subsequent rewards. Unlike your male counterpart, however, if you do falter, you're likely to indict yourself first. After all, you always knew something was lacking . . . something indefinable. You may become confused, then stumped, begin to doubt your own abilities, then question your own competence. In the end, you may seek to blame yourself for your own alleged deficiencies.

Not uncommonly, each woman believes that her experience on the job is exclusively hers. Given the excess of job responsibilities, however, you may claim you have no time to speak with other women about their doubts and anxiety reactions, or you just may not trust others enough to seek the validation you need. When you do fraternize with your peers and begin to understand that your powerlessness is a prevailing condition, many of your fears may be allayed. But you may still be stuck with professional impotence and feel you must continue to drive yourself toward perfection.

Some women may reason that if they "become like" those in the dominant power structure, they might be recognized as like kind and, though not completely accepted, they might at least be promoted and paid accordingly. Adopting the trappings of those in authority may temporarily provide you with the illusion of power and help you conceal your vulnerabilities. You may even be told to change your style—your pace, your manner of speaking, your clothes, your sense of humor. In a rush of determination, you might try to conform as suggested but soon find you're disoriented and are "becoming someone else." Even if you are successful in your attempt to ape the aggressiveness, the formidable competitive maneuvers, the shrewder manipulations, and join the underground of corporate politics, you still may not reap the expected rewards. Perhaps you'll be promoted but later find you're not making the same money as your male counterparts, and the powerlessness becomes numbing.

Either way, you may still be locked out of what many women call the "Men's Club" and continue to experience the subtle exclusions. Katherine stated:

"I'm very visible when we're meeting with clients, but I'm politely and systematically shunned at the watercooler. The men have their own private culture. When they won't let you in on the joke, 'forget' to inform you of how a deal turned out, or bond in special groups at office functions, you begin to experience a palpable alienation. After a while, the exclusions just wear you down . . ."

This kind of powerlessness metamorphoses into anger, frustration, and an all-pervading sense of futility. Many women, unable to find solutions, take the exclusion as personal criticism and look inwardly to consider their "flaws." This misguided accusation does not help to assuage the burnout momentum. Conversely, it has a galvanizing effect which propels women deeper into the latter stages of burnout.

BURNOUT AND THE DEPENDENCY/AUTONOMY CONTROVERSY

To overcome the powerlessness in your life, you may be attempting to sort out how much dependency is acceptable and how much autonomy is necessary. Over the past few years, autonomy has become a woman's synonym for salvation, and dependency has suffered a bad name. Colette Dowling's *The Cinderella Complex* gave a concrete voice to the frustrations women were feeling about not only themselves as the financial dependents of men, but also their own hidden desires for dependency. The message was clear. By taking charge of your own choices, you could "unlearn" your "helplessness," become a self-sufficient, spontaneous human being, and, in the end, learn to love yourself.

Women began to perceive Dowling's notion of "springing free" from all dependencies as the final solution to their painfully felt conflicts. Emotional liberation would be forthcoming through a good job and financial responsibility. By unleashing ambition, women would find the right way to alter old deferential modes of behaving and could then begin to live unfettered by powerlessness. Dowling's analysis was accurate, but the focus was limited. For many women, autonomy has become confused with "doing it alone," and dependency with the desire to "cling."

Over the past few years these issues have become more complex than initially expected. Many of you now find yourselves attracted by the idea of autonomy but repelled by the blanket dismissal of your dependency needs. New and unanticipated conflicts emerge replete with ambiguities and contradictions. The push for financial autonomy in the professional arena may have eased some of the burden for some of you, but the context —the environment in which women by necessity must operate—has not always proved to be compatible with your values or training. The same holds true in the private arena: personal relationships have not kept pace with the burgeoning feminist consciousness. While women have been reaching out for domestic autonomy and trying to alter the balance of power in their personal relationships, many emotional needs have been inhibited. "How can I say I'm hurt or threatened or feeling neglected when I'm trying to be independent and autonomous?" one woman said. "It's a real bind. I feel I must be consistent to be taken seriously, but I don't feel consistent . . . The vigilance is very tiring . . ." Afraid of what her contradictory feelings imply, she is trying to sort out the compromises she can allow herself to make without feeling she's regressed. Some women say they feel a sense of shame. Having done all the "right things," they speak of still feeling inadequate, angry, and often scared. Others feel the strain of being good adherents to the autonomy principle and yet are embarrassed by their need for what they call "something else." They fear that the "something else"—that basic human need for closeness and affiliation—is the old hated dependency coming up to haunt them.

Unable or unwilling to express their emotional needs—needs that are experienced as the enemy of independence—you may be denying your true feelings and pretending to fit into what appears to be the accepted mode of behavior. Often, you don't know how to ask for what you need, and when you can, you experience yourself, at home, as "demanding" or "nagging" and, at work, as a "ball-buster."

Cynthia, a 26-year-old financial analyst, who has been in her job for a little over a year, related an anecdote which highlights this conflict:

> "I've succeeded in creating an image for myself at work which is, I believe, appropriately professional . . . I know when I walk into the office who I'm supposed to be and how I'm supposed to behave. But once in a while someone says something which completely throws me. Just last week a male colleague said, 'I think you're going to be one of those career women who's never going to get married.' Suddenly I got very scared. I began to believe that I've made myself

too independent—is this how people see me? But then, that's the image I want to portray at work—in a business sense it's got to be a plus. But personally, well, he really got to me . . . It's terribly confusing."

Cynthia's story is not uncommon. Like many of you, she's struggling to sort out her roles and to accept her desire for a professional and a private life. When her need for intimacy is denied for too long; the cool demeanor she's so skillfully erected becomes threatened. Like Cynthia, some of you may also become easily undermined by external critics. If you're coping with this issue, you may fear that, on the one hand, you'll be seen as "too independent" and, on the other, as what another woman called "needy and desperate," and so the denial game gets rougher.

The need these women are attempting to conceal is that primary longing for affiliation. "Doing it alone" rings of sturdy individualism, but it doesn't satisfy the need for closeness—an intimacy with one, many, or a whole community. The desire to be understood, to be seen, heard, taken in, or simply to lean on someone else for a while, has become so thoroughly emmeshed with dependent "clinginess" that, when confronted with their own desires for affiliation, many women become frightened and often develop a phobic mistrust of their feelings. The conflict then is firmly established: to become autonomous you must relinquish the hold your basic needs and humanity have on you. This is the very basis for burnout.

Today when a woman speaks of her deep desire to be with a mate, if she suggests that she might feel incomplete without her own person, if she yearns for affiliation, knowing as she does the strength she gleans from it, she might do so with a shade of embarrassment. Her politics may not be consistent with her feelings. She may believe that to be truly autonomous she must live within an uncomfortable sovereignty, matching her male counterparts who, all too often, will not relate to their deeper needs.

Scrambling for some balance between what you want—the right to make your own choices, or autonomy—and what you need—the right to rely on others for satisfaction, or dependency—you may feel at odds with your life, at sea with how to proceed, and conflicted by the gains and losses each implies for you. Autonomy as defined is both attractive and threatening. It promises to make you a strong, self-confident person but could springboard you into aloneness. Dependency, as defined, is both repelling and desirable. It may have victimized you in the past, yet it's an integral part of close, intimate relationships. Can you be independent and still get the nurturing you need? Can you hope to rely on others and not lose the ground you've gained?

Bewildered by these unanswered questions, you may find yourself becoming too vulnerable to the external and internal demands of your life. Assessing each demand in light of the newer rules in our society may prove exhausting in itself. As a consequence, you may find that, at best, you're denying your conflicts and stuffing them away, or, at worst, disengaging from any source of intimacy. With the passage of time and the continual exercise of restraint, you may discover you've been catapulted into burnout.

As women move away from formerly imposed subordinate roles, and as the old norms slowly convert into new accepted conventions, the boundaries by which you have historically defined yourself become blurred. What is possible and feasible for you? And, what is excessive? The tricky part in defining the reasons why women burn out comes from the confusion over the demands in your life. What is considered "normal" and what is construed as "excessive"? When should you back off, and when should you carve out another piece of the pie for yourself? Only a close scrutiny can distinguish between the efforts of a healthy, "normal" challenge and the excessiveness which promotes burnout.

If you've been bumping up against a wall of limits and continue to bang your head against it at all odds without making a substantial dent, your expectations can be said to be "excessive" and you're probably an excellent candidate for burnout. If, however, you perceive you cannot penetrate that wall, back off, and look for alternatives—perhaps climbing over, walking around, tunneling under, or, failing that, changing your direction entirely—your expectations can be construed as realistic and your efforts as a healthy challenge.

Katherine described it this way:

> "Psychologically it's a very tiring thing to keep on pushing. But, until you come up against that wall, you don't believe you'll fail, at least consciously. What this means is that when any relationship starts failing—in work or in love—you've got to change it or leave it.

You've got to alter it or get out. Like a bad love affair, it's only a matter of time before you'll find yourself pushed out or burned out."

The difference then between a healthy challenge and the process of burnout can only be measured by the rigidity or flexibility, intensity, and degree of your control, judgment, or involvement. When you feel you're burning out on overnurturing, on aloneness, on loneliness, on powerlessness, or on too much autonomy, the only true yardstick you can apply is that of your own inner experience.

CHAPTER III

Some Family Dynamics
of Women's Burnout

"It's only been in the past few years that I've thought it would
be nice to have a daughter—it would be wonderful to have a
little girl who would grow up now instead of when I did . . ."

Barbara A.

Stop here for a moment. Do you ever feel that, although you're an
adult in an adult world, your inner life is duplicating your childhood? Do
you perceive the feelings with which you live to be draining and repetitive? The way in which you burn out can usually be traced to the family
dynamics from your particular past. Why not take a few minutes now and
look over the following list of questions. Before answering them, reflect on
each one and try to recollect accurately those scenarios from your past that
each summons up:

1. Did your parents make it difficult for you to think for yourself?
2. Were your parents overcritical and overdemanding?
3. Did your mother behave as if she was less important than your
   father?
4. Was your father distant, noncommunicative, or lacking in affection?
5. Was your mother or father an alcoholic, on drugs, highly neurotic
   or disturbed?

6. Were you ashamed of either or both of your parents?
7. Did your mother insist you do everything "her way"?
8. Did you have a brother who was given more privileges than you?
9. Did you have a sister with whom you were in competition?
10. Were you the only or favored child thrust into an adult role prematurely?
11. As the youngest or favored child, were you rewarded for being "sweet" or "cute"?
12. Were you reluctant to expose any feelings of hurt, disappointment, or sadness in front of your parents?
13. Did you feel compelled to keep your fantasies and aspirations a secret?
14. Were you rarely allowed any privacy?
15. Were you left alone to care for yourself and, as a result, did you impose your own strict set of criticisms on your behavior?
16. Were you ever talked about as being awkward, lazy, ugly, stupid, or inept?
17. When you wanted something for yourself, were you accused of being selfish and self-centered?
18. Did you feel guilty over being brighter than other members of your family, and did you hide your intelligence?
19. Were you never seen as "good" enough?
20. Did you develop a false front to cover your true feelings?

If you answered "yes" to more than six or eight of these questions, there's a good chance that much of your energy is siphoned off today by internal scuffles with the past. Understanding how your family interacted with each other, how that interaction affected you, and how it impacts on your individual worldview today can be critical to identifying and halting much of the *unseen burnout activity* in your present life.

All of us are guided to some extent by deep family impressions from the past. Whether you're a woman who has broken with tradition or one who has basically conformed, those impressions, the messages received and absorbed from the hands of mothers, fathers, sisters, and brothers, die hard. A family unit is much like a small culture with a language and laws of its own. It has its own unwritten philosophy which permeated the general ambience in your home and which dictated the ways in which you would survive in the larger world. That philosophy included the allegiances between family members, the roles each member assumed, the quality of communication in the household, and the family principles, spoken or unspoken, which are usually meted out as commands for proper conduct. All those complex interrelationships molded the patterns for how to behave, think, and feel toward yourself and others in the present. Sadly, too many of those attitudes fail in the adult world. Some were based on anxiety and fear and, when shifted onto new situations and people in the present, fall short of their expected return.

Do you ever feel debilitated by your own reactions and responses to people and events in your life? Part of that internal weariness comes from a constant reliving of old family themes. When attitudes and feelings you learned and adopted from your home of the past are shifted onto new people and situations in the present, you're engaged in what's called the process of transference.

TRANSFERENCE AND BURNOUT

That unseen burnout activity referred to earlier can often be linked to transference. The main characteristic of this psychological phenomenon is the experience of feelings toward another person that do not pertain to that individual but to someone from the past. A time warp has been activated. You're not relating to the reality of the person in front of you but to an old emotional trigger from someone else who influenced your feelings years ago. The transference reaction is usually inappropriate, unsuitable, and ill-fitting to the situation. Whether you find yourself overreacting or underreacting, when a historical reproduction of responses is distorting the situation, it becomes an issue of confused or mistaken identity.

Consider this. When you moved from your parents' home to one of your own, you would have thought it bizarre to use the same key to the new lock. The old key simply wouldn't fit. You may have held on to the familiar key for visits, but when you approached your new door you picked the appropriate key from the ring. The new key with its different serrations is needed for the new cylinder. This applies to people and situations in the present as well. Old feelings do not necessarily apply to new situations.

Transference reactions are not only difficult to put in check, they're difficult to identify. Sandra, a 42-year-old woman with children from a previous marriage, was trying to sort out the problems she was encountering with John, her fiancé. She told the following anecdote:

> "Both of us are always right. No matter who ultimately gave in, during our arguments neither of us wanted to budge from our positions. John would tell me I sounded like my mother, and I would counter that he sounded like his. He would yell, 'I'm not your father!' and I would yell back, 'No, you're *yours!*' One evening we were squabbling and it occurred to me that although he and I were alone, there were actually six of us in the room—his parents, mine, and us. We weren't seeing each other with our individual differences, we were seeing our own parents in front of us and rallying old defenses to protect ourselves from new threats . . . . His fear of me was a carbon copy of his past, and my basic anger at him predated our meeting by years. We have real difficulties, but we're both making an effort to address ourselves to the present issues now . . ."

Sandra's transference reactions are not limited to her personal love relationships. They also show up at work with figures of authority, competitive colleagues, friendships, and others in the world who have positions of influence. And they're not always repetitions of doubt, anger, and fear, but sometimes of wish fulfillment. Most of us can relate to areas of neglect in our upbringing. In an attempt to correct the past, transference reactions are sometimes triggered by a person or situation who is seen through past-colored glasses as an idealized savior. In this case, judgment is clouded, and disappointment, hurt, or feelings of betrayal often emerge.

Many women who are burnouts talk about the repetitive quality of their poorer choices of people as lovers, confidantes, or trustworthy colleagues. Others speak about the repetitive nature of their responses to older women, men in power, those who are officious or imperious, those who are wealthier or more impoverished, or those who are interior and inexpressive. The issues are infinite. What's important, however, is for you to understand that your specific issue can be broken apart and examined. If you're knocking yourself out by the same repetitive behavior and you're making no headway in your life, you might look to those transference reactions which are a direct result of old family dynamics.

One way to begin is to sort out who you allied yourself with in the family and how those relationships influence your attitudes today.

FAMILY ALLEGIANCES AND BURNOUT

Think about the allegiances within your family. They're frequently based on invisible contracts that were developed early, then refined, and over time became unshakable. These contracts determine the degree of loyalty or disloyalty you could allow yourself to demonstrate, and were probably based on identification with the parent who, for you, had the most power or offered the most support. For instance: Was your mother the one who bestowed warmth, affection, and understanding in your home? If so, you, as the daughter, may have been loathe to side with your father in a dispute, yet torn because you desperately longed for his approval. Thus, a conflict was erected. Conversely, if your father was encouraging and generous, and your mother critical and picky, the invisible contract may have stated you remain loyal to your dad at the expense of the more frequent, day-to-day relationship with mom. If the conflict was too unwieldy, you may have had an invisible contract with yourself which advised you to maintain the family equilibrium by expressing loyalty to both parents (or neither), and hold your own discordant views secret.

These are only a few examples. There are invisible contracts between sisters and brothers, and other family members. The combinations are intricate and set a tone, if not a pattern, for how you will act and react to situations and people later in your life. As you recall your own contracts with your mother and father, think about how those allegiances influence you today. Remember: history repeats itself.

Here are a few attitudes you might hold today in response to those past allegiances:

—When a dispute between a woman and a man flares, you tend to immediately side with the woman, right or wrong, out of an old allegiance to, and sympathy with, your mother.
—On the job, you feel emotionally pulled toward the man with the most power only because the transference reaction duplicates the old experience of trying to win approval from your father.
—You feel disloyal and guilty when you don't agree with a friend in a public dispute.

—To avoid being drawn into a conflict, you remain quiet when a confrontation between friends or colleagues erupts.

As you can see, the dynamics of family allegiances are carried into the present and act as ongoing stress-extenders. The contracts in your adult life may have become riddled with conflict and, therefore, are experienced as pressure situations from which you may need to disengage.

FAMILY ROLES AND BURNOUT

Do you remember the roles each member of your family assumed or was assigned? Were they carved-in-granite definitions, or were they fluid, changing as necessity dictated? Roles in family life are often specific and, to a great extent, influenced by the culture.

In your home, who was responsible for household chores? And who was responsible for delegating tasks? Were any delegated to male members? Were the financial burdens—making money, paying the bills—the private bailiwick of your father, or were they shared by both parents? Did your mother have to ask for household or personal money? And what about social functions? Who initiated leisure events; who invited friends over; who accepted invitations? Did one parent usually need to be coaxed or cajoled into a family outing, and then, again, into enjoying it? The division of roles and labor in your household has undoubtedly done much to influence your feelings about the "shoulds" and "musts" of your life—whether you've broken with or adhered to family traditions.

While these roles are usually predesignated, other roles are not as clearly defined. But they carry a lot of weight. Think back to how you identified yourself, or how you were identified by other family members in your home. It may be easier to recollect your role by recalling the interaction that took place over dinner. Dinnertime seems to trigger the most succinct and powerful memories for women.

Were you the family "appeaser," the one who quieted arguments or incipient flare-ups by giving in to demands? Or were you the family "neutralizer," the one who anticipated trouble, then diverted it with benign expressions of goodwill? If you were the "referee," you may have learned vigilance in discerning the rules of fair play and mediated balance at the table. Or perhaps you were the "care-giver," the one whom everyone depended upon for sympathetic support because you never made waves. Some women remember themselves as the family "sparkler," the one who learned to garner attention and disarm her parents by developing an enthusiastic personality and a repertoire of chatty school stories. Others acted the part of family "comedienne," the one who used humor to ward off confrontations, suspicion, or anger. On the other end of the role spectrum, you may have been the "troublemaker," the one who provoked family passions to gain attention, or the "leave-taker," the one who insured her position by threatening a hasty exit if trouble brewed. Many more women, however, have spoken of being the "quiet absorber," the family member who remained mute, and through her silence implied consent. This silent suffering may have served as a precursor for a future inability or unwillingness to speak out—often at your own expense.

These are the nonspecific roles within families, roles which are sometimes assumed in the spirit of cooperation and community, but just as often are taken on to maintain an identity, to offset anxiety, or to assuage a sense of peril. If you think about it, the roles you recognize as your own are probably still very evident in your relationships today. You may be seeking endorsement from men and women in your present life with the same overtones of that family dinner. Do any of these responses ring a bell?

—When a person or event is triggering situational anxiety, you tend to be a "sparkler," and turn on your personality to maintain control.
—At business meetings you're likely to focus much of your attention on those who are under the gun, and spend more time internally appeasing them than concentrating on the issues.
—When a confrontation threatens, you tend to make excuses and absent yourself.
—Although you may be gregarious in other circumstances, you tend to become mute in the face of threatened disputes and almost pretend as if you aren't there.

Once again, the roles you assumed in the past are remobilized in the present. But they aren't necessarily functional now. In fact, when you feel compelled to reenact the same obsolete roles over and over again in new circumstances, spontaneity is obliterated by those preconceived ideas of who you "should" or "shouldn't" be. You may be hooked into many transference reactions which are cutting into your energy and wearing you down.

FAMILY COMMUNICATION AND BURNOUT

The ways in which you and your family communicated are essential to understanding how your energies are meted out today. Communication between family members basically refers to the intimacies that were freely given to or withheld from you.

Families reveal their feelings through the affections displayed or withheld in the household, through talking or silence, discussing, or playing. Clues to who was comfortable or uncomfortable with whom become highlighted when you recall exactly how individuals communicated with each other. Did your family work as a cohesive, supportive unit? Or could the individuals be characterized as self-serving and self-centered? Was there a mutuality of interests, or did one person dominate the family and drain the others with excessive demands and criticism? Did you really feel a part of the family intimacy, or only as an onlooker? Did the discussions breed closeness, or did they promote isolation and fear? The degree to which communication was invited or rejected is important to understanding how much stress was engendered in you at an early age. You may be repeating futile and exhaustive patterns in the present.

To put together an adequate picture of the communication in your home, you might want to try this exercise. Write down on a pad of paper how you remember your family. Consider each member individually, and then in twos or threes. How did each communicate with you and with each other? What was the basic content of their communication and was it consistent? Did members change when someone else entered the room or answered the phone? And, how did you experience yourself in relation to each individual? Make as many notes to yourself as you can recall.

What were their styles of communicating? There are many different styles, and not all of them include talking. For instance, one of your parents may have had a repertoire of "looks," facial expressions which denoted approval, disapproval, ridicule, annoyance, or love. Another may have used silence to indicate authority or to mete out punishment. Sighs or grunts could have been signals of discouragement, lack of caring, or a postponement of a response, as in "I'll think about it later." Certain body language—tightly crossed arms, lowered head, hands on hips, or a wagging leg—could have been information leaks concerning accessibility or inaccessibility. There are women who have reported that their distant fathers communicated through gifts and money, while their mothers indicated love through food.

Try to remember the content of their communication. The content is as critical as the style. Parents who gave out mixed messages promoted a sense of unreliability. An anxious mother may have verbally communicated "I love you," yet continually criticized your method for attending to tasks, your clothes, your room, your friends, or your interests. The message could have been interpreted as "I love you, but only if you do it my way." The submessage may have been disparaging: "Don't think for yourself—you're inept and will never get it right." An anxious father may have ignored your personal life, yet hounded you about school, achievement, and academic excellence. That message might have been decoded as "My approval is just around the corner . . . but there'll always be another corner." The submessage may have been: "Your needs are unimportant, perhaps silly, maybe too 'feminine'—success and achievement will win you love." A classic mixed message for women is a simple statement, "Don't be selfish," followed by the refusal to listen to your conflicts. The submessage here: "Your inner life is not important, and therefore wrong," which, in many cases, increasingly distorts the content of your own thoughts and feelings.

Did your mother speak differently when you were alone with her than when your father was present? Was your father in collusion with your mother in her presence, yet a gentle intimate when she was away? Did you and a brother or sister have a special bond which changed in the presence of your parents? Were there enemy camps and safe places in your house? Did members gossip about each other behind their backs? Perhaps you learned to mistrust certain groupings of people, and now, as an adult, transfer those perceptions of mistrust onto new relationships.

How you experienced yourself with each family member is significant, as it will provide clues to your inner experience with people today. One woman remembers that she felt "incompetent and, I guess, lazy. My mother did everything fast; she was in constant motion, cleaning, shopping, gardening, cooking. She got angry when I read because that was 'sitting down,' and annoyed when I wasn't involved in a chore of some kind. I used to walk faster when she was around . . . turn up my volume and look happy. With my father I felt uninformed and frivolous, so I'd ask him what I thought were important questions about politics or sports, and with my younger brother, I felt like a baby-sitter. I was the oldest, and responsible for watching out for him, but he had more liberty because he was a boy." Another woman remembers feeling angry around her mother because "she was powerless," defiant toward her father because "he made the rules," and jealous of her sister because "she got the attention." In her adult life, she carries those same experiences with her and simply shifts the emotions onto men and women in her job, social life, and personal relationships.

Burnout and methods of communication learned and applied are closely related. Women are often battle-weary from unresolved skirmishes, if not all-out wars from the past, and enter a new job, a marriage, or motherhood, semi-depleted. The communication skills adopted from families are not always effective or efficient. Yet, even if those skills were discarded in favor of new, more reliable methods, the messages from the past linger on. Once again, the transference reactions may swing into gear, causing you to "see" and "hear" through sensory equipment from the past. Do any of these experiences sound familiar to you?:

—Criticism from a superior at work feels too much like a family "put-down" and is construed as an attack.
—When you push and drive yourself on the job, you'll ultimately win the approval of the boss who, you're certain, has the same criteria as your most demanding parent.
—When you're told you've done a good job, you feel a flash of pleasure, then wonder how you got away with it.
—You speak to your women friends in one way, but if a man enters the room, you feel a swell of anxiety.

These are but a few examples demonstrating the process of mistaken identity and how stress can subsequently make subtle but insidious gains on your mind and body. Communicating is not just a matter of what you say and do, it concerns what you hear and see and how those messages are decoded.

FAMILY PRINCIPLES AND BURNOUT

"Women in our family always marry" is an example of a family principle which intrinsically contains burnout potential. "Women in our family always marry young" is a subtle refinement of that principle and accelerates the pressure. "Women in our family always have their first child by 22 years old" further enlarges the demand of that principle, and "Women in our family never divorce" prepares fertile soil for an incipient burnout daughter. All four statements inform of the rules for obtaining acceptance and approval within the family constellation. When the principles or values espoused by your family are in direct opposition to what you secretly believe (or fear will not happen), they're often experienced as threats or rebukes. When you wish to do something that is emanating from your authentic self, you may perceive yourself as silently bucking authority, and consequently a sense of "wrongness" may pervade your feelings. A sense of inhibition may also prevail, making it frightening for you to act on your own behalf.

"We know what's best for you" is a family principle with subtle implications, yet frequently has blatant ramifications. This is the voice of power speaking, and since you may have not dared to question the power, you may have begun to pretend you agreed with it and, consequently, to believe your own perceptions were skewed. If you were a perceptive child, you may have understood intuitively that the fears of your parents were being transferred onto you; that your parents did not completely know what was best for you but what was best for themselves and the family image they wished to maintain. This is a guilt-producing dynamic for children. When a child begins to conceal what she is perceiving about her parents, she's usually at odds with what they're selling. By pretending she doesn't know what she actually knows, she begins to feel guilt.

FALSE SELF: TRUE SELF

In the attempt to maintain a façade of compliance and act as if you were in agreement with the family principles, you undoubtedly experienced a drain on your emotions and intellect. Over time, you may have actually lost touch with your own authentic voice and feelings. Worn down by the volume of your parents' "truth," and worn out by your own wary rebellions, you may have begun to accept your own learned deception as reality. In time, you probably began to believe that you believed their principles and values—it just may have been easier to do so. This is the genesis of the false self system.

The false self is a survival mechanism that allows you to remain benign and nonthreatening in life. It begins with the family dynamics and then extends itself into your adult life. The false self is difficult to shake.

One woman explained her false self system this way:

> "I can see it every time I have a smile on my face which denotes nothing; when I laugh and am not amused; when I act cheerful and am hiding disappointment; when I've just been hurt and am throwing out flinty and witty one-liners. All of these ways of being have nothing to do with the people I'm with . . . I used to act this way when I was a kid and now they're just automatic. Sometimes, I have to concentrate heavily on what I'm really feeling to get to the truth . . ."

As a young girl, this particular woman bought into the family principles and philosophies to such an extent that she barely remembers her own beliefs or her own true feelings. She does know, however, that she is anxiety-ridden and continually trying to please others—whether she likes them or not.

Do you ever find yourself in her shoes? Do you know how to become vivacious and "on" by an inner command?

Acting and behaving the false self system on the job, at home, with friends, lovers, and family may throw you into severe conflict. You're probably hounded internally to "do the right thing" by the adopted false self, while your true self system—your own authentic feelings and beliefs—teeters on the periphery of consciousness, threatening to break through. A significant conflict emerges between the two selves, which is exacerbated by the energies needed to maintain the hollowness of the false self. When the false self continues to win out, that's when you're more than likely to burn out.

The false self system functions as a conscience whose voice obliterates your authentic perceptions and judgments. You may feel at times you're dancing to two different rhythms or living two opposing lives. The habits of living, working, and loving with the false self are not easily discarded, especially when you don't know exactly what your true self consists of, what it feels like, or if it's even real. Monitoring your true self takes a tremendous effort of self-observation to perceive the subtle clues that seep through. However, the true self sometimes does inadvertently leak through, especially when you're burning out and are beginning to feel disengaged from your surroundings. The impulse to lash out or "say what I mean for a change" is often discharged. At that stage, because you've deprived yourself of so many true needs, the true self is usually cynical and disenchanted. The idea here is to catch the false front long before you're launched on burnout and begin to utilize your true feelings.

What you've been achieving and accomplishing in your life through the false self system never feels quite right. Your victories are experienced as Pyrrhic—too costly to allow the feelings of joy; you feel compelled to achieve more and more, and triumph over all odds. What you want—a firm footing in the rational, concrete world—begins to eclipse what you need emotionally. The false self dictates that you behave scrupulously correct. Since it provides no deep level of gratification, women often present themselves as deceptively happy, in charge and in control. This double life whittles away energy reserves and subsequently is felt as an exhaustion of will.

If you're on the burnout cycle, you probably don't recognize the real limitations on your physical or mental capabilities. You're probably dominated to a large extent by the "musts" and "shoulds" of the false self and are pushing yourself beyond the perimeters of your personal endurance. If you were engaging your true self system, your reality judgment would be on target. You'd be judging and perceiving people and situations accurately and authentically—*you'd know when to back off.*

As a long-term burnout woman, you may have a harder time delineating just when and how your true self—your own values, principles, and feelings—was stifled and superseded by the false front. As a short-termer, you may only know that recently—perhaps in the past few years—you've been consumed by old voices which direct you to "do the right thing." In this case, "the right thing" means taking on any and all responsibilities and censoring your needs. It would be of great value toward combating burnout to understand that the "right thing" is usually culled from ersatz values refracted from the family dynamics of your youth. Both the long-term and short-term women, however, come to burnout with a set of responses implanted from childhood. Both of you can learn much about the what and how of your absorbed false systems by "watching" yourself in action.

If you feel you've lost the capacity for recognizing your own needs, for discerning the false from the true, yet you know much of your behavior is self-defeating and out of sync with your feelings, there are plenty of techniques in the second half of this book which will assist you. The invisible contracts you made with your family, the role-playing, the styles of communicating, and the inculcation of family principles may have become an invisible web which traps you into unwieldy feelings of guilt and resentment. You may be transferring them onto the players in your adult drama. Once you've retrieved an alliance with your true self system, you may be astonished to learn just how thorough your adjustment with the false self had become. You'll probably be astonished as you realize how tired, depleted, irritated, and anxious you were, and may even perceive yourself as someone who has been out of character for far too long.

FAMILY PHILOSOPHIES AND BURNOUT

If you remember, the family philosophy is the umbrella theme of the family unit. Let's take a minute and look at two examples of those philosophies, and learn how they inflicted both internal and external burnout reactions in two women.

Both examples are long-term burnouts who come from families where one parent had an extremely negative influence. You'll see how the true self slowly becomes eclipsed by the false self system, and how and why a woman may be trained into denying her very basic needs.

1. *"I had it bad, why should you have it different . . ."*

The father of Barbara A.

Barbara is one of these long-term burnout women who has been married for seventeen years and has two children. Currently, she works as an administrative assistant for a large food company. At 37, she is now coming to terms with the stress engendered in her as a child—stress which has caused her high anxiety, illness, and, ultimately, burnout. Both her mother and father were immigrants who came to the United States embittered and angry. Quite sadly, they offered Barbara a rather loveless home. Here's what she said about her childhood:

"My parents weren't warm, loving people. My father only knew how to work and yell. He was a cranky, moody, angry person. He loved me—I realize that now—but I sure didn't know it then . . . That's when I really needed to know—it could have altered my life. I remember I'd bring home a report card with a 98 on it . . . real proud . . . and he'd say, 'So, what happened to the other two points?' Because he'd had such a tough life, he didn't want us to suffer . . . but he was so insecure and jealous, he didn't want us to get any 'special attention,' either. I used to apologize for everything to keep the peace, right or wrong, and I either made myself as scarce as possible or tried to look busy and useful.

"My mother was a joyless, troubled person. She never touched or kissed us . . . she just couldn't express herself. I think she secretly disliked her life, and my brother and I added to her burdens and disappointments. She and I were silent adversaries . . . she either didn't know a lot about mothering or was scared of it. But my grandmother lived with us, and she was wonderful . . . my saving grace. She wasn't verbal in her affection—I just knew she loved me. She was always there for me in silent ways.

"People sometimes ask me why I didn't leave home and get an apartment. It's hard to explain. My father's tyranny was such that I could only move out if it was to get married. Otherwise, he would have considered me a 'whore.' It was a real trap. And there were so many arguments those years . . . every occasion we ever had in the house was precipitated by a fight. I'd just back off and look busy. That's what my mother taught me to do in her own way—that's what she did. My father would go on a tirade and she'd stand there and not say a thing. That's what I did too. I'd go silent, and maybe cry some.

"I cry when I'm under stress now, too. I carried a lot of those old patterns of coping into my adult life. After I got married, because I didn't get pregnant immediately, my father still wasn't satisfied. I was *supposed* to have a baby . . . that's what women were about. He kept after me: 'You're not pregnant yet? What's the matter with you?' I didn't want to have a baby then . . . I was ready some years later, but I wasn't then. So, because I was pressured and needed his approval so badly, I got pregnant prematurely and, as a result, I wasn't a very good mother myself. I didn't know what I was feeling —I never had any space to think for myself. I just raced around taking care of everything—keeping the house clean, keeping the baby quiet when my husband was home, keeping everyone fed, keeping my jobs going, keeping the peace according to some imagined blueprint in my head. I felt scared and I felt stupid, and I covered all those feelings up with a lot of hollow activities.

"As I got older, it was hard for me to believe that women who had careers and were smart and intelligent would think much of me. I'm still a little intimidated and a little jealous of them. There weren't any women in my life who operated in what to me was the man's world. I had a number of jobs, but they never meant much to me. Yet, I know, the fact that my husband and I struggled through those early years together, that we have a good marriage that's lasted this long, and that my two kids are so bright and even happy is something of an accomplishment. We worked at it—we both have proclivities toward burning out and have learned to spot the signs of it in each other. Some of my newer women friends say they're a little in awe of our longevity. It's amazing. I've felt so incredibly exhausted most of my life.

"I think I'm beginning to understand it all now. I know what I need, what I value, and, most of all, how to avoid going silent and isolated. But I needed help to learn all that . . . and I really feel everything is changing for the better . . ."

When Barbara first sought counseling, she appeared deceptively in control. She said she occasionally suffered bouts of depression but didn't know why. After exploring her history and probing her detailed accounts of her daily activities, it became clear she was in a state of both emotional and physical exhaustion. Her depressions were the result of disengagement from herself and a desire to fill up the emptiness inside with incessant mind and body activity.

Prior to seeking treatment for burnout, Barbara totally feared men and coped with her fear by becoming something of a servant to them. With her male bosses she was indispensable; she never argued or opened her mouth. Her transference reactions turned all men into her father, from whom she desperately longed for approval. And she job-hopped. If a new authority proved to be warm and kind, the intimacy scared her; she wasn't familiar with it. She had to leave before she disappointed him, which, in her mind, she was sure to do.

When Barbara was first married, she was silent and couldn't imagine any life other than one of devotion to her husband's needs. She had no belief in her right to do anything differently. And she constantly sought his reassurance that she would not be left. The ultimate punishment was abandonment. Since the family philosophy was "pull yourself up by your own bootstraps" or "nobody helped me and I'm not going to help you," there was no thought of warmth or support. Her true self system was totally blocked off by the frightened false self which dictated that she be a service. There was no room in her family for demonstrations of need or for feelings. There was only survival.

Women who were brought up in emotionally deprived homes often feel inept as adults in social or professional settings. When a child grows up watching out for trouble, circumventing anger, avoiding hurtful and punitive confrontations, there's little time for fantasy, absorbing intellectually, or having the calm required for the subtleties of creativity. There is also an absence of attention to detail. The verbal, social graces between people, the subtler politics of perceiving or judging accurately, are never freed from their inner distortions. There is, however, a very adept and singular ability to sense threats and incipient danger in relationships. As a nurturing anticipator, the child learns to sidestep what could be trouble by perceiving then predicting the ungovernable event way before it turns cataclysmic. Women who were raised with such dynamics unconsciously devote themselves to picking up sensorily the minutest of signals—like the wind whistling down the river before a storm breaks—as a means of surviving. But they neglect to pick up the ways in which people relate to each other without fear. They may have the accoutrements of socialization but nothing to support them—no learned knowledge or confidence. Consequently they develop a deep sense of inferiority, inadequacy, and, most always, the lack of courage to test reality. A woman from this background usually responds to her life by adopting formalistic, ritualistic, or rigid behavior patterns. She doesn't trust her impulses. She only trusts her rigid, self-imposed system which is replete with inflexibility. Self-sufficiency becomes a mainstay of that system. Competence, being of service, and perfectionism become essential ingredients in her life and express themselves in her work, daily toils, and interpersonal relationships. She frequently burns out on labor, fear, and anxiety.

Barbara hid her exhaustion deep inside for years. She quietly worked, raised her son and daughter, helped put her husband through business school, and, like her mother, kept her complaints and her needs to herself. "I took on the role of everything to everyone," she said. "Besides, I needed to do everything myself. I needed to be busy, doing something all the time. When I didn't have chores to do, I'd watch television . . . I became a television addict to blot out my racing thoughts and feelings . . . and, as I think about it now, to rest my mind."

When she was 30, she began to experience attacks of panic:

> "They were awful. I'd feel a rush inside of me, then light-headed, and my heart would pound. My legs would lose feeling and my vision would blur. I really thought I was physically ill or dying. I didn't believe I should lean on my husband, so if I began to panic during the night, I'd get out of bed and maybe scrub the kitchen floor . . . anything to keep me occupied. Later, I did become quite ill . . . I had pneumonia several times. The doctor told me I needed consolidated rest . . . he said I was utterly worn out."

Barbara's story is extreme, but as such it illustrates how those early family dynamics, if not checked, can follow you through life. For Barbara, her "saving grace" was her grandmother. This was the only person with whom she felt a loving allegiance. The other unwritten contracts in her home advised her to stay away. Neglect and abuse were the provisos. Her role was that of "quiet-absorber," the one who implies consent through silence. Family communication was done through raised voices and emotional abandonment, and the content of that communication relayed that she was in her home on sufferance. The family principles were clearly stated: "Until you get married you're nothing, and if you leave before, you're a whore." Barbara's transference reactions were severe. All men were to be feared; women were to be mistrusted—they were in silent collusion with men.

Barbara not only carried those dynamics with her into her adult life, but also, in the absence of cruel criticism and stern judgments, superimposed them on herself. The stress and pressure to earn her right in the world almost cost her her life. Ironically, those sudden panic attacks acted as signals. If they hadn't instructed her to stop and get some help, she might have, indeed, been critically afflicted.

Today she says:

> "I've really integrated a lot of what happened in the past with my present life. But sometimes I still tend to lose sight of it. That's when I let people hurt me . . . that's when I hurt myself. I know I can't live in that depleted state anymore . . . I have to stop, back off, and remember who I am, what I want to be, and what my needs are. I've given up a lot of that rigidity about getting things done. I just don't let myself get as scared . . . I don't drive myself as much anymore . . . I don't feel the need to prove . . ."

2. *"My way is the only way . . ."*

The mother of Julie R.

Julie began her interview by saying, "I don't think I'm the burnout type," yet garnished her conversation with many burnout references. She preferred to define her symptoms—frequent colds, lower-back pain, anxiety, and exhaustion—as "my character weakness." Like many women, Julie didn't completely understand the basics of burnout and felt squeamish admitting it had affected her life. She suggested that calling herself a burnout gave her an excuse for not functioning perfectly. Fatigue and illness were initially tossed off as pedestrian concerns. She felt that giving in to either was "acting irresponsibly," something her mother had instilled in her at an early age.

> "My mother was hypercritical and picky, verging on hysterical. The house was her life . . . everything had to be done a certain way—there was no altering it. There was a way to hang clothes on the line, a way to wash lettuce, a way to fold sweaters . . . a way to put on clothes. She even believed there was one way to wake up and get out of bed. She was annoyed with the way my brother slept—the covers were pulled out from the end of the bed in the mornings.
>
> "She was really always busy. Her day began with a list of responsibilities and, damn, she carried them out with a kind of supreme efficiency! If she wasn't ironing, she was shopping, chopping, washing tiles, vacuuming, bustling. I see her always with a sponge in one

hand and a dust cloth in the other. People were judged as to whether they 'set a nice table,' if their kids were clean, if their lawns were tidy. There were a lot of rules . . .

"I tried to please my mother by looking busy and happy. Sitting and thinking was not well received—it looked 'lazy.' Reading was an act of aggression—unless it was schoolwork, and that had to be done in my own room, very neatly. I was really afraid to be sad or down in front of her . . . I knew it was upsetting. The point was, as long as she was busy and I was busy and my brother was busy . . . there was no problem. She would glow and this wonderful smile would come out. But she couldn't deal with anything emotional—anything that had to do with my feelings or inner thoughts . . . I guess I just buried them . . . I thought they were wrong.

"My father adored her and tended to explain her virtues to us. Why not, though? She made no demands on him—he was the 'man' and, I guess because of biology, he was privileged . . . He could be lax. He worked all day, sold insurance, and there was a very definite message: 'Stay away from your father, he's had a tough day.' If he left a towel on the bathroom floor, she'd smile knowingly, pick it up and, almost by sleight-of-hand, have it washed and on the line in two minutes. My father had the power by night—she had it by day. He really felt she was the perfect woman and often told me he hoped I'd be just like her. As I grew up, the comparisons, at least to me, were really startling. I felt inept and oafish next to her. His intimacy with me was based on my relationship with her. If I was depressed or sad, he'd talk to me very personally, very privately . . . He'd tell me how lucky I was to have such a model mother. Those were the only times we spoke seriously, but I always felt we had a shared secret and that did make me feel special . . . no, more than special . . . okay.

"My dad and I had a kind of silent agreement as well. I only realized a few years ago how clear that contract was . . . I would never make trouble, I'd be helpful and sweet, and then I'd get a special wink from him. He had a soft, compelling voice and I used to think he was protecting me because of the sound. The words I was actually hearing meant less than the voice, because what he was teaching me were lessons in how to be a better person—how to be grateful and cute . . . I smiled a lot for him . . . and for her. Looking happy all the time made a difference . . ."

In her adult life, Julie suffers from continual stress. At 42, she smokes two packs of cigarettes a day and, when she comes home from work in the evenings, has "around three vodka-and-tonics to cool out . . ." Divorced for four years, Julie works for an electronics corporation in a lower-middle management position and supports two teenagers.

The majority of her married life was spent grappling with her critical "internalized mother"—trying to sort out what values were hers and which were imposed as a false system. This has been a complex task. She's never been quite sure "where one ends and the other begins." She's never had that maternal permission to be a separate person, to explore her own rhythms, timing, and, of critical importance, her own needs.

If you come from a home where judgments and criticism were omnipresent, like Julie, there is a good possibility you will experience the world at large as a stern and demanding parent. Julie doesn't trust herself. She finds it difficult, if not at times impossible, to make decisions for herself or for anyone else. Passive and careful in her behavior and thoughts, she checks out the opinions of everyone and anyone. She continually questions herself and is riddled with self-doubt. When she does make a decision, she seeks out airtight justifications, "just in case anyone questions me."

After putting herself through college, Julie became a teacher and then married. "Teaching small children seemed to be right for me," she said. "I knew the material and was in control of the kids. If the kids exhausted me with their demands, I thought of it as a character weakness on my part. I mean, I was supposed to be able to tough-out anything. I felt guilty and ashamed when they irritated me . . . I wanted to be a strong, positive shaping force for them. I wanted to be remembered years later as a kind of moral Jean Brodie." Julie not only internalized her judgmental mother and set her up as a critic of her life, she found herself "becoming my mother" and enforcing strict codes of behavior on the students. "I would drive myself to make sure I was on top of each and every kid's problems. In a way I became as intrusive as my mother."

After she had her own children, she tells this anecdote:

"When my son and daughter were small, I decorated their room like a real kid's room. There were lots of things they could play with and really use. Not like my childhood room which was there to be seen but not used. I wanted them to feel ownership. But, at the same time, I wanted the room to be magazine-picture perfect. I had an image of them sitting in their little chairs at their little desks all very neat and tidy. When the 'look' of the room was spoiled by their activity, I'd get this terrible feeling of disorder—it wasn't the way it was supposed to be. It made me nervous and unsettled. I'd compulsively clean it up and order them to keep it neat, *just like my mother.*"

Julie is constantly striving for the perfectionism which will ultimately, in her mind, give her maternal approval. She carries the illusion of failed virtue in her feelings and suffers bouts of burnout depression born of incessant self-demand. "I have a lot of guilt about my kids," she stated. "I feel I should be doing more as a 'mother.' There's a conflict between being a 'mother' and what's really me. Unless I'm being strict and conscientious about my children, I feel I'm letting them down . . . When I'm being strict and absolute, I feel I'm nagging."

The continuousness of her inner battle drives her to burnout. Women like Julie set impossible tasks for themselves which dooms them to overextend themselves and overwork their minds and bodies. They cannot relax for a moment and can only fully enjoy spontaneous personalities if they are distanced—on television, in films or books. The unpredictable personality threatens the order in their minds and their control over the environment. The old family dynamics loom in the recesses of thoughts and feelings threatening to lash out if they succumb to the spirited but uncontrolled impulsive moment. Like Julie, they may smile a great deal, but the smile masks the deeper desire to rebel, to emancipate those darker, true self feelings. Because Julie cannot free herself, she drinks in the evenings to loosen and perhaps kill off the binds of childhood.

When her marriage threatened to collapse, she decided to leave the school system and go into the private sector. Her skills at organizing and administrating were superior, but she was filled with doubt. She had enough outward ability to land her present job, but on an inner level found it difficult to relate to female peers or authorities. Seeking constantly to please, her relationships with women were faulty. She presented a false self which was too eager, too self-effacing, too insecure. But she did her job well.

"I had the same feelings on this job. Everything had to be neat, tidy, orderly. I'm meticulous about detail, yet never sure I've done the job the 'right way.' I worried every night about what I hadn't finished and who would find out. My immediate supervisor was this terrific woman, but I was always tense around her . . . I was sure she didn't like me . . . or would find me out . . . or was about to fire me every time she asked me into her office. I was much friendlier with the men in the office then . . . but only men who were at my level or lower . . ."

For years Julie refused to relate to the feminist movement. She felt she remained a "good girl" by rejecting the cultural changes. Leaders in the movement threatened what she'd attained. And, of course, her mother and father accused her of being a "libber" when she voiced any self-assertive ideas. Her transference was so complete, even those who would have offered support were seen through the critical mother filter. Compounding her fear of investigating women's groups was her father's "soft, compelling voice," which demanded that she be grateful and sweet. His double message confused and alarmed her. He seemed to be offering her paternal warmth and love, but his words, when separated from demeanor, were guilt-instilling. Since he was the only figure from whom she felt comfort or support, she internalized his communication and was loyal to the memory of those private talks.

Of course, Julie's loyalty to her father was an indication of what she expected from men. She still seeks out men whose remoteness is disguised by a gentle demeanor, who appear to be emotionally present, but who, in fact, cannot or will not relate to her needs. "I'm not sure if my needs are legitimate," she said. "I don't really know how to distinguish my baby needs from my adult needs, or if that matters . . . I don't know what's fair to ask for, much less demand . . ." During her marriage, Julie avoided asking or even inferring she needed anything "personal," yet felt the need "to anticipate all his moods and be a good listener." In the aftermath of her divorce, she began to understand that "he never knew who the hell I was, and neither did I." But when they split up, she was "devastated" and felt she had "died." When the man disappeared, so did she, and the critical mother reappeared inside of her, mentally belittling her inability to "hold a man." To Julie, a man's attention provided her with feelings of worthiness, value, and *normality*. When she's not in a relationship, she immerses herself in frenetic activity to hold her "awful feelings" at bay.

Her burnout proclivities weren't difficult to locate. She incessantly races from her own internal voices—whether it be on the job, as a mother, with men, or with friends. Working on the premise that "a moving target can't be hit," she keeps herself in perpetual motion. She continues to live out those contracts with her family, alternately playing the role of "appeaser," "sparkler," and "quiet absorber." But the connectedness between her symptoms—chain smoking, lower-back pain, constricted muscles, frequent colds, anxiety, and exhaustion—and her emotional life is beginning to make sense to her. She's beginning to back off from the race against her feelings, and from her need to rev up to block their impact. She concluded:

> "I'm trying to nurture myself. I've learned to trust myself much more—to trust what's inside me—and I'm more comfortable with the idea that I'm changing . . . I still feel that extra pressure to perform and to be the perfect woman, but I'm trying to compromise. I can see that that strong push to be perfect ends up in misused energy and, in the end, nothing gets done the way I had wanted. I want to learn to accept that things can be done satisfactorily, they can be lived with that way, and they don't have to be done perfectly. I guess I have been a burnout personality, but I like to think I'm changing all that now. You can't feel burned out when you know you're growing . . . Knowing you're growing signifies hope."

Both Barbara and Julie came from homes where turmoil and confusion alienated them from their true selves and demanded they behave with learned deception—the embryo of denial. It became critical to their survival that they deny the disturbances they witnessed in their parents, and unconsciously absorb the strain.

Not all of you were subjected to such extreme parental domination, yet most of you can relate to specific kernels of their experiences. The extent of your own denial can be measured against the distress you experienced in your own particular family culture.

FAMILY DYNAMICS AND
THE EVOLUTION OF DENIAL

The techniques, habits, and feelings of denial were discussed earlier in Chapter I, but how does denial begin? What dynamics in your household encouraged this process?

If, as a child, you were overprotected, spared the details of reality, sheltered from conflicts—be they in the home, with relatives and friends, or in the larger world—you were probably not prepared to face either the common stress of the adult world or any unexpected dissonance. You may have been encouraged to deny as a means of preserving yourself from the ruder realities of life. As a result, you may have developed the instincts for self-guardianship but learned to deny your vulnerabilities and limits.

If you grew up in a home where antagonism and continual arguments prevailed, your denial may have evolved, like Barbara's, to block out the evidence of danger. In order to survive, you may have learned to "go dead" and avoid the cacophony of frightened feelings which emerged too often to be tolerated.

Perhaps you came from a home where one or both parents presented themselves as arbiters of moral rectitude. Religious principles or codes may have been used to instill a sense of ethics and honor. Your parents may have projected themselves as models of incorruptibility, but those openly expressed values may have been betrayed by their observable, antithetical behavior. The double message you received may have urged you to deny your true perceptions of this confused reality in your home. You may have learned to suppress your awareness of these contradicting parental messages to maintain an equilibrium.

Were you overwhelmed by events in your home? Was there a broken marriage and a stream of new faces with whom you had to cope—your mother's boyfriends, a new husband; your father's girlfriends, a new wife? Perhaps events, situations, and people changed too quickly to digest. You may have been unable to deal with the swiftly shifting personalities, with their highly charged emotions, or with the push-pull of allegiances. In this case, you were not conditioned to respond adequately to stress. Denial of these fast-shifting scenes may have evolved as a method of remaining rooted and maintaining an imaginary continuity.

We all learn to embrace and deal with life through direct mastery of its vicissitudes. What we aim for is sometimes called "the goodness of the fit," a unity between what is wanted and what is needed. Achieving what you want and what you need are contingent upon your abilities, capacities, self-expectations, opportunities, and efforts. When your efforts to gain mastery are successful, a sense of competence ripens, which in turn heightens self-esteem. If a solid sense of self is to be achieved, it must be given space in which to mature and develop. Only then can the process of mastery be completed.

But "the goodness of the fit" will go askew if that process is interrupted. When consistency and stability are intruded upon, or when assurance and affirmation are not forthcoming, burnout will become an issue. You might experience the inclination then to isolate yourself, to deny the absence of critical supports, to steel yourself against the perilousness of unpredictability, and to act "as if" you cannot be hurt.

Denial which evolves from disturbed family relationships fosters a splintered sense of self. Connectedness between memory and the here-and-now breaks apart. The self "splits." The remembrance of things past is consciously limited to that which will not intrude upon the intensity of your pursuits or bring you pain. Because of the firmly entrenched habit of denial, you may not understand that your perceptions and judgments of reality can easily become distorted and that you may be inflicting avoidable damage upon yourself. Like Julie, you may see yourself not as a potential burnout, but as a woman endowed with a "character weakness," and unconsciously promote further denial in your life.

"The goodness of the fit" has strong implications for women who are burning out. Since most women were raised with enforced gender limitations, that "fit" may feel awkward, out of sync with the needs of the true self. Anxiety over who you should and shouldn't be, over the internalized "mother voice" and your authentic voice, over achieving an identity in the "man's world," over how much autonomy and how much dependency can be demonstrated in work and love, and over conflicts between apportioned time for work and apportioned time for leisure can create stressful emotional pulls. For many of you the traditional training of your families is at odds with the new social options. Women familiar with long-term burnout know that these are serious considerations which are constantly in a state of flux but which hopefully will provide a better "fit" for younger generations of women. As Barbara said: "It's only been in the past few years that

I've thought it would be nice to have a daughter. It would be wonderful to have a little girl who would grow up now instead of when I did . . . There's so much more I'd want her to have . . . At least she'd know she had some choices and a sense of herself as a whole person . . ."

If you think you may be burning out and you're caught in old patterns and attitudes, you can begin to help yourself by exploring your past in an attempt to distinguish between the values you learned which are true and seem to "fit" and those which are false and have not worn well. It will also be helpful for you to begin to identify just how burnout manifests in your adult life, what it feels like, and how to distinguish the symptoms. Remember, when you're coping with burnout, self-awareness is half of the battle.

CHAPTER IV

The Symptoms of Women's Burnout

"I had only one desire which was ongoing: I wanted to sit in a corner, put a paper bag over my head and say, 'Leave me alone, world, 'cause I'm not here.' "

Cass J.

At the height of her short-term burnout, Cass stopped feeling.

"I thought I was dead inside. From being an emotional, animated, loving, warm person—I suddenly couldn't feel. I felt useless, like a mass of depression . . . and totally disoriented. I didn't know what to do with myself. Worse, I didn't know what I wanted to do. My life had always been busy, filled with activities and appointments, but suddenly I was mixing everything up. I couldn't get on top of my schedule or my thoughts. What I thought were logical notions about my businesses, or my family, were actually irrational, 'off the wall' judgments. The disorientation scared me. This was the first time in my life I actually experienced fear . . . fear and futility.

"I gained a lot of weight during that year. I'm not sure if that was because of the burnout, or because I had become so celibate and was eating a lot for oral satisfaction . . . but I just felt dead. One night I went out with a new man, someone I had been very attracted to.

During the evening he kissed me. I didn't feel any rush—I didn't feel anything. I had lost my interest in men, in sex, in relationships.

"Also, for the first time in my life I started crying. I mean, I had cried at funerals or in sad films, but I wasn't one to go around weeping—I didn't think it was becoming to women. Men expected us to cry and I wasn't going to give anyone that satisfaction. Then, an old friend of mine who was worried about me came over. As soon as I saw him, I ran into his arms and started crying. While he was holding me, I realized I was starved for affection—I was starved for someone giving something back to me . . . for someone patting me on the head and saying, 'Good girl.'

"I really had lost control of my life. I was easily distracted, restless, and totally exhausted from spinning my wheels all day. I couldn't understand this because I've always been filled with energy. I've been married, divorced, raised a son, managed three businesses at the same time, supported my family . . . but a lot of things happened all at once and I couldn't get a grip on them. My mother became very ill and I had to visit her in the hospital every day; I was in the process of moving to a new apartment in a new neighborhood; I was doing a lot of business traveling; and then the man I had been seeing broke off with me . . . I guess it was all too much. I couldn't focus on any one thing but was taking care of them all.

"I started getting a lot of colds, back pains, and odd aches, but couldn't get a good night's sleep. For a while I thought I would die of weakness. This just wasn't me! And then, one night, while trying to fall asleep, I became aware of my aloneness. I suddenly sat up and heard myself say out loud: 'I don't know what I'm doing! I need help!'

"But the only people I was attracted to then were people who needed me. All I wanted were people going through a divorce, an eviction, a depression, and I'd jump right in. I began to realize that the people who needed me reconfirmed the fact that I was worthwhile. I could pour out all this stuff and watch them grow, but I couldn't do it for myself. There was no 'me' left for me. So, if no one asked for my help, I felt useless again. I felt I was a failure to myself, and that hurt—I'd always been such a success. My sense of independence, which is very strong, just left . . . I wanted everyone else to make my choices and decisions for me, but I didn't really trust anyone.

"For a while I thought I was going through an early menopause . . . you know, the over-forty thing. I figured I was really finished and, worse, a has-been. That word, by the way, 'has-been,' kept creeping into my vocabulary. So did the word 'bored.' I felt bored all the time. I had only one desire which was ongoing: I wanted to sit in a corner, put a paper bag over my head and say, 'Leave me alone, world, 'cause I'm not here.' "

What Cass described is a woman in the final stages of a *short-term burnout*. It was difficult to correlate the story she told and the woman she described with the vibrant, ebullient person relaxing in a plush, floral easy chair—they were as alike as winter and spring. Admittedly, however, Cass has become much more reflective about herself than she's ever been in her 48 years; her bout with burnout has changed her thinking and altered the style of her life.

She's always been a very active woman—vital, smart, with an abundance of stamina, a joyous sense of humor, and an authentic desire to maintain a flow of people in her life. Men and women alike flock to her warm, inviting home seeking out her company. Lively and energetic, Cass likes to be "on the move," directing, managing, and administering to her multiple businesses, supporting causes, being a mother to her 21-year-old son, caring for her aging parents, maintaining a bustling social life, and, most important, nurturing the myriad individuals who tap her generous spirit most every day. Since her burnout, however, she's begun to realize that she cannot respond to every public, personal, and professional cry for help. Her reservoirs become depleted and there's no self left.

Cass's symptoms began about a year before the period she described. They emerged slowly, almost imperceptibly. When the external circumstances of her life began to disintegrate, the symptoms blossomed into an intricate network of physical, intellectual, and emotional protests. One night while struggling with sleeplessness, she turned on the television and heard a conversation concerning burnout on a cable health show. "I was actually elated," she said. "I finally knew I wasn't going crazy, I wasn't over-the-hill or dying. I identified with the burnout problem immediately." The next day she called the office and made an appointment for a consultation.

BURNOUT: PHYSICAL AND MENTAL

Not all women suffering from burnout are as physically active as Cass, nor do they all find themselves with her particular external exigencies pressing in on them. Many women who seek treatment complain of fierce mental activity; their professional and private activities are comparatively circumscribed and predictable.

A woman like Cass who is a physical doer and has stepped onto the Burnout Cycle, often speaks in terms of time schedules but thinks in terms of self-doubt. She lives two succinct lives. One is her outer world of optimism, her overtone of enthusiasm for digging in and accomplishing. The other is her inner pessimism, her undertone of doubt, insecurity, and the fear of breaking down in any one of her many important functions. She may operate on this split-level of demand and accomplishment quite smoothly for a period of time, never fully acknowledging the slow fatigue that is beginning to overwhelm her. But, when external conditions place their additional burdens on her life, the serious short-term burnout stages are not far away. Like an ill-functioning pressure cooker, the steam she's built up backs up on her and eventually bursts.

It's quite common for a woman who is undergoing the beginning stages of burnout to sense that she is not mentally functioning as smoothly as she once did. Her inability to concentrate, to attend to details, to feel present in a conversation or business meeting subtly makes itself known. Her mind drifts, she wanders off for moments at a time, and may even find herself daydreaming. All of these symptoms highlight her wish to remove herself, to gain some respite, to take a momentary break from the ever-present sense of externally or internally imposed pressures.

Another woman may not experience actual demands on her time, or even any external crises, yet live out a mental agony of real or imagined expectations and judgments. She may view the world with suspicion and mistrust, worrying over excellence, if not perfection, and experience the ravages of unspecified guilt. Men, money, disenchantment with a job or a relationship may justify her belief that she simply isn't enough: she doesn't think fast enough, isn't smart enough, pretty enough, socially desirable, witty, sexy, or accomplished. Her mental activity is excruciatingly exhausting, but it isn't new to her. *She's suffering a life-style of long-term burnout.*

You will remember that long-term burnout is a consequence of a life-long inattention to both physical and emotional well-being. You may have evolved a mode of functioning wherein the doing, the accomplishing, and the becoming are of paramount importance, but you've probably paid little heed to the consequences of your intensity. This life-style gradually encroaches on your social, sexual, creative, and recreational life. Little time is set aside for real enjoyment or pleasure.

Both of these burnout modes—the physical and the mental—are equally debilitating. Where the physical doer may need to stop her body from running, the mental agonizer may have to check her thought patterns. Typically, however, they overlap. Women who suffer both simultaneously are subject to a severe blend of distress, yet whether the burnout manifests in short-term, long-term, physical, mental, or both, the symptoms may be precisely the same. The only measurable differences are the intensity and degree to which they intrude on functioning.

Alice, in contrast to Cass, is less a physical doer. She's always been a reflective woman with an active, alert mind who works at home alone as a graphics artist. She's a long-term burnout with a lifetime compulsion to prove herself. Each time she approaches a new project, she's propelled deeper into the Burnout Cycle. At 37, she almost stopped functioning:

"I really can't remember when I didn't feel some degree of burnout—I just didn't know then what it was called. But, when all of these symptoms were rushing me, I knew I had to do something or I'd be dead in five years. I was too irritable and anxious to continue to go on as I had been.

"Recently, I'd gotten a large job designing posters and brochures for a bank and, since I work free-lance, wanted to impress the agency. Later I understood that this was not a unique situation for me . . . Every job I've ever had affected me similarly. I'd become obsessive and scared, almost driven with the desire to be approved and accepted.

"I felt totally alone with this assignment and kept thinking if I failed—if I blew it—my career would be over. I was having trouble thinking then . . . I began to have chest pains and headaches but quickly dismissed them as the usual stress that comes from working too long and too hard. Friends would say, 'You have to get out

more,' but I'd refuse to go. I was becoming bored with idl
tions . . . or even important ones. I couldn't listen and react appropriately. I was clipped, flip, and brittle. One night I did go out to a party and saw myself overreacting to everything. I laughed too hard at mediocre jokes and exaggerated the significance of casual remarks. It was impossible for me to separate the essential from the inessential because nothing but my anxiety was coming through.

"On the other hand, everyone was annoying me. I didn't like this one or that one, privately criticized everyone, yet would brood and suffer when a friend didn't treat me with kid gloves. I was in a rather insignificant relationship with a man then and gave it much more importance than it deserved. It became paramount that he adore me and overlook my flaws . . . but I wasn't overlooking his . . .

"The only two activities I enjoyed were eating and sex. I kept gaining weight . . . Every time I'd do a sketch that didn't work, I'd end up stuffing myself.

"As far as my boyfriend was concerned, I didn't want to talk to him, I only wanted to get into bed. I thought I was just sexually hungry, but now, retrospectively, I understand it wasn't sex I wanted, it was the physical closeness . . . I felt it humanized me, at least for a couple of hours.

"During the day I'd catch myself biting my cuticles, wagging my leg, smoking incessantly, and worrying over my job, who was angry with me, who I hadn't called back, or money. I had headaches every morning, would take Excedrin, have several cups of coffee and then get a caffeine rush which would accelerate the anxiety. Then I'd be dizzy and disoriented and my worries would turn to my health. I was a mass of insecurities and anxiety . . . The more I'd worry, the less work I'd do and the guiltier I'd feel. Also, I couldn't sleep. I used to write in my journal at three in the morning . . . Everything I recorded was either negative and self-abnegating or was a diatribe on the many ways I should improve myself—my weight, my clothes, the ways in which I spoke . . .

"I guess I reached a breaking point, because one day I became completely exhausted and just sat down and cried. For the next month I cried incessantly. My perceptions were blurred. I was hideously fatigued and began to sleep during the day. I remember going to the supermarket and, while being checked out, my knees caved in. I think I just wanted to fall into oblivion. I didn't know it then, but I was almost beyond burnout. I had depleted all my energies; my tank was on empty. And, if my body hadn't been smarter than my head, I think I might have had a coronary . . . something too serious to play with.

"What I really wanted was for someone to come in and take control of my life—tell me what to eat, what to wear, when to sleep, what to say. I couldn't bear any responsibilities, even something as small as picking a restaurant. Everything I did publicly was a performance and I couldn't wait to leave so I could be by myself again. I knew how to behave and did just that—behaved for people. But it was all surfacy. I had no real emotional moorings.

"When I finally started to sleep at night, it went from four hours to six, then to ten, and for about a month, on and off, I slept sixteen to eighteen hours a day. Part of that was exhaustion, but part of it, I'm sure, was escape from myself. In either event, a friend told me that it didn't matter—sleep was healthy—so I indulged. I think all I needed was permission to rest.

"I did try to tell a few friends what was going on with me, but I've always been so in control, so competent and confident, they just didn't believe the depth of what I was saying. I guess it blew my image, or it scared them. But that didn't help me; it just threw me deeper into isolation. I think that was the most frightening of all . . . that feeling of aloneness, of alienation from the world. That's when you start toying with suicidal fantasies."

Again, the friendly, open woman who told this story betrayed few of the symptoms which she poignantly addressed. The Alice who agreed to be interviewed had a ready smile and a sensitivity toward her environment. There was nothing "clipped," "brittle," or "suicidal" about her. Looking very fresh in an Indian print dress and low-heeled boots, she spoke thoughtfully about her lifetime inclination to absorb herself in self-doubt and to punish herself for her imagined failings. "I have to remember that no one is doing this to me," she said. "It's me who gets in the way of myself."

The loneliness and aloneness Alice experienced began to severely intrude upon her perceptions and judgments and helped to throw her deeper into the Burnout Cycle. In her isolation, she had no one to validate her thinking. Her thoughts of suicide were a result of her increasingly helpless and hopeless feelings. Like many women who have chosen work which isolates them, Alice confessed to aloneness as an occupational hazard, but went on to say that she's now learned she must balance her work schedule with a social life and physical activities. She now plans lunch or dinner dates with friends and has taken up tennis and aerobics. And, she's learned that affiliation—maintaining closeness with her friends—is critical to remaining balanced.

Alice came to recognize she was not experiencing a nervous breakdown but was in the throes of burnout when her continual fatigue and jumpiness drove her to seek medical attention. Her doctor put her on vitamin therapy and offered her information about burnout. Later, remembering the book *Burnout: How to Beat the High Cost of Success* (Freudenberger and Richelson), she bought a copy that afternoon and, after a thorough reading, began to understand that "the craziness I was feeling might just be something manageable."

Many physicians would diagnose her reported exhaustion as depression and treat it as such. As was discussed in Chapter I, this is often a mistake. Depression can emerge as one symptom of burnout, but it is not a main component. The level of exhaustion that Alice had reached was, in a sense, as she said, "almost beyond burnout." She had continued to deplete her energies and resources over a long period of time. When she finally did seek help, she was beginning to lose her capacity to survive.

Alice's symptoms had been percolating most of her life, but she was too close to them to see them clearly. Her anxious thought patterns and habits had become a normal way of living for her.

> "It was like a private life I led," she said, "one that no one knew about but me. Telling friends about my constant agitation—the need to be perfect, to excel, to be better—made me feel like I couldn't cut it. You know . . . being a woman in our culture isn't easy. There's a hidden demand to look strong, controlled, and in command."

Not every woman prone to burnout will undergo the formidable experience of a Cass or an Alice. Since the burnout concept has infiltrated our popular language, many women are now able to decipher their symptoms before escalating to those extremes. Today, many of you have educated yourselves and are beginning to perceive that point at which your bodies and minds have succumbed to overuse and misuse. It's not uncommon to hear women exclaim, "I think I'm burning out."

Yet there are countless others of you who are unaware of the burnout trap and just what constitutes a symptom or series of symptoms. Guided by the mythology of perfection, many of you often express the notion of being hounded by contradictions in your feelings and your experience. As a lamentable result, the most glaring manifestations of burnout are at best perceived as predictable developments of normal life or, at worst, as evidence that you aren't measuring up to the standards perpetrated by the demands of this decade.

Both short-term and long-term women burnouts are prey to what Alice called the "hidden demand to look strong, controlled, and in command." The short-termer may be thrust suddenly into a series of dramatic circumstances and become disoriented by a barrage of unpredictable events. The long-termer wears down over years and may be surprised when, like Alice, she discovers one day that she just can't cope. It's not unusual either to hear of women who are overburdened and harassed by external and internal demands quite suddenly spraining an ankle or succumbing to a physical illness which forces them into a rest period. The body *will* break down under stress. If you refuse to follow the instructions from your conscious mind to retreat, back off, and unload some of the pressure, your unconscious may, paradoxically, instruct you to get sick to survive. The body says no, but the head says go. The body refuses to continue to acquiesce to the demands of the mind and, as a result, breaks down. Often an accident occurs or a set of symptoms emerges which requires rest and removal from the prolonged, imposed stress.

THE BURNOUT SYMPTOM CYCLE

The progression of women's burnout can best be illuminated by the twelve-stage cycle described below. These particular stages are not clearly separated or delineated one from the other but often blend and overlap into each other with no conscious recognition. The stages apply to both long-term and short-term women burnouts. The degree of intensity and length of time one stays in any particular stage is dependent upon the specific circumstances of the woman—her personality, her self-perception, her previous history, and her ability to cope with stress.

Please remember and note: It is important for you to understand that the symptoms delineated here are often experienced as a natural part of one's life. Many may be normal, human responses to events.

You may *not* be burning out but may have suffered a setback—a disappointment, an illness, a loss, or some of the other harsh vicissitudes of everyday life. In that case, you may be experiencing one or many of the symptoms for shorter or longer periods of time. The symptoms here are compressed into a continuum for the purposes of describing the burnout process. They may not necessarily all apply to you. You'll note that there are steps that can be taken immediately to help you reverse or prevent the momentum.

If you do suspect you may be burning out, don't be alarmed. Identifying the cause of your malaise is half the battle. Once you understand that you're suffering from burnout, you'll be in a very good position to alter and reverse those aspects of your life that are adding to your stress. Further, once you've begun to learn to identify the signs of burnout, you'll be able to offer some assistance to others who are demonstrating symptoms but who don't as yet understand what they mean.

For now, take a look at the Burnout Symptom Cycle, its subsequent descriptions, and immediate steps to take, then identify the stage which best characterizes your particular experience and feelings.

STAGE 1: *Compulsion to Prove*

Historically, the desire to prove oneself in the world, to have impact on one's peers, has acted as the impetus for achievement. For this reason, Stage 1 is the most difficult to distinguish on the Burnout Symptom Cycle. The desire to prove initially emerges as beneficial, but if it gathers too much momentum, it can ultimately prove injurious. In fact, when the *desire* shifts to a *compulsion* and a nagging discomfort is perceived within yourself, the first stage of burnout has defined itself and may be coming into existence.

Stage 1 is rooted in a series of accumulated notions concerning self-esteem, expectations, and value. It is often characterized by an obsessive

THE BURNOUT SYMPTOM CYCLE

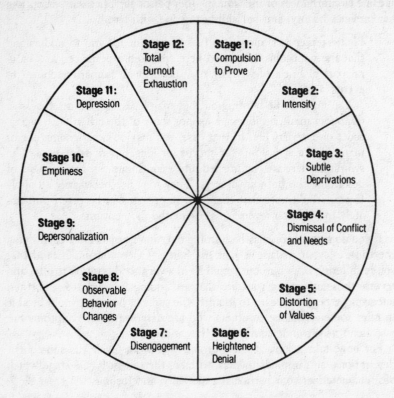

determination to succeed, to excel, to conquer, feelings of loneliness, and is launched by excessive expectations of yourself. Often there is a vaguely "delusional" sense to the anticipated challenge which is highlighted by an unwillingness to envision any limits or setbacks. Stacey, a woman fairly new to the academic community, put it this way:

"I think my compulsiveness is in wanting to be able to do everything right . . . to really be superwoman. Most of the people in my field have gone through all that Ph.D. work and have been rather compulsive to start with. We have that quality of overdoing, overworking, overinvolvement, and overextending ourselves. It's just very hard to set limits when you want something."

Stacey's compulsiveness was not confined to her academic work. She had a husband and an infant child at home and "felt I had to be superwoman with them all. At the beginning, when I went back to school and had my son," she said, "I had this fantasy of doing everything perfectly."

Other women who have been through the Burnout Cycle speak now, and with some regret, of their initial zeal and vitality—of their high intentions to become the exemplar model of best mother, most sensitive friend, ideal wife, sexiest lover, cleverest negotiator, greatest revenue gatherer, the most fashionable, the thinnest, prettiest, smartest, funniest . . . Often they aspired to all of these models, across the board. In time, their thinking became linear, their language seasoned with superlatives. They fused up with their aspirations and compulsively set out to prove they could achieve them all, at all costs—including their health and well-being.

Where does the compulsive need to prove come from? Often those desires are outgrowths of swollen expectations implanted either in childhood by demanding parents, or as adults by one's political, social, or professional milieu. Further, quite typically, print and electronic media play an important part in shaping one's assumptions concerning self-worth and set unrealistic models of that to which women should aspire.

The compulsion may be spawned by an absence of external expectations, as in the case of a woman whose parents retreated from supporting any of her expressed or unexpressed aspirations.

Stacey tapped the source of her problem when she said: "My mother is so uncompulsive that my own compulsiveness seems to be a reaction to her lack of direction." In this sense, Stacey's position on the Burnout Symptom Cycle was a compensatory response to a parent who made no strong statement of self-definition or structure. This is a common reaction for a woman who grew up in a permissive and seemingly uncaring atmosphere. As she matures, she places more and more compulsive, self-demanding expectations upon herself. Her driven quality becomes self-imposed. She is harder on herself than anyone else, and leaves little time or space for pleasure or gratification. In this way, paradoxically, she denies how little she was either cared for or was expected to achieve.

A woman will be less likely to find herself heading for burnout if she was rewarded for her autonomous decisions and helped to gracefully separate from her family without any hidden, unverbalized agendas. However, a woman who was rewarded for clinging to her family's values and punished for separating from them will need to seek out self-definition and may become compulsive in her need to prove herself autonomous.

For many women, the compulsion to prove may be studded with defiance and anger, culturally justifiable when placed within the context of masculine privilege. Penetrating what has typically come to be called the corporate "Men's Club" and being accepted on equal terms for equal or superior work can be enormously frustrating. Women in this position are often forced to continually substantiate their talents and abilities. The superhuman effort to establish parity with men—and often with women in superior positions—can also propel women onto the Burnout Cycle.

Quite commonly, Stage 1 is heralded by an unarticulated need for accomplishment which is born of low self-esteem. When love, respect, recognition, approval, or equality have not been forthcoming, they leave a hungry void. Low self-esteem, a floundering sense of confidence, a poor self-image, loneliness, or powerlessness can be temporarily propped up by "fusing" with or becoming excessively involved with a job, a child, or a mate. But if you are "fusing" up only to escape a bad feeling about yourself, the gratifications will be short-lived. When you conquer a role, your rewards may only touch you superficially. You could readily find yourself burning out through lack of substantive nourishment.

The many variations on this theme are discussed in greater detail in Chapter III, about family dynamics. What's important here is to understand that the first stage of burnout often blends into the second with little fanfare.

What You Can Do—Now: Make a concerted effort to become aware of your own compulsive and perhaps self-demanding patterns. Try to identify the point at which your desire to achieve or to win changes into a compulsion. Begin to pace yourself according to your own natural rhythms and responses. This could harness the burnout momentum immediately.

STAGE 2: *Intensity*

If that compulsion to prove gains a foothold, an urgency regarding the job, relationship, or project may begin to smolder. The compulsion becomes confused with conscientiousness, dedication, and commitment, labels that legitimize the new intensity. A surefire signal that Stage 2 is in effect will be the unwillingness to delegate work, responsibilities, or domestic chores for fear of losing perfect control. It's not that the other's abilities are mistrusted, it's that no one is as finely tuned to the details and ramifications of the job or relationship as you—no one else will give it the full attention it requires or deserves. You may feel if you do relinquish even a piece of the responsibility, you'll lose credit or status when the end reward comes along. As a consequence, pressure builds and your focus becomes even further intensified and concentrated. Again, the need to prove oneself is paramount.

When questioned about the issues of intensity, Deirdre, a 29-year-old banking executive, said this:

> "I often think that when I dig into something new, my take-charge attitude becomes rather manic. I get an idea about how something should be accomplished and absolutely pursue it. Once I've bitten in, I'm like a bullterrier—tenacious, unflappable, inflexible. There's no deviation for me. I have to do it and do it by myself. That goes for my job or a man. Once I've decided I'm in love, that's it! I don't let go. I'm really very, very conscientious."

This unbudgeable position usually goes unnoticed in Stage 2. Others, peers and family, may only acknowledge you as a woman who is vigorously pursuing a goal. But under the push, a number of anxieties may be percolating which seem to threaten your goal. Fear may manifest in the sudden idea that you don't think fast enough on the job, that you're not attentive enough to your child, not sexual enough with your mate, not quick enough, brilliant enough, attractive enough . . . or that without that intensity, life is meaningless and lonely. In short, some nagging suspicions rear: You're not keeping up with your standards of excellence, real or imagined—standards that have been gleaned from parents, men, the media, or even older, more experienced women, or that you may not have anything substantial enough in your life to take its place.

To quell these anxieties, you may dig in deeper, urgently pressing harder to compensate. Deirdre illuminated this issue further:

> "I think I become obsessive when I feel I'm doing something wrong. I turn things against myself, then become tenacious about wondering what it is I'm actually doing wrong. When my now-broken relationship was just beginning, I kept worrying about losing fifteen pounds, changing my hair, and whether his friends truly

approved of me. Nothing had happened, but I needed to make certain nothing would."

Another woman, Janet, a 30-year-old housewife with two small children, had a similar response. She spoke of becoming compulsive about the safety of her children and demonstrates just how the anxiety intensifies:

"I had just had my first child and was so happy but needed to prove I was a perfect mother, that nothing would ever hurt him. A few months after his birth, I began to get anxious over what I may have been doing wrong. I'm always looking for the 'something wrong'—I'll keep looking till I find it. I can't just say, 'This is fine, I'm doing okay' . . . I have to do even more. I couldn't let go of the idea that I had to prove I was a really devoted mother. Everything else in my life at that time just sort of slipped away."

This is the process of Stage 2. An intensity develops toward the project or relationship which often acquires an intolerable urgency. Along the way, long-repressed insecurities reemerge, and to circumvent suspicions of incompetence or intimations of dependencies still unresolved, women press harder and push further. They are now engaged in a beginning cycle of real denial.

What You Can Do—Now: Begin to delegate some of your responsibilities to others. This may prove difficult, yet it will alleviate some of the stress, quell many of your anxieties, and break the intensity binds.

STAGE 3: *Subtle Deprivations*

When, however, as Janet said, "Everything else in my life at that time just sort of slipped away," the next stage of burnout was ushered in. *Stage 3 is characterized by a waning attention to one's self—to one's personal needs.* With the project or relationship dominating your internal landscape, the subtler duties and pleasures of everyday life are often viewed as interferences—unnecessary intrusions—and tend to be forgotten or postponed.

You feel jammed up by time and demands, and the more mundane daily tasks are neglected. Bills go unpaid, clothes are left at the cleaner's another day, grocery staples are not attended to, telephone calls go unreturned, birthday cards or calls to friends or relatives are forgotten, prescriptions remain unfilled. One woman spoke of forgetting to deposit a check in the bank for over two weeks, another of not balancing her checkbook for months, and another of overlooking her medical and car insurance payments until she received notices of expiration. All of them commented, "I just didn't have the time." The day-to-day habits and necessities of living are readily put off for another day. Postponement is one of the major signs of a burnout process.

Along with these omissions, in Stage 3, wants begin to eclipse needs and women begin to subtly deprive themselves of emotional pleasures. Linda, a married woman in her mid-twenties, recently promoted to a middle-management position in an advertising company, spoke to this problem:

> "I don't have any time for myself now. I would love to take a break and go away for a weekend with my husband, but I just can't fit it in. I'd love to go home after work and play tennis with him for two hours, or go out for a nice leisurely dinner, or to the theater . . . but recently there're just not enough hours in the day. I bring a lot of work home and, when I don't, I'm preoccupied with what I have to prepare for the next day. When my husband tells me about his day, I'm usually thinking of something else. By the time I've done everything that needs to be done in the house, I'm exhausted and fall into bed. Or, when my husband wants to make love, I've usually just thought of three things I forgot to do that day . . . I'm not very interested in sex these days—it just doesn't seem important . . . When I do get sexually involved, I tend to become quite mechanical. I am also having difficulties having orgasms."

Other symptoms which may emerge here are related to feeling states. Feeling intensely driven, you may develop a serious demeanor, begin to lose your sense of humor, and become annoyed when others detain you with a joke or funny story. Where you might otherwise be alert to the ironies and inconsistencies of everyday life, in Stage 3 your earnestness may eclipse these lighter moments. Often there is an absence of hearty laughter and, in its place, thin, superficial smiles. You may feel pushed to acknowledge the conversations and interactions of those around you but find yourself indicating the appropriate responses only. You may also begin avoiding social contacts under one pretense or another. You're too "tired," they're "boring," or, "it's just a waste of time." As Linda noted, you may also find yourself turned off sexually. Anything that doesn't apply to the focus of your attention may be considered an intrusion.

Habits, too, may begin to subtly or more dramatically change in Stage 3. You may find yourself smoking more than usual, perhaps drinking too much coffee, or consuming too much alcohol, and begin to experience hangovers or suffer from insomnia. Some women speak of overeating or eating poorly—junk and fast foods. Janet, who is home much of the day, spoke of preparing her family's meals: "Everyone ate at a different time and I found myself eating all their leftovers. I stopped making a plate for myself."

As a single woman, you may just grab a bite in the corner or from the deli on the way home from work. The desire to give to yourself becomes less and less important.

In short, Stage 3 can be identified by the waning focus on your own needs—the tendency to subtly deprive yourself of personal attention and care has begun to take shape.

What You Can Do—Now: Try to reverse your patterns of denial. Once you've admitted you're denying, make a list of those necessary tasks you've been avoiding. Make a point of completing one, then another, and on to the next. When you stop postponing, many of your anxieties will diminish. Additionally, take a look at the foods you've been eating, how rapidly you eat, and the amount of rest and attention you provide for yourself. If you've been taking quick showers, change to long baths. Begin to pamper yourself. And, try to regain your sense of humor without using it as a denial tool. It will help you to relax and perhaps regain a balanced perspective on your very real needs.

STAGE 4: *Dismissal of Conflict and Needs*

This stage is crucial to understanding the progression of the Symptom Cycle. It's usually at this point that you become aware that a conflict within yourself has emerged, that your feelings and behavior are out of sync. Fugitive thoughts concerning your health—sleep, nutrition, exercise, and diminished energy—may begin to provoke your attention. You may begin to wonder why you're disgruntled, why that cough is not going away, why you're feeling "fluey," out of sorts, perhaps even put upon, when ostensibly you're doing everything "so right."

Logic dictates that you step back and assess the conflict, but, typically, women heading for burnout make every effort to conceal it from themselves and from others. The conflict is regarded as meddlesome—an intrusion which, if allowed, will jeopardize the compulsion. Therefore, instead of acting as a positive deterrent, the conflict manifests as a threat. As a consequence, coping mechanisms are swiftly erected which serve to block awareness, deny and control anxiety, and to dismiss it, along with your needs, as unimportant. More and more your own needs are postponed in favor of the "larger," *wanted* picture. The research project, the job, the product, the brief, the proposal, your family, are all more important than you.

Behavior in Stage 4 varies. But when the compulsion is threatened, you tend to marshal your defenses and dig in with renewed determination. When friends or family or mates express concern, perhaps by stating that you seem "unavailable," "preoccupied," "tired," or "not there," you're inclined to put them off. You may hear yourself saying that you'll ease up, "as soon as I get my promotion," "when the new budget is completed," "as soon as my child is in school," or "after the holidays are over." The words are sound but the intentions are specious.

When Linda's husband began making demands on her to ease off a little, her compulsion to prove herself on the job was threatened and her conflict blossomed. She had to stave off his concerns by creating false deadlines:

"I'd tell him that as soon as the immediate campaign was completed, I'd take a few days off and we'd go away. But I knew that I was already involved in a proposal for a new client and that I'd eventually have to make up a new story to satisfy him. *I would vacillate between anger and guilt:* I knew he was right and was being very caring, but I didn't want to be reminded of it . . . I just wanted him to leave me alone . . ."

None of the women who had been through the Cycle took their own statements seriously and, in retrospect, understood that they were rationalizing their conflicts away. Sadly enough, they knew, too, they would continue to do so. The desire for aloneness subtly crept up on them. They began communicating less, had little energy for intimacy, and felt easier being "left alone."

Other women displace the conflict. They throw themselves into vigorous exercise routines, continue to eat improperly and inconsistently, or find that they have little or no time to eat. Excessive worry over weight typifies the displacement syndrome. By focusing on unwanted pounds, harsh diets, obsessive calorie counts, the real conflict is eclipsed. Overspending is yet another displacement symptom. It may suddenly become imperative that you buy something new to diminish the real feeling of self-neglect—a blouse, shoes, the perfect suit. Spending money one can ill afford often acts as a spurious justification for frustrations and should signal you're developing an increasing array of false cures. As Deirdre noted:

"When I hit that irritable place in myself, I go right to a department store and buy a silk shirt . . . then I break out into a sweat and am really upset because I've overextended myself some seventy dollars. That money should really go for my car payment or the rent. But at the time, I really believe this will bring me solace . . . I mean, I've worked hard and deserve something for myself . . ."

Another symptom indicative of Stage 4 is the sign of genuine fatigue. Often you cannot get enough sleep and then worry yourself into bouts of insomnia. Or you may sleep restlessly and unsatisfactorily all week, then sleep through the entire weekend or even through a vacation. Stacey observed:

"I was physically just exhausted—too tired to catch up on sleep on the weekends. At first I could make up for my missing sleep on Saturday and Sunday, but after a while there wasn't time on the weekend to catch up with it. I was only sleeping four or five hours a night and it just wasn't enough. But I didn't want to admit that to myself or anyone."

It is at this stage that the potential for *physical* breakdowns is most evident. Caring less and less about your body forces you to become disenfranchised from your self. As you separate mind from body, each is left to its own devices and ultimately pushes toward collapse.

Women in Stage 4 of the Cycle ultimately find themselves searching for new and better ways to submerge their needs and dismiss the conflict. When the attempts are successful, they're led straight into the next stage.

What You Can Do—Now: Do not dismiss your friends, colleagues, or family members. Listen to what they are saying. There are those times in life when you must trust other voices of concern. It is imperative that you

begin to take time for sleep, for talking to others, and for so
reflection. This is not the time to jump into a harsh diet or take up new
exercise regime. Do not add any further pressure on your mental, physical,
or emotional stamina.

STAGE 5: *Distortion of Values*

Once the conflict has been perceived and put on hold, it becomes
difficult to distinguish between the essential (the real) and the inessential
(the unreal) in your daily life. As was discussed at the beginning of the
Cycle stages, it's not easy to capture the precise moment changes begin to
occur within oneself, yet when women dismiss their very specific needs,
they do begin to speak of discovering rather disturbing alterations within
their perceptions and value systems.

Characteristic of Stage 5 is the distortion of values which often
manifests in a distorted concept of time. Women in this stage commonly
compress time into the present. The past and the future are sealed off by
that same intolerable urgency. It's not unusual for a woman to toss off
casual statements indicative of her growing anxiety: "I have no time for
relationships for the next two years," "I've got little time for friends now,"
"I can't take a vacation this year," "I just can't get away for the weekend," "I'll have to skip the holidays this year," or "I'll just have to miss my
niece's birthday, or my parents' anniversary party, but I'll make it up next
month or next year." The need to sever relations with the past and the
future is a blatant and critical symbol of the burnout process. Linda described this dilemma in her own life:

> "I've been terribly dedicated to becoming the youngest middle
> manager in our company, and that's good. But I *know* I'm too
> committed to this career. I *know* I'm too involved. I've sacrificed a
> lot of my personal life, but the job seems to have become all inter-
> connected in a way that's hard to extricate neatly from the personal.
> I'll have to deal with this sometime, but I can't do it now . . .
> there's too much to lose."

The notion of loss, as Linda indicates, is one of the demons which
haunts the burnout bound, especially women. Losing ground, losing that
foothold in the company, losing hard-earned power, or losing the relationship, losing desirability, losing youth, losing an image in the community—

these are anxieties often viewed through a cloudy prism of death or survival. Given those two choices, of course, the survival becomes a necessity. In Stage 5, the other life-gratifying options are eclipsed and cannot be seen as possibilities. The survivalist, then, also by necessity, makes a slow shift in a significant part of her value structure.

Values here become distorted by placing the measure of your worth on how you are reflected back and validated through your children, mate, family, house, clothes, acquired goods, or competence on the job. Children are often viewed through the judgmental eye of the community at large and criticized for mispronouncing a word, making noise, or basically acting their age. Housewives speak of the obsession with cleaning their homes and the guilt which nags them after severely chastising a child for dropping a crayon, marking the walls, spilling milk, or acting up at someone else's home. "My family embarrasses me," Janet said. "I don't like people coming over because my kids won't behave properly. I know this is wrong, but I just can't help it. They make me a nervous wreck." The need for control over yourself and others, to have everything in order and "just right," becomes paramount. Control is a way of avoiding that intolerable, nagging anxiety which is becoming more and more intrusive.

As values in Stage 5 become eroded, other symptoms occur. Often, relationships themselves are misperceived. A child who is unable to express an insecurity may be perceived as underfoot and a nuisance; a friend who wants to talk about a problem as smothering; a mate who wants alone time as demanding. While these situations can and often do smack of truth, in Stage 5 the experience is frequent and questionable. Sensitivities toward the outside world become blunted and to some degree deadened. Priorities become confused. People who don't qualify for attention get it, and those who do, are often left in the shuffle. Women who become fused up in a new romantic relationship are sometimes swept up in the passion and their friends are temporarily jilted. When the throes of excitement and obsession have calmed, or when the relationship breaks off, she may recognize that because of her inattention she has lost friends and may not be able to pick up where she left off. Some friendships are redeemable and can be renewed. At that point the woman may begin to understand what she almost lost and just how distorted her values and priorities had become.

For this reason, the feeling stage of Stage 5 is often described as "disorienting" and "confusing." Stacey explained herself this way:

"I remember that my schedule around that time was very busy—even a phone call had to be scheduled in. I felt mentally hounded. When I was going full-speed ahead, I felt hyper: too overworked and overburdened. Everything was distorted around me. I was yelling at the wrong people and acting polite and nice with the ones I should have been yelling at. In order to keep the pace going I started using cocaine to give me a 'lift,' and then grass to level off."

Another woman who sought treatment for a severe case of burnout exhaustion gave an extremely apt description of Stage 5: "I didn't seem to know myself anymore," she said. "I seemed to have lost something within myself that I used to value . . ."

What You Can Do—Now: Today, take at least a half hour to reassess your basic values. Write down what is important to you and who is important to you. Sift through the connections you've made with other people in the past and, given their availability, make a concerted effort to reconnect with them. It is critical that you avoid aloneness and isolation. The lonelier you become, the less clear your thinking will be. Without feedback from others, your own inner thoughts will reverberate with ongoing confusion. You need closeness and intimacy to revive your sensitivities.

STAGE 6: *Heightened Denial*

Denial is a most significant feature of the burnout experience. You don't purposely set out to deny feelings, strong emotions, fears, or frustrations, you employ it unconsciously as a defense against the impact of life's harsher realities and demands. However, in Stage 6 of the Cycle, *the concept of denial takes on unwieldy proportions and acts to obscure the burnout path.*

This stage is referred to as Heightened Denial, as it's here that the Subtle Deprivations of Stage 3 are magnified and spread out to include a variety of situations, people, and perceptions. Whereas in Stage 3, the subtler pleasures and duties in a day are avoided and treated as interferences, by Stage 6, your world vision has become significantly circumscribed and limited. It's here that you go one step beyond the dismissal of your human needs. You begin to deny them and, along the way, you also begin to deny the reality of events outside the fixed framework of your compulsion.

When you begin to perceive yourself as behaving in situations but not feeling anything commensurate with the event, some denial is at work. In this stage, you may not be able to fully grasp the grave implications of your ongoing situation. And you may be unable to recognize the impact they're having on your psychic life or on the lives of those who care about you. Further, you cannot allow others to have impact on you. This defense is demonstrated by the woman who repeats the same story again and again, fixed in her focus on her job, a man, her weight, money, family, loneliness. She sometimes becomes a compulsive talker who relates to only one issue. Nothing else in her life is awarded conscious meaning. Another woman may shut down and close off any social intercourse with the outside world. More often, she will behave or act as though listening to others, offering just enough attention to respond correctly, but, in fact, she has drifted off into her own private thoughts. *Her denial has now become an essential ingredient for her survival.* If she gives it up, she might not be able to function. Therefore, denial serves as an excellent tool to avoid, dismiss, or discourage any possibility of another person making an inroad into her life. She is now experiencing the beginning of a critical aloneness and is heading for isolation.

Women engaged in Heightened Denial arrived there first by a massive denial of their own needs. *The perpetual nurturer is most susceptible to this stage.* Having shut down so many of her own needs to satisfy those of others, and seeking to be accepted, her anger festers. Unconsciously she doubles up on her need for denial. In order to continue functioning, by necessity, she shuts down even more of herself and, as a result, has less energy to expend on what she's come to consider the "peripheral world."

Stacey recalled her inability to tolerate social exchanges:

> "I didn't want to go anywhere where I had to talk to people. To preserve myself, I'd walk into a party, say hello to the hostess, find the closest bookcase and read titles. If there were no books around, I'd pick up a magazine or the newspaper to read. I was behaving like a real bore, but I didn't have the energy or patience to deal with new people. I just didn't want to be bothered. I felt I was fulfilling my obligation by just being there."

Intolerance is one of the major symptoms of this stage. Without the energy, interest, or ability to listen to or engage others, new ideas, fresh concepts, or interesting suggestions are experienced as demands and are usually rejected. As a consequence of heightened denial, you may acquire an inability to tolerate ambiguity or contradiction and become nonreceptive to the external world. Thinking turns rigidified and inflexible, eventually creating an even smaller universe. In fact, at its extreme, you may find you're either hard put to include international, national, or local events in your constellation (you don't have time to read the nonessential), or you intellectualize your denial by including little else. Either way, there just isn't enough time or space to attend to what is now ever increasingly viewed as mundane or unimportant. The inability to absorb is usually reflected in your impatience to return to that which you do consider important and pertinent.

To justify the tension and irritation, some women will find themselves projecting their anxieties and insecurities onto the outside world. By belittling suggestions of subordinates or superiors at work, lashing out at those who offer concern, or generally denigrating the interest and intent of others, the compulsion is protected. As a consequence, women in Stage 6 can find themselves losing their network of support and building an ever alone and lonelier world. Angry and weary, they may shut down even further, denying themselves the new critical needs for affiliation, affection, comfort, and friendship.

Without the clarity to penetrate the morass of angry and confused feelings, a woman may begin to experience a sense of isolation and be propelled into the following stage.

What You Can Do—Now: Listen carefully to your own language. When you hear yourself spouting cynicism and bitterness, take it as a sign of burnout and not as a reality. You must begin speaking with others about your feelings and your need to isolate yourself, and you must back off from assuming another overly responsible task. The intolerance you're feeling is symptomatic of overextended energies.

STAGE 7: *Disengagement*

When the denial of needs is intensified, it's a very short path to the disavowing of emotions. To compensate for being stretched too far and expressing too little, you can become psychically detached from your surroundings and, as a result, disengage from yourself. Ellen, a bookkeeper for a recording company, described this stage thusly:

"I felt I was looking in at a party—from outside, through a window. It was a little dizzying. I knew something was wrong with me but was so resentful that I pushed harder to maintain control of my actions. At work I'd sit in meetings silently disliking everyone, thinking how bored I was, how stupid everyone sounded, how no one was recognizing how smart I was. *I felt like a robot* . . . like a service . . . maybe like a machine . . ."

A critical symptom of disengagement is the sense of disorientation and diminished hope. In Stage 7 you often begin to speak a language of cynicism and behave in a loner's mode. Like Ellen, cynicism emerges as a function of protection. Fatigued by the continual effort to control yourself in what by now is perceived as a hostile world, in Stage 7 you're likely to insulate yourself in a cocoon of contempt for the ideas and behavior of your colleagues, family or friends, or society.

Your cynical attitude, however, is usually a disguised plea for help. This is demonstrated over and over again by the continual nurturer who, though drained and distanced, nonetheless can only define herself by how much she's needed. The more disappointed she feels, the more she nurtures others—she covers up her own needs by anticipating their needs. But, as she becomes disengaged from herself, she may either drive others away, or be too depleted to respond to outside demands and, as a result, experience herself as unneeded, valueless, nothing. Her judgments continue to be distorted; she may misperceive who is loyal to her and who is not. A subtle paranoia creeps into her thought processes.

Another woman in Stage 7 may avoid appearing troubled by being "on" in the company of people. She may click into overdrive and push her waning vivaciousness and humor to their peaks, then close down and click off when she shuts the door to her home. Ellen, again, underscored this experience:

"I'm naturally up and talkative—people expect me to be 'fun and happy.' It's really easy for me to move into high gear—you know, tell jokes, be funny . . . But when I was feeling miserable, it was a real drag. I worried if I didn't do my number, no one would like me. That was my value. For a while I stopped going out . . . I just stayed home glued to the TV set."

For the woman who is disengaged from herself, television, music, books, or the movies can often act as a best friend. Life is distanced and safe. Women have spoken of watching the screen "without really seeing" as a method for staying in life without experiencing the demands. A young woman in finance spoke of buying "ten to a dozen sleazy novels to escape" from her "anger and disappointment with the world," while a junior high school teacher said, "I would fall into a narcoleptic sleep the minute I got home each day. I couldn't concentrate on anything."

Ritualistic and stylized behavior is another aspect of disengagement. Internal loneliness freezes spontaneity and may propel you into formalized versions of living. Conversations become mechanical transmitters of information; sex is solemn and often academic; eating is automatic and joyless. You remember the correct etiquette for human functioning, but you've lost the heart for it.

At this point in the Burnout Cycle, you may begin to act out the disillusionment you feel and may begin to speak of dropping out. The disappointment is followed by anger and rage, which is then transformed into a sense of impotence. It's here that one woman experiences a rawness of emotion and finds herself depressed, giving vent to frequent crying jags, while another will find she has developed an inability to cry and perceive herself as "hardened" and "tough."

Fear over the inability to make real contact with others may lead you into false cures—alcohol, sex, tranquilizers, food, amphetamines, grass, coke—anything which will give you temporary solace from the real alienation which nags most of the time. Simultaneously, your behavior may now become more noticeable to yourself, to your colleagues, friends, and family.

What You Can Do—Now: If you've begun to use "false cures" to regain energy, do remember that they are masking your true feelings and physical condition. Back off from alcohol and drugs—they are not the appropriate antidote to your inner desolation. Very often, the disengagement can be reversed by seeking out affiliation with others. Do avoid, however, pushing your personality further to prove you're "fine." Pick someone to talk to who has proved sensitive in the past. This person could offer you the support you need while you revamp your perceptions about yourself. And, again, remember, you need rest, relaxation, and, above all, something pleasurable to feed your spirit. This can be reversed.

STAGE 8: *Observable Behavior Changes*

Women this far along in the Burnout Cycle do not like criticism. One of the first observable changes in your behavior may be the inability to distinguish between what you fear most—an attack—and what you need most: attention, support, closeness, and intimacy. You become more withdrawn, something of a loner, and more of an isolate. Your judgment may have subtly become impaired; you may interpret concern as assault and will most likely be difficult to approach on any intimate level. As a consequence, in Stage 8 you may retreat both metaphorically and literally. You may become difficult to reach by mail or phone, install an answering device to avoid contact, and require several phone calls over a period of days or weeks before returning the call. You may offer intricate excuses as to why you cannot attend a party or social gathering, or you may cut people off with a clipped and annoyed response. Perhaps you'll intimate that you're profoundly involved in a project, your family, a man, or a new group of friends to get those concerned off your back, or, you may have begun to suffer some further paranoid feelings and convince yourself that no one authentically likes you.

Often, in Stage 8, you are experienced by friends as manicky and unable to settle down. Conversations have little content—you may flip from topic to topic unable to maintain a continuity without experiencing boredom. Your language itself may indicate how you perceive people: "He really pisses me off"; "She's a pain in the ass"; "They're jerks, incompetents, wimps, stupid, nothings . . ." At this point you may have little space within your feelings to assess people or situations accurately or with compassion. Flexibility has vanished.

You may smoke more now, often lighting cigarettes one after the other, allowing them to burn away in the ashtray. If you stopped smoking some time ago, you may suddenly resume, explaining this lapse away by saying, "I have it in control; I can stop again whenever I wish." You may drink much more now, too, stopping off after work at the local watering hole, or buying a bottle of wine to drink by yourself at home. Conversely, you may choose this most inappropriate time to stop smoking, to launch a severe diet, or break off a relationship with a mate. In this case, you may reason that if you place stronger strictures upon yourself, you will become "a better person." Your search for false cures to burnout is now becoming rather intense and, to some degree, even frantic.

Another observable symptom is a verbal change in attitude. If you have previously been given to weighing situations and appreciating the value of human connectedness, you may now express your cynical opinions openly. A deep disillusionment and disengagement may be revealed in statements like "It's a dog-eat-dog world"; "Get 'em before they get you"; "I had to learn the hard way, now she has to learn it too"; "Why should I help anyone? No one helped me . . ." Feeling undervalued and angry, you may be obsessed by those in power, and display anxious behavior in their presence. As a consequence, you may act cold and distant, or, on the other hand, overtalk to compensate for your uneasiness.

Most important here is the desire to control your fragmented vision— your feelings and attitude. In the process, your behavior will usually alter significantly enough to alert others to the seriousness of your condition. Concerned about the extent to which you are jeopardizing your mental and physical health, friends or colleagues may try to help, but to little avail. In Stage 8, unless others broach this topic with kid-glove care, they will be dismissed.

What You Can Do—Now: It is critical at this juncture that you do not shut out and shut down on other people. LISTEN TO WHAT THEY'RE SAYING! Someplace inside of you, you have space to allow the benefit of the doubt on their observations. Instead of imposing stronger strictures on yourself, you must loosen your need for control and take in what others are seeing, hearing, and saying. In the same position, you would want a friend who is burning out to listen to you. Try to separate criticism from concern. This is of vital importance. As you begin to recuperate and regain your perspective, you'll wonder why you didn't accept concern and caring earlier.

STAGE 9: *Depersonalization*

Whereas in disengagement a woman can still be approached with extreme sensitivity and soft caring, in Depersonalization you have gone beyond understanding that which you need. Depersonalization is a more serious form of disengagement. By Stage 9, logic and reason may not be available to you. Self-negation is the prime symptom here, and it manifests in the disavowing of your body and person. Linda described this stage quite accurately:

> "My face had broken out in horrible cysts . . . I went to my doctor, who prescribed both topical and internal medications but warned me that my blood pressure was way too high, that I had an abnormal EKG, and that I needed to cool out. I was much more concerned with the cysts and followed that advice but completely disregarded his advice about my blood pressure and heart. It didn't seem to have anything to do with me at the moment . . . Anyway, I had way too much to do. I had to fly out of town that weekend for a major convention. By the time I returned home, I had completely forgotten what he said . . . I didn't want to hear it."

Linda's story perfectly captures the depersonalized mode. *A woman at this stage loses contact with herself, with her body, with her priorities,* with the sense of a personal future, and what neglect can and will eventually reap.

Janet also reported a depersonalization anecdote:

> "I had put on about thirty pounds over a year and continued to see myself as slender. My doctor told me I was a borderline diabetic, and if I didn't start losing weight I would eventually be put on insulin. I went home that day and ate half a Sara Lee cheesecake, one of my kid's chocolate bars, and a bowl of popcorn . . . I guess just to prove it wasn't so."

In Stage 9, little impact is felt by the conscious mind. Unconsciously, women may become frightened but block that fear by continuing to indulge in those habits which are destructive and dangerous to health, well-being, and survival. Time is eclipsed. People are experienced as specters of life—not sufficiently real to make impact.

Priorities at this point are meaningless. You may be drinking every evening and experiencing severe hangovers the next day, yet, while vowing each morning to stop, resume drinking again at night. Where you may have previously either rejected or used cocaine recreationally, you may now seek out friends who can supply it or acquaintances who deal. You may have a series of meaningless affairs which are exciting in fantasy but fall flat in reality. Time is now compressed into the moment—the immediate present. There is little sense of how your behavior may affect your future. As a consequence, the needs of others, which were previously overvalued, are now significantly undervalued and dismissed. A child's need for attention may go unnoticed; a friend's plea for help with a problem may go unheard; a mate's desire for intimacy may be neither felt nor given a response. In short, in depersonalization, others do not exist. But worse, you, yourself, do not exist.

The feeling state here is one removed from reality, and the behavior manifests itself as cold, aloof, drifting, and untouchable. You function, but by rote. There is little sense of connectedness or meaning to your life.

What You Can Do—Now: If you've lost contact with yourself and perhaps your surroundings, it's not as hopeless as it feels. There's still a part of you that understands you need some help. It would be wise at this point to seek out professional counseling with an expert who understands burnout. It might also be appropriate for you to see your physician in order to ascertain the status of your physical functioning. You may need to back off from many of your responsibilities for a while and attend to your physical needs, or you may want to revamp your life-style and explore some options for yourself which will alter the compulsiveness. However, you will need assistance. You must admit you are unable to tackle this alone.

If you are a friend, family member, colleague, or lover of someone who is demonstrating depersonalized symptoms, do urge that person to seek professional help. You might suggest accompanying her on the first visit to provide her with support. This act may also provide the burnout with a new insight on her propensity to "do it all alone."

STAGE 10: *Emptiness*

The depersonalized state is a breeder of emptiness. Women in Stage 10 speak of feeling hollow, cleaned out, drained, useless, void, and depleted. There is a feeble desire here to fill up, but the cures employed are typically false, nonreplenishing, and ultimately unfulfilling.

Excessiveness is a key to this stage. In order to assuage the frightening feeling of emptiness, women tend to fill up on that which is temporarily gratifying to the senses. Ellen related the following story:

"I would come home from work completely depleted. But I'm supposed to be the 'fun' party girl . . . I started using coke to get myself up, then I'd go out to a party, get crazily drunk, come home with some guy, and, in the morning, wake up in bed with this utter stranger . . . I'd have no idea how he got there . . ."

The feeling of emptiness is not pleasant. To most women it signifies what Ellen later called "the failure of my life." Filling up on alcohol, work, drugs, and sex was a means of tricking herself into believing her life was full and exciting. However, the empty feelings became so acute when she wasn't on the run that she soon found it impossible to spend any time alone with herself. She'd be thrown into what she called "unendurable emotional pain and panic." It was a torture to be alone because being alone meant having to look at herself.

Other women speak of developing severe phobias around this stage. Agoraphobia is a symptom of inner emptiness. Women who are unable to go out on the streets, enter banks, supermarkets, drive in traffic, take a bus or subway, are often suffering from the desire to have a reliable person—a nurturer of their own—to give them some support in their lives. Backed up with unexpressed anger and frustration, the outside world becomes frightening and foreign, causing them to experience what are called spontaneous panic attacks.

Janet described this symptom:

"The first time it happened I was in a department store with my youngest son. I suddenly got very dizzy, then my face became hot, my heart was beating crazily, and I thought I was going to faint. My legs felt like jelly and I didn't think I could breathe. I was scared to death. I just wanted to run. All the counters were blurring and I actually didn't know how I was going to take care of my son *and* myself . . . In a short time it passed, but I still can't go back to that store. I'm terrified it will happen again."

This is the experience of a phobia attack. Aloneness coupled with emptiness feeds the symptoms and forces the woman either to keep running or to retreat to her home to maintain a safe place.

"My overriding concern," Ellen said, "was to make sure I had every moment filled. If I couldn't find people to go out with, I'd take a tenmilligram Valium to knock myself out so I could sleep the time away."

Food plays an important part in the emptiness stage. There is the feeling of nourishment from stuffing foods which symbolize home and

warmth and gratification. Some women binge on sweets—ice cr[e]
candy—others on the carbohydrate uppers, or fast-food taboos. Stacey
spoke of downing two Big Macs, French fries, and milk shakes, while
Janet referred to pizzas, fried chicken, and potato chips. During the binge,
these women reported that they felt "guilty, but powerful," as though
they had some control—control over what they chose to eat to quell the
empty feelings.

Sex also plays a significant role here. As Alice stated at the beginning of
this chapter: "The only two activities I enjoyed were eating and sex . . .
I thought I was just sexually hungry, but now, retrospectively, I understand it wasn't sex I wanted, it was the physical closeness . . . I felt it
humanized me, at least for a couple of hours." In reality, she was becoming increasingly dehumanized. In Stage 10, sex may act as a narcotic, a
substance with which to fill up and temporarily relieve the numbness.
Another woman who was interviewed said: "I was getting so sad and
disoriented, one Sunday morning my boyfriend and I had just had sex and
five minutes later, when he went into the bathroom, I had totally cut off
again and forgot he was there . . ."

Since the empty feeling creates a void which wants to be filled, women,
like Cass and Alice, speak of wanting someone else to come in and take
control of their lives. Unmoored, and running on fumes, it's a short distance to the following burnout stage.

What You Can Do—Now: If you've reached this stage, you may feel
some alarm as you identify with the symptoms. However, please remember, recognition and identification are part of the authentic cure for
burnout. The emptiness you're experiencing is a direct result of deprivations imposed on yourself and, again, it can be reversed. You will need
someone trained in burnout and who works with phobias to guide you
back to the initial cause of your symptoms. It's strongly suggested that you
make the phone call and arrange an appointment with a professional. If
you feel unable to make the gesture, enlist someone else to make it for
you. You'll have taken the first step toward healing yourself and regaining
your spirit.

STAGE 11: *Depression*

By this stage, many women reach the point of simply not caring anymore. Although you may temporarily snap back in a new situation, per-

haps with new people, life seems futile, hopeless, and joyless. Despair and exhaustion are the primary feelings, if not the only feelings made conscious. Whereas in Stage 10, Emptiness, you may have looked to fill yourself up with false cures, in Depression you may use drugs or alcohol simply to regain your lost spirit. At times you may feel beyond hoping for respite. A major symptom here is the desire for continual sleep. Incentive and motivation are usually obliterated, leaving only the wish for escape.

Stage 11 is most serious, as it's here that some women begin to toy with suicidal notions. On an unconscious level, you may take too many chances —while driving, crossing streets, walking in dangerous neighborhoods. On a conscious level, you may mentally play out the suicidal gesture. One woman spoke of fantasizing her car crashing into a brick wall, another of "drugging myself into a lasting sleep," someone else of "leaning out the window of my office until I lost my balance."

If you're entertaining suicidal notions, remember they are not self-contained and unconnected to the buildup of symptoms. They are the handmaidens of self-flagellating, self-brutalizing thoughts. When women begin to regard themselves as nonfunctioning people, their entire lives are felt to be sucked into a vacuum of failure. Self-esteem is diminished to the point of nonexistence.

All too often, women in Stage 11 are unaware that they are depressed. Despair and self-hate are so extreme, they cannot separate their true value from their feelings. In essence, they become their feelings, and see no other option. As such, caring for themselves in any way is difficult, if not impossible. The refrigerator and cupboards may be empty for weeks, and while they may feel the need to eat, it's too much effort to run out to the market. They may fall into a deep sleep instead. The laundry may not get done, and because there's been no continuity in daily tasks, there may be no clean underwear, run-free stockings, or unsoiled clothes.

During Alice's interview she stated that her depression was so consuming she didn't have the energy or the inclination to put on makeup or perform any grooming tasks:

"I would forget to wash my hair, and then hated the way I looked. I'd avoid mirrors because they proved I was right about the way I was feeling. When I'd stop and actually look at myself, I'd think, 'Well, there it is—this is the real me.' I was becoming a total slob—like a shopping-bag lady. If I had to go out, I'd realize at the last

minute that I had no clean clothes and end up rummaging through
the laundry hamper for a pair of pants. I know this sounds awful, but
I just didn't care . . ."

During this stage, many women are beyond comfort. Some women are
also beyond tears. Others, as in Disengagement, cannot stop crying. One
woman may cease eating here; another may gorge herself on a quart of ice
cream, be unaware she's eaten it, and, of course, taste nothing. Numbness
and rawness are often interchangeable, causing certain periods of wrench-
ing emotion and others of deadness.

Relationships are often in serious jeopardy during Stage 11. Since
women here are beyond comforting, they project a sense of inconsolabil-
ity. Threats from the outside—from a mate or a boss—have little impact
on depression. One woman reported that her live-in lover told her if she
didn't seek help he would have to leave her. Although she was very attached to him, she replied, "Well, do it now and get it over with . . ."
Another woman whose job was on the line didn't have the energy or
judgment to perceive the politics working behind her back. After repeated
warnings from her friends, she was finally fired. "I didn't give a damn at
that point," she said. "I just wanted to be left alone."

Stage 11 is extremely serious and should not be either ignored or regarded as a condition which will "change by tomorrow." Women here
essentially have burned out and most usually do not fully grasp the critical
implications of what their condition has wrought.

It is of the utmost importance for women seeking professional care to
make certain that not only the depression is treated. **Burnout exhaustion
must not be overlooked or dismissed.***

What You Can Do—Now: The wisest move you can make at this
point is to make a visit to a medical doctor to ascertain the extent of your
exhaustion and what steps you should take to physically attend to yourself.
If you haven't as yet contacted a psychologist, psychiatrist, or social
worker, do so *today*. If you live with someone, enlist his or her help, and if
need be, have that person accompany you on your first visit. Many people
are experiencing similar burnout depressions, yet do not understand that
the depression can be lifted. You're in a position to alter that confusion.

* When you make an appointment with a professional, ask if this particular person is familiar
with the treatment of burnout. Currently, there are many professionals who are training
themselves in the dynamics of burnout. Whether you make the call or someone else makes it
for you, make sure the professional is advised of your symptoms.

At this point, you are in the process of endangering your physical and mental well-being.

STAGE 12: *Total Burnout Exhaustion*

This stage is the culmination of the previous eleven stages in the Cycle. While not every woman will arrive at this final stage, those that do have totally depleted themselves. There's no "me" left—the fuse has blown. At this point, the value of that original compulsion or series of compulsions has lost its magic. Life seems meaningless, without texture or tone.

Stage 12 is a life-threatening situation. Physical and mental exhaustion may be imperiling your survival. It must be understood that you have a legitimate right, if not responsibility, to seek professional help and care for yourself. This includes a complete medical examination and hospitalization if recommended. Your immune system may be malfunctioning, and you may now be predisposed to any number of stress-related illnesses, from the cardiovascular to the gastrointestinal. It is imperative that you listen to friends, family, lovers, or colleagues, and that you allow yourself to be helped.

When total burnout exhaustion sets in, you may be completely unable to make the appropriate judgments about your condition. The seriousness of Stage 12 is of crisis proportions. *It should be judged as a red-light emergency situation.*

SOME LAST THOUGHTS ON THE SYMPTOM CYCLE

Again, it is urged that you remember: *Many of the symptoms described in the twelve stages may be normal and even healthy responses to the vicissitudes of modern living.* You may be experiencing some paranoid feelings concerning your job, or you may be run-down and in need of time off, a vacation, a chance to spend time with a husband or lover, yet not be in the Burnout Cycle. You could simply be reacting to an event or a series of events which, when resolved, will catapult you back to your normal emotional and physical condition.

Additionally, please bear in mind: Not every woman suffering from burnout will experience the severer stages of the cycle. It is possible to be stuck in a particular stage for a short or a long period of time. Conceivably, a specific situation may have occurred—the loss of a job, an illness in the family, a move from one city to another, abandonment by a mate—which could springboard you into any one of the stages. Once that changes or is resolved, the symptoms may vanish. Conversely, if the circumstance is not altered for the better, and if sufficient attention is not paid to the emerging symptoms, the propensity for remaining in that stage or moving deeper into the next stage may become operative. What transforms these symptoms into indicators of burnout is based on both the intensity of their feeling and the length of their duration.

As you begin to identify your own particular symptoms, try to ascertain the degree to which you are being affected. If you find you're becoming emotionally, intellectually, behaviorally, and physically impaired, you must then begin to give yourself the appropriate attention.

Equally important is the identification of the symptoms as an education in the burnout process. Once you're familiar with the signs, you'll be able to offer your help and support to someone else who is stuck in a stage or series of stages. You may already have noticed suspicious burnout symptoms in a brother or sister, father or mother, husband or lover, your youngster in school or college, a member of your staff or a colleague, or perhaps a good friend. As you must take heart from the concern others will show to you during a burnout run, so will others want to take it from you.

HOW TO "UNLEARN" DENIAL

Before moving into the professional and private aspects of your life, there are some additionally immediate steps that can be taken to begin reversing the burnout process. And they're all directed toward "unlearning" and "undoing" the patterns of denial in your life. Many of the symptoms you've just read about can be prevented by understanding that denial can be halted. Let's begin:

1. Right now, admit to yourself that you may be burning out. Now, try to identify the feelings, behavior, and attitudes on the Symptom Cycle that directly relate to your inner experience. Do not dismiss any "pings" of recognition! Remember, you're beginning to undo the habit of denial.

2. Exhaustion breeds even more denial and distorts your judgments

and intuitions. This week, make it a point to get some solid rest. Attend to yourself physically and nutritionally. It's too difficult to identify old patterns when you're fatigued—your perceptions will not register accurately. Think of taking vitamins to build up your depleted system. Seek out a professional who is knowledgeable in the area of nutrition. Learn to once again eat a balanced diet.

3. Now, take a good look at the ways in which you've been functioning recently. Have your attitudes toward people and situations become rigidly fixed? Is your behavior unusually inflexible? Is irritability running high? Have your days become a series of routines and rituals? Are you having any fun—any laughter or pleasure? Try to avoid justifying your answers. What you want to do now is to get an accurate "fix" on the cost of your denial.

4. Next, begin to evaluate the models you've been using to promote your denial. Whom are you trying to please? What image are you trying to present? Is your desire to legitimize yourself overwhelming an expression of your genuine needs? And try to distinguish whose voice speaks to you with the most authority in your head. The "musts" and "shoulds" probably belong to someone else from the obsolete past.

5. Denial can be "unlearned" by reducing your inner controls. Think about what you've been holding back from friends, your mate, from family members. What would you like to tell them about yourself (if you could)? What myths have you been perpetrating to maintain those relationships? Begin to loosen up a little.

6. Think about what you'd do with a "free day." If you've been functioning automatically, this is your chance to reclaim your enthusiasm by admitting what is authentically pleasing to you. Don't back off from this step because what you enjoy isn't compatible with what you want to accomplish or prove.

7. Now, try to locate the triggers in your environment that kick off denial—those in your work world and your personal world. Are you denying that you're bogged down in a job you dislike or one that's become a dead end? Is your marriage in a holding pattern of politeness or sexual deadness? Are you seeing someone who is married, unavailable, or unsatisfying? Are you denying your need for intimacy or love because you're afraid you might not find it, or that it

might intrude upon your career plans? Take this opportunity to answer with abject honesty.

8. Think about the ways in which you might reorganize your life so as to include people with whom you can feel unrestrained and who have time for you. Don't dismiss this step because it seems impossible. Use your imagination, then set some new goals.

9. Do not dismiss the connectedness between your irritability and your exhaustion; between your aches and illnesses and your over-extensions; between your loneliness and your desire to control. If you're tired, admit it. If you're angry, declare it. If you've had enough, say so. If you need to detach somewhere, begin to back off. If you're tired of giving out, start pulling back. If you want to be given to, ask.

10. Avoid isolation! Even if your inclination is to creep away and hide, begin to seek out support and clarification from others. No one person will have all the answers, but someone may provide you with insights which could prove strengthening, clarifying, and encouraging. Friends usually offer interesting perspectives that can expand your consciousness and sometimes, through the talking, inadvertently suggest fresh options. Ventilate your thoughts. Admitting denial is the step which precedes change.

11. Today, when your friends ask how you are, try to restrain yourself from saying, "Fine." You don't have to speak an essay, but you can begin to answer with some truth. The closeness will act as a catalyst for "undoing" much of the denial.

12. *Make new mistakes.* Devotion to the old ones squires you directly into burnout activity. New mistakes are indications that you're stepping out of the old molds and breaking the habit of denial.

And, lastly, remember: When denial has become a way of life, you've become emotionally "stuck" and probably feel helpless to alter your inner controls. Paradoxically, although you may *need* to change, a part of you may not *want* to change. The more you're told you "must" give up something, the more tenaciously you may cling to the old cognitive patterns. This dynamic is called resistance. Popularly, it's referred to as the familiar "stuck place."

This book is not intended to make you change your attitudes or feelings. No one is making demands or insisting you become "unstuck." However, it is strongly suggested that, although you may be "stuck," you can still move.

—You don't have to leave your job. Just find out what else is available out there.

—You don't have to give up a relationship. Just continue talking to new people.

—You don't have to stop overextending. Just stay alert to what others are thinking and saying.

—You don't have to give up anything. Just learn to pace yourself.

You're going to be living for a long time. In fact, a recent study from The Aging Society Project, a special project sponsored by Carnegie Corporation of New York, tells us that women can expect to live until eighty-nine—seven years longer than men. What are you going to do with those years? How are you going to treat your body, your mind, and your emotions to ensure you'll reap the pleasures of this life? Try to live with moderation, not exclusively with extremes and excesses. By learning to pace yourself, allowing yourself to have time for leisure and love as well as work and accomplishment, you'll avoid the displeasure of burning out.

Change often occurs by simply staying open—by listening to new information from a variety of sources. And burnout is often arrested and reversed by allowing yourself the privilege of hearing.

Part II

WOMEN'S BURNOUT
IN ACTION

CHAPTER V

Business Burnout

"It won't happen immediately, but in a few years the words 'business' and 'woman' are going to be thoroughly compatible. Until then, we're all going to be very tired."

Diane V.

Do you ever hear yourself using these expressions?:

—"I'm compulsive about my work."
—"I have to steel myself everyday."
—"I keep things bottled up too long."
—"I feel guilty if I don't push myself to the limit."
—"I don't know what my limits are."
—"I always feel under the gun."
—"I feel a pressure to surpass myself and keep achieving."
—"I must keep proving myself over and over."
—"I won't settle for less than perfection."
—"I think of myself as a survivor."
—"If I keep going this way, in six months I'm going to be completely burned out."

This is the language of women's business burnout. In conversations with women at all levels and in many different types of work, the burnout candidate liberally garnishes her language with phrases of this kind. You

may already have heard yourself intentionally or even unexpectedly voic-
ing one of these laments. If so, you may be either seeking some advice on
how to alter your situation, or making an unconscious plea for help.

Women's business burnout is perhaps the easiest type of burnout to
identify, yet for many women it's the first to be denied. The professional
or business arena is double-bind country. Given the strides and advance-
ments of the past two decades, there is a reluctance to voice dissatisfactions on the job. As a woman, you may feel you must be in continual
control and command, for to reveal fallibility or limitation could be construed as weakness and score a mark against you.

When a man enters the job market, he is confronted with the familiar
sets of stresses. However, he isn't compelled to justify his sex—only his
capabilities. Women often experience themselves as being forced to prove
themselves on both fronts. It follows that women will tend to deny their
needs, their energy depletions, and their dissatisfactions until they're well
into the Burnout Symptom Cycle.

If you feel the crunch of burnout symptoms encroaching upon your
performance, your attitude, or your personality, alterations are in order. If
conditions cannot be changed, you may require a job change. Or you may
decide to alter the way in which you perceive yourself at work, and perhaps learn to balance out what you want from the job and what you need
to sustain yourself. Many of you are probably denying that burnout symptoms exist. You may feel that reluctance to admit to debilitating psychic
drain or to job pressures which are contaminating other areas of your life.
You may not be fully aware of what you're experiencing. You may only
know that you went into your job with exuberance, ambition, and optimism, and now you feel somewhat disgruntled, used up, disenchanted, or,
worse, that your professional life has, without warning, become hollow and
meaningless.

The feelings and perceptions concerning your job dilemma may be
influenced by the notion that your friends and colleagues are made of
stronger stuff, that everyone else is doing their job well and getting the
approval, rewards, recognition, and credit you are missing. You may feel
testy and unfulfilled in your work or with your working environment and
perhaps, on a certain level, betrayed by your own waning enthusiasm. A
lot of you came to your jobs well seasoned and experienced. You're good at
what you do, you know that, and chances are the experience you've
chalked up is a strong testimonial to your worth. And yet you may be

caught up in the very common lament "If I'm so successful, why aren't I happy?"

Meredith, a 36-year-old assistant media relations manager put it this way:

> "I think there are a lot of women walking around out there with a lot of rage. We're disillusioned and worn-out. I bought the idea of the career woman and I'm doing it big. I'm living on my own, I'm considered successful, I make a very good living. And . . . I curl my hair, dress very well, use Pearl Drops . . . and something's still wrong with this picture. I really do work like a dog and put in incredible hours. I like the work . . . but I'm beginning to sag. I'm not being affirmed somehow . . . something's missing . . . my personality is changing. I don't feel good about it all. So, why am I doing what I'm doing? What's the point here?"

What *is* the point? When you spend over half of your life in job situations, and you're unmotivated, listless, angry, or, worse, you're feeling increasingly meaningless, the money may be the economic bargaining point, but the work itself may seem emotionally pointless. Like Sisyphus, you see yourself pushing that job rock to the crest of the hill every day, only to press yourself harder on the next with a discernible loss of spirit.

What does happen to that initial exuberance, ambition, and optimism? For some of you, it may be a case of job tedium, but for others the center of that argument doesn't hold. Too many women with challenging and stimulating careers are questioning why their spirit is being whittled away and why they're beginning to feel cynical and lethargic—major signs of incipient burnout.

Meredith is struggling with the "whys" of this issue. The balance between what she wanted and got—an exciting, challenging job—and what she needs—being "affirmed somehow"—is out of sync. Her needs are on the downside of the slant. They've been abandoned by the more compelling force of her professional ambitions, and she's now beginning to "sag." How did this happen to her, and what can she do to change it?

WOMEN'S PERFECTIONISM AND BURNOUT

When you're on the Burnout Cycle, you usually enter a new job with an outsized ideal in mind. An old knapsack of internalized images is harnessed to your back which dictates who you *should* be on that job, how you *should* perform, the time you *should* put in, and the excellence you *should* achieve. Perfection is the keynote here, and the reigning *bête noire* of your professional life. Being perfect the first few weeks on the job initially seems to earn you the right to be on the payroll. But anxiety and tension run rampant. Typically, the first months on the job, you set up unrelenting standards for yourself and an obligation not only to match them indefinitely, but also to surpass them. The approval and attention generated by such excellence, however, becomes a mixed blessing. Meredith recalled:

> "I was super good the first few weeks on my job. I had a lot of good contacts and knew who to tap and what favors to call in. I was full of marvelous ideas and solutions to ongoing client problems . . . and just couldn't stop. I was on overdrive, humming along . . . I could do no wrong. Then my performance leveled off and I realized I had set up mammoth expectations for myself and about myself. I felt compelled to keep duplicating that experience . . . I kept pushing to compete with my own successes. I knew I couldn't keep it up, and not long after, I was working fifteen to sixteen hours a day just to stay ahead . . ."

Women who become workaholic burnouts can be said to have put all their identity eggs in one job basket. Their worth is measured by tortuous standards of excellence which betray an inner world of self-doubts. If you suspect yourself of being or becoming a workaholic and there are no commensurate pleasures in your life, your nonstop activity may be concealing a cluster of inner fears gleaned from both your family dynamics of the past and cultural criteria of the present. This is not a problem unique to you. Numbers of working women are addressing themselves to those fears and criteria and are beginning to sort out the distinction between fault and fantasy.

As a workaholic perfectionist, you're probably terrified of being seen making mistakes. The mistake defines you—not the effort. Many women speak of the fear of looking "stupid." Yet it's not anxiety over having made a "stupid" mistake which is troublesome. It's being defined as a "stupid" person. Quite commonly, a woman will choose to forget or to deny her past successes. Her collective achievements are not integrated with the day-to-day experience of herself; therefore, they aren't valued as proof of competence, talent, and originality. But she'll take her mistakes quite seriously. She'll relate to them as a measure of her identity—not as a measure of the moment—and use them as a terrifying endorsement of her incompetence, mediocrity, and predictability. To the perfectionist, a mistake is the dreaded evidence of what's been feared all along: there's a fraud lurking underneath. Often, the doubling up on hours and responsibilities is an unconscious act of contrition. The perfectionist feels she's on parole and must prove through an overextension of her energies that she is willing and able to pay her debt to the corporate culture.

Another perfectionist may fear her work life is teetering on borrowed time. Robin, a market research manager, spoke of her doubts the first six months on the job:

> "I felt as if I had a certain amount of time in which I was allowed to make mistakes. After that, I had to be perfect. You know, the first couple of days or weeks it's okay to be wrong. It's acceptable to make a few blunders—you don't know the ropes. During that time I wrote a proposal which was lauded and gave me a great deal of attention. My boss wanted to make me known to all the big guns immediately . . . I was excited and energized and felt I had broken some female stereotyping about myself. But, in the wake of that event, I began to feel an expectation to be better than I normally am, as if there was a time limit out there—a border I had to cross which would signify the end of my allowable mistake-making time. I can't come to terms with the fact that I'm not perfect and that that's not the worst thing in the world. I'm continually waiting for the ax to fall and to be told I'm fired. Every day I believe my time is up . . ."

To compensate for the mistakes she makes (which often can be reduced to "not being assertive enough," "not remembering the name of a contact the moment I'm asked," or "not returning all my calls the same day"), Robin worries excessively and walks around "with a sick feeling in my stomach." She consumes her energies working overtime at her office, and then, much later at night, "worrying about it all before I go to sleep."

Unfortunately, perfectionists such as Robin and Meredith never authentically believe they're right. They have trouble trusting their own instincts and hand their power over to whoever speaks with a voice of power. There is an interesting conflict percolating underneath their self-doubts.

As a perfectionist, you probably are of a dual mind. You tend to formulate two internal messages at the same time. One message tells you to take a chance and find out if your instincts are right. The other message dictates that you play it safe and only trust outside voices. You might think of this conflict as a struggle between your dependable ego, or true self, battling for ascendancy against the harsh-conscienced, superego of your false self. The battle between what you really believe is the correct way to proceed and what you believe others expect of you leads to a denial of the true self and squires you into perfectionism. When you slide into perfectionist habits, you no longer think through what you're doing or reflect on the consequences. The pressure to perform, in time, depletes your energy reserves. It would be prudent to remember: It's the harsh conscience that dictates you pay penance for mistakes, that you victimize yourself with overwork, that you continue to strive toward the spurious virtue of perfectionism. If you were relying on your dependable ego to guide you, you'd question your perfectionist obsession. You'd begin to perceive when it's time to detach, or when you need to be nourished by emotional ties outside of work.

The paradox of perfectionism rests on that double message you give yourself. Think about the dialogues carried on inside your own mind. You will admit you cannot be all things to all people, that you cannot single-handedly change your work environment, that you cannot gamble with extra responsibilities, or that you cannot survive in isolation. Yet the harsher voice tells you you can and you must—it stands to reason if you push harder you will surpass yourself. This notion is encouraged by the new popular seminar culture. You may have attended several training seminars, or read the myriad brochures offering techniques and skills on how to "get ahead in the company," and have internalized too many unrealistic career development lessons. Perhaps you believe if your female counterparts can manage the long, grueling hours, a monumental list of responsibilities, frequent business travel, clothes shopping, hair appointments, exercise classes, plus being continually creative and responsive to their social lives, their families, and their love relationships, if you just press harder, you'll match them in high achievement and juggling skills.

But each woman has her own unique rhythms, her own inner clock, her own stamina center, and her own true self. When you jump into the overzealous perfectionist mode, you may be unaware of the abuse you're heaping upon your own resources. You can "have it all," but you may end up giving out more than your "all" can withstand. Somewhere along that line, if you're becoming disenchanted and slightly deadened, a significant need has been abandoned, and, more likely than not, observable behavior changes have emerged, signaling a serious stage of burnout.

—Do you frequently address yourself to the "weaknesses" in your performance?

—Are you psychologically battering yourself into believing you're maybe not as bright, talented, skilled, or quick as the others?

—Are you trying to match someone else's rhythms or style?

—Do you often worry about others judging your competence?

—Are you in a race to win the prize for "the one who works the longest hours"?

If any of your answers are "yes," your high-standard's ante is getting upped higher and higher. The workaholic perfectionist ultimately becomes rigid in her thinking, then married to the idea that excessiveness is the answer to her self-doubts. When concerned friends comment on how "drawn" you look, or how "moody" you've become, they may be dismissed as interferences. You may find yourself "yes-ing" them to death when they offer suggestions for alleviating job stress, but continue to drive yourself. If so, that's a surefire signal that you've gotten out of control. The job compulsion has jelled and you're no longer in touch with your needs. You're probably giving less and less time to a personal life and are depriving yourself of significant attention. Additionally, you're most likely *not* being affirmed by your colleagues. By setting up a grueling standard for the entire office, you may be creating an atmosphere of resentment, hostility, and indifference toward your hard work. This is the time to begin to back off.

CREDIT THEFTS, RECOGNITION LOSSES, AND BURNOUT

That much needed affirmation that potential burnouts require can appear in many guises. Receiving credit for ideas that you have generated, or for work that you have accomplished, is an important source of validation. A woman, especially one conditioned to nurture, is highly sensitized to fair play. She knows whose "baby" is whose, and is vulnerable to injustice whether it be directed toward herself or others whose work is being unfairly "lifted." This issue is not limited to giving credit and taking it when it's due; more specifically, it focuses on expecting credit when it's deserved. Dismay, hurt, then anger are the emotional prices one pays when credit and the subsequent recognition are stolen away. Credit and recognition identify you as a valued employee and as a worthy competitor. The open acknowledgment of your talents, skills, and successes equals affirmation, which we all require to fuel self-esteem.

Potential burnouts do not volley the loss of credit or recognition smoothly, nor do they protect themselves from hurtful repetitions. Most women are not comfortable with legalized corporate deceit—it's not compatible with their conditioning. When it occurs, there is often an unwillingness to believe that the credit for a project, a deal, a proposal, or an idea has been appropriated for another's advantage. "I feel betrayed . . . stunned, when it happens," one woman stated. "It's not the kind of ethics I adhere to. Maybe I'm a fool, and maybe I'm overly concerned with how the other guy feels, but when I see someone lifting the credit, it eats away at me. I think that's a part of my burnout—that slow eating away that drives you crazy." Women tend to operate with a more humanistic approach to their working environments than do men.

Credit theft is demonstrated in a variety of situations and affects women in many different kinds of work. While the events which precipitate the theft may differ, the resulting stress, anger, and impotence are equal in felt intensity. Here are four variations of that experience:

  —"I'm told by my boss what a 'genius' I am, how fast I assimilate, how creative my ideas are, how quick I am to absorb the market trends, or to anticipate volume and implement solutions. But when

it comes time for public credit and recognition, I hear her saying
how 'she' gave that season a lot of thought, how 'she' predicted the
big new seasonal trend, how 'she' was responsible for the success of
the new lines. I swear, it feels as if I'm being 'raped' . . . I slowly
began to understand that the flattery she gave me was a weapon to
keep me cranking it out, but in my place . . ."

Sally F.—Department Store Buyer

—"There's nothing subtle about the way credit is ripped off in my
school. The principal will yell at me, tell me my idea sucks, that it
lacks vision, and that I'm not seasoned. Then at a staff meeting, if a
sticky situation arises, he'll use the idea, take the credit and the
applause . . . I'm enraged and quickly losing all my incentive . . ."

Sharon O.—High School Teacher

—"When I put a proposal together and it's greeted with enthusiasm, my bosses inevitably say: 'We told her to put that together—
she's good at following through.' When I do speak up and confront
them, I'm told I'm too sensitive . . . This adds to my burnout
problems. I mean, it's palpable. I get headaches, drink too much,
and feel utterly used . . ."

Tanya K.—Social Worker

—"Landing a plum account when you're selling advertising space is
a coup. On one occasion, I had wooed the clients, knew the ins and
outs of their operation, understood the personalities involved, and
had developed fine working relationships. Just as the deal was about
to be clinched, the bosses stepped in to close it. When it was successfully brought to fruition, they took the credit. But, on another
occasion, because they hadn't done their homework and hadn't
taken my word, the deal flopped and I was blamed."

Gayle L.—Advertising Space Sales Person

These situations are classic no-win situations. If you do speak out, you
may be labeled a complainer, overly sensitive, unprofessional, petty, pee-
vish, or a poor sport. If you don't speak out, the feelings of outrage are
stuffed down, bottled up, denied, suppressed, tranquilized away, neutralized by alcohol, or they escape inappropriately in unprotected loose talk.
"It's just very frustrating," one woman said. "My morale is killed. I wish I

could slough these things off, but it's just not okay when my ideas are usurped. It matters very much to us . . . very much. I mainly let these situations slide, especially when it's credit-stealing. It would probably be politically expedient to be more brash, but I'm not comfortable with that sort of point-system competitiveness. I guess it's a lesson in solitude and loneliness that women receive in a big corporation."

That particular "lesson in solitude and loneliness" is not an asset to the day-to-day burnout problems. It breeds apathy and remoteness, prime enemies of the basic need for affirmation. Although stolen credit is but one of the many project-to-project, meeting-to-meeting stress factors which cumulatively feed burnout momentum, it is persistently addressed by women in business as a critical energy depleter. Some women have learned to combat this situation through self-promotion skills. Kim, who works in public relations for a major network, said:

> "I'm not without problems getting credit for myself, but I refuse to remain silent about my successes. Before someone can nab the credit, I make sure everyone hears about it. I've been known to walk around the hallways saying, 'Guess who I just lined up? Isn't that terrific!' Or, before I implement an idea, I go to my boss and say, 'I just had this wonderful idea . . .' Even if it's a team effort, everyone then knows I generated the idea, and I don't fume and rage alone in my office. It's become natural. I'm so public about it, no one dares snatch it away."

Kim's method has been successful for her. However, her style is uncomfortable to many other women. Typically, women feel embarrassed over touting their own successes and tend to wait for the expected return. Margaret, who works with a market research team at an advertising company, stated:

> "Expecting credit is an idealized notion of the world, but I could never walk around advertising myself, either. Someone taught me how to use memos to protect myself. After every meeting I memo the files and my boss; before implementing any of my ideas I memo the files, my boss, and two vice presidents. And I let everyone know what I'm doing and how it's progressing on paper."

In other jobs, credit and recognition thefts may be inescapable. For many of you, Kim's method may add a pressure to act as someone you're not, and Margaret's method may be unsuitable to the way in which your particular company functions. Both are practical solutions which have lessened the strain for these two women, but what if you're mired in personality entanglements which you believe will worsen if you take action? Do you tend to absorb the slights without experiencing additional stress? Do you have enough support, affirmation, emotional honesty, and closeness in other areas of your life to balance off the strains? If your answer is yes, this is a burnout issue you need not address. However, if your answer is no, you may have to rethink your options.

Quite often, women keep their sense of options limited. The company is made into the image of homes and marriages. A commitment to a particular mentor, boss, group, project, or company goal is welded to their identities. Responsibility, coupled with a keen sense of loyalty and, often, gratitude, are powerful adherents which prevent you from realizing your own negotiable worth. Distinctions between home values, family values, and business values remain undifferentiated. Usually, if a woman is given to toughing out bad situations in her personal life, or if her family philosophy includes such ideals as "We're not quitters," she'll bring that same spirit into her business life. A woman who feels unappreciated, unseen, impotent, and stuck usually rallies her defenses and consoles herself by thinking, "It's okay . . . I know I did the job, and the people I care about all know." By denying her emotions, she hopes to defeat them. It's not unusual for her to have come from a family where her mother equated modesty with femininity and where her father espoused—but not necessarily acted upon—the virtues of humility. That double message advised her to achieve, but to remain humble and dependent. Her intellect informs her that her anger is a healthy response to an unjust situation, but her harsh conscienced superego tells her that her anger is an unlovely aspect of her self. When the superego wins out, she can envision an absence of options and begin to burn out.

Gloria, an executive assistant to the president of a computer corporation, suffered a severe case of burnout exhaustion. While in treatment, she initially spoke of the "heavy demands of my job, the pressure of maintaining control of the myriad functions and people . . ." She acted as liaison for all departments, which meant "understanding each personality and keeping track of their individual responsibilities." She also "covered" for her boss, initiating solutions, making his decisions, and generating ideas which "he then publicly projected as his own." For some time she assumed that all of these responsibilities "just went with the territory." She had no sense of what an asset she had become to her boss or the quality of experience she was racking up. "Al was quite skilled at subtly ingratiating himself as a savior," she said, "and, perhaps because I secretly wanted to be saved, I wanted to believe him."

Burnout symptoms began to manifest in Gloria's attitudes toward her body and health. Within a year and a half with Al she had gained nineteen pounds. "The more frustrated I became," she said, "the more food I popped in my mouth." She also began taking "uppers" for energy, and Valium to calm herself. "I was becoming an irritable wreck, quick-tempered and sarcastic with everyone but Al. I reserved the 'wonderful me' for him." Friends and colleagues suggested she change jobs, find a position in which her skills would be acknowledged, but Gloria put them off. "I didn't feel competent enough . . . I was so emptied out and exhausted, my judgments were all off. All I wanted to do was watch television and eat."

When Gloria sought counseling, she discovered that she secretly believed she had no other options, and no real negotiable worth. Ultimately she contacted a headhunter, "just to find out what the realities were. I called from a phone booth on the street," she said. "I had such an awful feeling of disloyalty." She found she had many options, that her experience, talents, and skills qualified her for a number of positions. In time she did change jobs, but only after she made the connection between her résumé and herself. Once she understood that she had an autonomous identity solidly established and refined through her own efforts, her sense of time and continuity assumed realistic proportions. Gloria had viewed her accomplishments as random flashes of luck. She had no sense of the past as belonging to her, or of the future as expanding for her. The urgency of the moment was all that she counted as significant, and when each individual crisis had passed, so had her part in the situation. Like that of most burnouts, Gloria's intensity blinded her both to her options and to hope.

Before Gloria could gain the recognition she deserved or stop the systematic usurpation of credit, she had to come to terms with not only what was wanted, but also what she needed to maintain her equilibrium. When she finally admitted to herself that she needed more than covert approval and that she was unsatisfied with "ghost" accomplishments, she was able to put a stop to much of her burnout activity and begin to reverse the process.

BURNOUT PREVENTION: REINFORCEMENT AND AFFILIATION

Perhaps at this point the affirmation you need, as well as an honest exploration of your job compulsion, can best be served by speaking with other women in similar circumstances. Potential burnouts don't usually like to ask for help or to reveal themselves as troubled. Yet, one of the top burnout preventive measures for women is the reinforcement from other women. Talking over job problems and the accompanying symptoms of stress, anxiety, and self-worth is not simply a clarifying experience. The responsive reinforcement and support from others who are not only familiar with your conflicted inner landscape, but also seeking answers for their own, offers what burnout candidates *need* the most and receive the least: closeness, caring, and affiliation. Support systems are an invaluable aid to combating burnout. Like the consciousness-raising groups of the seventies, the effects of female affiliation in this decade are strengthening, regenerating, and self-validating. It is of utmost importance for you to remember: *Isolation and aloneness are dangerous breeders of burnout.*

Several of the women interviewed for this book spoke of the insights gained through such support groups. Nicole, a sales rep for a New York–based magazine publisher, talked about a group "of five or six of us who got together at an out-of-town convention to discuss business." Inevitably the conversations moved into other areas of their lives and the mutual good feeling compelled them to meet again as a group back home. Nicole went on:

> "I'm not sure what I'd do without my women friends. I used to believe that banding together with women was healthy but that it threw up a wall and separated us much further from men. I've changed my mind. I work for two men, and while I've never had any problems with male domination before, these guys are my nemesis. I've been standing on my head to please them and getting nowhere. But my problems, I discovered, are not unique, and it's such a joy and relief to be able to dump them. Each of the women in this

group contributes something different—some sort of expertise. One is good at time management; another often has psychologically astute insights and comes up with new strategies and tactics for dealing with people. Another woman has made me realize the value of networking, and when one of us is stumped, she offers great contacts and solutions. And the other is an inveterate care-giver whom we all yell at. She's changed tremendously this year. The beauty of meeting with these friends is how invigorated we can feel afterward. When the group works best, I feel confirmed and validated . . . I don't feel as isolated . . . as depressed. There's a lot of laughter and good feeling . . . it puts my work life into a perspective I can handle . . ."

In an atmosphere of congeniality, trust in yourself can be regained, anger diminished, and some solid tools, skills, and techniques for self-preservation learned. As Nicole stated: "When you're growing, being nourished, and laughing, you can't be burning out."

THE "MEN'S CLUB"— EXCLUSION AND BURNOUT

Not surprisingly a large group of professional women have recently been addressing a frequently overlooked burnout issue: the hidden stress of working in a male-dominated work environment. They speak of the sense of exclusion, of a discreet but significant lockout from casual gatherings where information and decisions are informally disseminated, and of a clannishness which restricts the steady flow of important communications. "This is an extremely difficult barrier to break," Diane, a regional manager for a fast-food chain reported. "It's like attending a very civilized party to which you haven't been invited. No one tells you to leave, but they won't refill your glass."

In an atmosphere of subtle exclusion, the pressure to excel and the desire to prove oneself as both remarkable and exceptional become paramount. "The trick," Diane continued, "is to learn how to hang on to your femininity but *never* let them accuse you of being a woman." The issue also stands as a critical stress-producer and stress-extender, acting as it does on the ability to do the job with efficiency and to perform as someone other than yourself. While most of you have good relationships with either your male peers or your male bosses, usually one avenue is stifled. Some women have been denied the relaxed encouragement of a male mentor in a superior position. Others are invited in by the man in charge, but not by their male colleagues. Katherine, who spoke in an earlier chapter of her corporate life, put it this way:

> "It's all very subtle. A woman works very, very hard in an environment which is and has been historically male. American capitalism was started by men and while the whole business enterprise is beginning to open up, and while there are many wonderful men with whom I work, I'm tired of having to validate myself every day. If I was in the most fantastic environment in the business world—and mine is admittedly much better than many women I know—I'm still not in my environment. A lot of us are far more tired than we even know."

This conflict will not disappear by tomorrow. Numbers of women on the Burnout Cycle address this issue from the sides of their mouths with the implicit understanding that they know it exists, but they also know they cannot change it single-handedly. "The workplace is fraught with exclusions," one woman said, "but they're not the kind of thing easily typed up in a memo for files. I steel myself every day to ward off the feeling of invisibility."

If this is a persistent issue in your work life, you're probably familiar with the pressure to measure words, to monitor specific "female" responses, to silently absorb attitudes of condescension or thinly veiled patronization. It takes enormous amounts of energy and fortitude to keep a lid on escalating anger while behaving appropriately neuter. And, whether you deny the invisible shield or consciously attempt to penetrate it, it takes its toll in a daily drain. Additionally, it's equally enervating when, as Katherine stated, "you're left out of the camaraderie walking to and from meetings, conventions, parties, and in front of the watercooler. Or when you watch them all stop talking as you walk into one of their offices. It's just demoralizing. You don't realize how debilitating it is until a deal you've been working on comes to a climax and you're never told."

The dynamics of exclusion are basically acted out in a cycle of denial, self-recrimination, anger, then impotence. The cycle continues to repeat itself. Along the way, women begin to experience an increasing emotional

distance and a driven desire to excel. Exclusions promote emotional isolation, and within that landscape, burnout is awarded fertile soil on which to
grow. Without the affirming voices of those in your daily constellation,
the healthy challenge of the work is clouded by the compulsion to beat the
female stereotyping rap. The sense of being an "outsider" prevails, and
many women begin to question their own perceptions.

When Diane was promoted to manager, above and beyond the normal
anxiety which accompanies such a move, she experienced a loss of faith in
herself. Many of those early self-doubts are still with her:

> "I worry about my decisions. Are they based on rational judg-
> ment, or out of my fear of being female? Am I being judged harshly
> or leniently because of being a woman? Unfortunately, women like
> me are very busy using the man as the standard . . . but this is a
> fallacy. Yet, I find myself questioning too often, 'What would *he* do
> in this situation?' "

Initially Diane worried herself into a critical stage of burnout. She developed the intense tenacity which was characterized by an inability to
trust anyone else, the dread of not being smart enough, the fear of not
keeping up with an imagined standard of excellence, and the need to be
perfect "to prove they'd made the right choice in me." Her life became
obsessively focused on her new role as manager which she translated into
"doubling the revenues in my department." She began to avoid social
contacts, developed a joyless demeanor which was steeped in earnestness
and fierce purpose. Her sleep was often interrupted by frustrating bouts of
insomniac mind dialogues. Irritable from lack of rest or pleasure, she
found most conversations "intolerable and boring," especially if they concerned topics external to her industry. Her friends and husband grew
concerned, but when they attempted to approach her, they were nipped
in the bud with defensiveness bordering on abuse. " 'I don't need criticism right now!' was my main position," she said. "I felt as if people were
trying to take something away from me, and I had enough of that in my
office."

Diane, like many other women in her situation, didn't know what was
happening to her. Burnout had touched the interiors of her professional
life and her marriage. The intimate aspects of her relationship with her
husband, including her sexual life, were in a cool stasis. "I couldn't manage both worlds," she said. "I felt like I was on the rack being pulled at

both sides and didn't have enough to give to both. So I put my marriage on hold."

Prior to her promotion, Diane and her husband had been trying to work out the wrinkles in their dual-career marriage. After the announcement and the celebratory excitement had settled down, she began to resent the bargains they had struck. Working late into the evenings, and arriving at seven-thirty in the mornings, "I was spent . . . I was frazzled and put-upon and wanted him to understand how important this test period was for me. I just didn't want to hear his problems then . . . They were annoying me . . ." Diane began to unconsciously lump him in with the "Men's Club" clique from her office. Though she felt impotent to assert herself on the job, she felt she had free rein at home. Much of her anger was displaced where she thought it wouldn't hurt her.

The need to maintain a firm hold on that sense of job urgency was familiar to Diane. If she relaxed, ironically, she feared she might lose sight of her goals. What she wanted and what she needed had become blurred and unfocused. She needed closeness, affection, laughter, intimacy, and *support* from her husband and her friends to sustain herself through the period of adjustment at her new job. Instead, she became a closet "loner," acting as if she was involved with people, when, in fact, she was shutting them out and distancing herself further from herself. Affirmation of herself as a woman at home and with friends could have offered the sustenance needed to withstand the alienation at work.

Often, the "locked-out" experience on the job is intensified by your own family dynamics. Diane's father never achieved the professional status he had envisioned for himself, and found it difficult to encourage a daughter. "Nothing is for free" was his philosophy, which Diane internalized as a bitter truth. She firmly believed in paying her way but never understood the emotional economics involved. Her interpretation of his words was based on the premise of "earning the right," which meant bartering herself as a service function, not as a person. In Diane's home, mistakes were paid for through silence. Her father communicated displeasure by withdrawing and shutting her out. She could only re-earn the right to his attention by playing up to his narcissism through flattery or by becoming a sterling reflection of what she thought he, himself, wanted: to be revered, respected, and, above all, recognized by his colleagues in the business community. However, while she knew she could earn his attention by building him up, her efforts to win his approval through her own achievements only created tension between them. Diane could not see that her successes threatened her father; she believed she just hadn't accomplished enough yet.

That dynamic was transferred onto the men in authority at work. The more they excluded her, the greater her desire to excel increased. After a particularly successful deal was clinched by her department with Diane at the helm, she said:

> "I was utterly elated . . . but quickly cut down to size again. I expected that camaraderie that comes from high team spirit. I did get a modicum of recognition—you know, a quick 'Hey, good job'— but I didn't feel good about it. After the discussion meeting that day, my male colleagues shut down on me again. They were laughing and joking among themselves, but it wasn't something in which I was included. I became the invisible woman who's treated with politeness but with no professional intimacy. There's no way to fight that kind of behavior. I was furious. I kept vacillating between wanting to cry and wanting to scream at them."

What Diane did do was to harness her anger and dig in deeper. Burnout candidates often employ vendetta tactics to assuage humiliations and snubs. But their vendettas boomerang, for ultimately they turn their anger against themselves by assuming many more responsibilities and isolating themselves further. The sense of powerlessness is not easily muted. If it doesn't pop up itself in emotionally charged words, it will reveal itself in a fierce intensity. Diane doubled up on her intensity, driving herself, her marriage, and her creativity on the job further into the Burnout Cycle.

Women on the burnout path quite commonly view male bonding patterns and behavior as a test they must pass. Feeling goaded and challenged by the exclusions, they simultaneously feel compelled to break the masculine code. But that code is ancient and steeped in exclusivity. In many companies men are now cautiously welcoming talented, skilled women, if not into the inner sanctum, at least onto the team. In other companies, the rules are fixed. The male establishment is inflexible and rigid. Promotions are few and anonymity for women is typical. The overdriven, highachieving female burnout is fine fodder for the latter type. Veiled promises give rise to false hopes; a promotional carrot dangles on the end of the corporate stick which cannot be grasped. Many women have had to make some hard decisions about their business fates—the price of attempting to penetrate the "Men's Club" is too high. They realize that their emotional temperatures are too sensitive to the daily heat and understand that if they don't get out, they will, indeed, burn out.

Other women, and you probably number yourself in this group, continue the battle, determined to find methods for ameliorating the systematic depletion of positive energies. Another woman in this situation might refuse to admit to the significance of the small stresses she incurs, either by suppressing her conscious perceptions, or by denying their validity. The information is too burdensome and too dangerous. "Just do the job and get on with it" is her typical response to female colleagues and to herself. Eventually, as a result of bottling up her feelings and pretending she doesn't know what she knows, she begins to experience a number of burnout symptoms. One such woman began to feel disoriented by her persistent denial:

> "At times I feel something alien happening to me and I get scared. I feel I've lost touch with my personal world—certainly what's acceptable to me in my personal life. I have different standards for work and for outside work, and I don't think that's necessarily good. Sometimes I feel as if I've become a caricature of myself. I become larger than my own self. I bend over backward to act as 'a person in business' rather than as a woman or even a human being. I act as though I'm impervious to the realities and shuck all feelings for humanity in order to concentrate on what I'm contracted to do. It would be better if I stopped trying to be so cool, stopped splitting myself in two, stopped being so snappish or distant when someone else complains . . ."

The woman who spoke did seek treatment for her symptoms and in the course of discussions revealed she had been suffering from an ulcer and frequent headaches. The demands of her job, the added stress-extenders of her "split" life, plus the refusal to ventilate her concerns put a lid on her spontaneity. While male exclusions were only one part of her burnout function, that issue became a symbol of her methods for staying in control.

RESOLVING THE MALE "DIFFERENCE" BURNOUT ISSUES

The differences in female and male training and conditioning are underscored in the workplace, and perhaps for this reason women are more acutely attuned to the imbalances in both privilege and behavior on the job. As business options for women expand, so does the knowledge of historical inequity. The psychodynamics of women and men are profoundly different. Most men do not experience the compulsion to validate themselves as men on the job; the opposite is true for women. Most women do feel compelled to legitimize themselves—and on a daily basis.

At a small gathering of women employed outside of the home, four critical male "difference" issues were raised, with one eye toward resolving some of the conflicts they inspire, and the other on preventing emotional burnout on the job. The ideas and perceptions concerning these issues were related spontaneously, with an attitude of "this is the way we know things to be." They reflect many of the same issues women in treatment for burnout are addressing:

A. *Legitimacy and Entitlement*

"Men aren't trained that they *have to* make it; they're trained that they *will.* They're told: '*When* you go to college,' '*When* you become a doctor,' '*When* you become president . . .' Women are told: '*If* you go to college,' '*If* you become a doctor,' '*If* you . . .' Men are given the definite message; for women, it's the conditional . . ."

The fact that most men absorbed a "definite message" concerning their futures, while women absorbed the "conditional," takes its toll in female attitudes toward entitlement. In general, men are advantaged in that their abilities were encouraged. Business aptitudes and acumen were strengthened as a prelude to entering an industry. Until recently, most women were not prepped for career development. They were encouraged to esteem qualities of warmth, politeness, sensitivity, and attractiveness. Unless you had a father who promoted your abilities, or a mother who encouraged self-expression and individual identity, you probably developed a fractured sense of entitlement.

The notion of a "career" for women has traditionally been provocative and laden with conflict. Acknowledging your ambitions and your wish to marry and have children is still cursed with emotional underpinnings of serious proportions.

—Can you "have it all" without burning out?
—Will a child interfere with your career plans?
—Will your company support maternity leave?
—Should you rise to a certain level before your first pregnancy?
—What will you do with your child while you're at work?
—Will you be comfortable leaving your baby?
—If you already are a single parent, can you request time off for emergencies?
—What will you do with a sick child at home?
—Will you be able to work late?
—Can you travel?
—Because of these unknowns, are you viewed as "conditional"?
—In spite of your skills, talents, and perhaps your experience, are these "feminine" ambiguities held against you?
—Do these unknowns authentically prejudice your sense of entitlement?
—And, how much of that attitude have you absorbed and converted into negative stress?

"I'm overwhelmed by the child issue," said Anna, a 35-year-old attorney in therapy. "I can't think about it anymore. There are three women in our firm and I'm the only one facing the biological age problem. I'm constantly being asked, in an offhand way by male partners, 'You're not thinking of getting pregnant in the next six months, are you?'—the implication being that if I am, I won't be given important cases. As a result, I play down my 'womanness' and play up my availability."

Anna makes herself available for momentary travel, late night hours, Saturdays and sometimes Sundays, "to ensure high billing hours." She views each working moment as pivotal for her career and insists she's "chalking up invisible but significant credit." Time is compressed into the present only. There is no future, and past accomplishments are forgotten. Driven to legitimize herself as a nonconditional associate, she embroiders her areas of responsibility and volunteers her services indiscriminately to her colleagues. "When I decided to go to law school," she said, "my dad kept repeating, 'If you become a lawyer, it's going to be a lot of hard work and a lot of sacrifice . . .' That was okay by me then, but now I'm ready to snap . . . I rarely see my husband, and when I do, either I can't switch my mind around, or I'm falling asleep." On an unconscious level, Anna is making up for her "womanness" by convincing her father and her colleagues and those in charge that she hasn't let them down. Her professional life is one uninterrupted test period. The "conditional" message for Anna has become a self-fulfilling prophecy. She only accepts herself with conditions which dictate she keep running, even if the tank reads "empty."

What can you do to diminish your need to legitimize yourself and begin to perceive yourself as entitled? Can you "have it all" without becoming a victim of burnout? At the outset, *you must begin to increase your self-awareness.* If you're anything like Anna, your wants have almost completely eclipsed what you need. That high intensity, characteristic of burnouts, is camouflaging your need for replenishment. Fatigue, incessant busyness, and maybe years of denial have most probably impaired your perceptions and judgment. You may have trouble distinguishing between the essential and the nonessential and, as a result, your authentic value system may have become distorted and lopsided. It is critical that you begin to reacquaint yourself with your needs. What you consider a waste of time may be exactly what your senses are crying out for—an immersion in playfulness, leisurely dinners with a loved one or friends, music, the theater, films—activities which will feed and nourish but above all provide you with closeness, caring, and affiliation. Self-awareness—the acknowledgment of what you're feeling and what you require to refuel—will lead you back to the person you may believe you've lost. By listening to your reliable ego, your authentic true self, you'll hear the wish for relief from incessant overextension. Perhaps by allowing yourself entitlement to your needs, the sense of entitlement on the job will, in time, find its own legitimacy.

B. *Power*

—"Men go after power and feel comfortable using it. Women want power, but it's not in our experience and we're frightened of what it implies. I'm willing to accept responsibility, but the power concept throws me off."

What makes the concept of power threatening to women? Many women have said they don't like to use the word "power"—it connotes manipulation and tyranny. To them, power is seen as masculine, an attitude which can be traced back to dominating and demanding fathers or domineering and controlling mothers. It symbolizes the totality of the person to be feared. Responsibility, on the other hand, is seen as a competent and benevolent attribute, one which is accepting of individuals and their differences. It symbolizes aspects of a person which can be admired and respected but which do not necessarily overwhelm or frighten.

Often, a woman will perceive herself as having power, or as being power-full, but back off from exercising or demonstrating it for fear of losing femininity. If the notion of power is welded to aggression and intimidation, will it change your personality and will you be seen as too definitive, too masculine? There may not have been any female models of power in your background to whom you can now relate, or you may have heard the women who did have power bad-mouthed and judged as "hard and cold" by your parents or influential acquaintances. If you utilize your own power, will you alienate and antagonize men and other women? You may feel quite ambivalent about the image of power. You may timidly try it out, but pull back when trouble, real or imagined, threatens to erupt. "If you're a 'good girl,' " one of the women said, "you don't want power. You'll insist it's shared responsibilities you're after, and recognition based on the authority of your expertise and competence . . . I say I don't want it, but I've got it and hold it back. And I'm angry with myself for deferring so often to others who use it . . ."

C. Deference

—"If a man is told, 'Keep your hands out of the pot,' on a project for which he's partly responsible, he'll fight back. He may say, 'Nothing doing—that's my baby,' or, 'Get rid of someone else—my input is invaluable,' or phone someone from the upper echelons to back him up. When I'm told to keep my hands off, I listen and defer."

If power has been traditionally prohibitive for women, deference has been traditionally approved. Deference is a defensive tool which provides an area of safe retreat in the face of a sticky situation. Silence, persistent smiling, apologizing when you know you're right, displaying enthusiasm for ideas you believe to be dull, and backing down when your position is arguable are all properties of deference. When they are consistently used to avoid your inherent power, to circumvent confrontations, and to maintain the false self system, they become dangerous contributors to emotional burnout.

Consider the range of emotions inspired when you defer out of fear. First, there's a shot of irritation, followed closely by frustration, then impotence. A sense of humiliation emerges, followed immediately by anger which is suppressed or denied. Where does the anger go? It eats into your energy reserves and in time is converted into habitually felt hostility. Often, the anger immediately converts to tears. You tremble, clench your jaw, dig a nail into your thumb, bite your lips, and fiercely fight back the swell of tears threatening to erupt. The emotions are exhausting.

A habitual denier will state: "I'm not angry at him or her, I'm not angry at all . . . it's too petty to deal with . . ." But in time something snaps. In an unexpected outburst, you may lash out inappropriately, frightening yourself and everyone around you, or begin to experience a void within yourself, a worn-out core which has lost its elasticity and its spirit. Both modes are the outcome of systematically suppressing or denying the significance and utility of your power. Typically, a woman burnout will tend to "protect" herself by holding a tight rein on her denial mechanisms. In this way, she reasons, she can have some measure of control over the environment. She may bury her head in paperwork, appointments, and meetings as a method of reviving her old intensity, or she may lose feeling for the work, become lethargic, let down, disinterested, and find herself "even further behind."

These are serious burnout issues for women. The most obvious solution would be to take a risk and try out new modes. But this brings up another conflict.

D. Risking

—"Men feel free to take risks. I tend to be much too conservative, basically because I'm involved in too much gratitude and fear."

Why gratitude? The germ of that feeling extends back to the notion of entitlement. If you're not entitled, then you must have been granted a favor, or you're an unwanted legacy, or a company freeloader. Sadly, too many women secretly feel grateful for "having-been-given-this-opportunity-to . . ." The appreciation is limitless; "thank-you's" are extended indiscriminately, with little thought to who should be on the grateful end.

The issue of gratitude is a transference reaction from the past. Parents who communicated a message of martyrdom encouraged a measure of guilt. As a child, your activities, your conversations, your needs may have been treated as burdensome and responded to with irritable resignation. Your expectations as an adult may reflect that early experience. You may have so thoroughly inculcated the lessons of gratitude, you don't know how to respond to those in your professional life without it.

It follows, if you're swathed in gratitude, you won't make waves, even if those waves could be beneficial, and perhaps profitable to the company or yourself. Risking implies winning and losing. It's an axiomatic truth that you cannot win anything without risking a loss.

It might be enlightening and aid self-awareness if you looked to your patterns of responding when the question of risk emerges. What do you tell yourself—and perhaps your colleagues—to justify the avoidance of risk-taking? You may be stuck in the intimidated mode and fear the ramifications, either real or imagined. Or you may have become trapped in denial and rely on defensiveness to get yourself off the risk hook. If you're a procrastinator, you probably avoid by habitually postponing action.

Take a look at this guide and try to identify which style is most recognizable:

Intimidated	Denial	Procrastination
I'll antagonize someone.	It's not important to me.	This isn't the right time.
I'll threaten someone.	I'm not concerned with changing anything . . .	I have to think about it some more . . .
Someone will retaliate.	I don't care . . .	As soon as this season is over . . .
I'll lose my support . . .	I don't even know how long I'm going to be here.	When X gets her promotion, I'll be in a better position.
No one else has done that . . .	None of this means anything to me, anyway . . .	After the convention I'll give it more thought.

Intimidated	*Denial*	*Procrastination*
I don't like confrontations . . .	I'll be fine . . . just fine . . .	I've got too much going on right now . . .
I'll hurt his/her feelings.		After the vacation.

Risking is a critical issue for women who are burning out. Above and beyond the risks you might want to take which are directly related to your present job, you may be avoiding changing jobs. Perhaps you've become sufficiently disenchanted working for others, or have "topped-out" in your present company. To regain your spirit, you may be considering the entrepreneurial route, taking your skills, talents, and experience and going into business for yourself. Intimidation, denial, or procrastination will only prolong the Burnout Cycle.

Of immediate concern is the risk of taking a solid, hard look at what you need, right now, to maintain your mental, emotional, and physical health. To change your life, if not to save it, you may have to take some tough stances. Saying "no" to others can be construed as a risky act of aggression, or it can be interpreted as a sane and efficient act of sound judgment. But before you can say "no" to others, you must begin to say it to yourself.

The habit of overextending, of thriving on intensity, of feeling alive only in crisis can be unlearned, but you must stay alert to your own conditioned responses. Do you put off or postpone vacations because someone has intimated "it's not a good time for you to leave . . . too much work has piled up"? Do you work through holidays because someone else took that week off? Do you break doctor and dental appointments, skip lunch, work at your desk through dinner, miss the aerobics class, postpone the hair appointment, beg off from the cocktail party because you got caught in the quicksand of demands and "didn't dare say 'no' "? Or are you usually just too busy to take the time to attend to your needs?

Men will frequently feel freer to cater to specific needs, and although the self-care may be spotty, they nonetheless take advantage of certain opportunities. In this case, risking also means saying "yes." One of the women said:

"At out-of-town conventions, you're up at six-thirty and not back to your hotel room until maybe one-thirty or two in the morning.

That's a full day of intense, concentrated work. Th̶
the time to get a massage, go to the health club, go̶
The women won't. It's just wacky . . . We're all af̶
bad, or that we'll be accused of using expense account ...ᴄy for the
wrong purposes . . ."

If you have an expense account, do you take advantage of it? If you're
allocated dinner money for working late, do you take yourself out to a
good restaurant, or order a container of yogurt or a hamburger and eat at
your desk or in your hotel room?

Burnout exhaustion can often be defeated by making the small lifesaving gestures. As the cumulative stress and strain of your work life feeds
burnout, the cumulative hours of self-care can heal the damage that's been
done, and ultimately reverse the habits of your life. If you're afraid to risk,
remember to ask yourself, "what do I fear?" To live without risking is to
live without life—it becomes joyless.

The differences in male and female attitudes and behavior will not
disappear in short order, but by incorporating self-awareness, you'll have a
better chance to learn what you can change and what is unalterable. Self-
awareness is a three-pronged process. It includes *anticipation, identification, and comprehension.* As you learn to acknowledge your own perceptions and needs, you'll be able to anticipate which situations are poten-
tially loaded, identify your feelings about them, and gain a better
understanding of why they aid your burnout functions. This does not
mean to imply that you'll become impervious to the conditioned inequities, but it does suggest that many of your reactions will eventually be
resculpted. You'll be in a position to choose your battles and take charge of
your psychic and emotional resources.

Diane put these conflicts into a concise perspective when she stated: "It
won't happen immediately, but in a few years the words 'business' and
'woman' are going to be thoroughly compatible. Until then, we're all
going to be very tired. The pressure we all feel is an objective reality which
should be taken very seriously. If we don't, too many of us will be lost to
burnout."

CHAPTER VI

So Little Time,
So Little Love

"I have a very satisfying career, a growing sense of autonomy,
and I work like hell. But . . . I'm not enjoying it like I used
to . . . there's got to be something else . . . Can you burn
out on an absence of the personal in your life? I think that's
the core of my fatigue . . ."

Joanne W.

Do you ever feel you might "erupt" if you continue to live without
an intimate connection? Do you steel yourself when asked, "How's your
personal life?" Are your days so rigidly structured by time that you've
excluded the area of the personal, perhaps even in your marriage? Do you
feel compromised by the need for a close relationship because of the gains
you've won in your career? Or have you forfeited the personal because
"there are no men out there," or because a love relationship has proved so
hurtful, you've now backed off for fear one might "take you over again"?

Burnout is the by-product of neglected needs. When feelings and emotions have been systematically deprived, efforts to deny that neglect or to
compensate through work are increasingly ineffective. Control, compe-
tency, and even excellence in one critical aspect of your life rarely provide
authentic gratifications for what one woman called "that unlived sense of
self I've kept concealed for far too long." Burnout is indiscriminate: it

feeds on starvation of any kind. In this particular instance, it grows on that inharmonious equilibrium between work and love.

THE "CRISIS IN CLOSENESS"

This has been a sticky issue for women to address. You may be justifiably reluctant to point a finger of blame at your job for a number of significant reasons. At the outset, not all women are working for personal fulfillment. Supporting yourself, your children, and perhaps providing for ill and aging parents are indisputable economic realities. Satisfying work in itself is a goal we all aspire to. It endows us with definition and it provides an anchor and a sense of security in an otherwise chaotic and imprecise world. For numbers of women, the challenge of work has allowed them to shed the female stereotyping which traditionally kept their mothers—and threatened to keep them—in half-life roles. Many of you chose to reject those conventional values scripted for the typical fifties woman and opted for growth opportunities—a stronger voice and fuller participation in all sectors of our society. The pioneers of feminism struggled to open those avenues previously barred to women. Although frustrating inequities still linger in politics, the workplace, and relationships, those hard-won victories must *not* be made the scapegoat of the new, often painfully felt "crisis in closeness."

Take a careful look at your particular conflicts. Are you suffering from aloneness or loneliness burnout symptoms? Aloneness burnout often emerges when you're missing a closeness with yourself; symptoms of loneliness burnout will appear when there is an absence of closeness with others. If you're experiencing either one, you may be feeling more of an isolate, an internal recluse in a frazzled world of external bustle. In many instances, those symptoms are not caused by your professional aspirations. They are an outgrowth of delayed or denied emotional gratification.

Women across the country are seriously addressing and attempting to untangle the confused strains between work and love. For some of you, there's an expressed uneasiness surrounding the issue, an underlying fear that the autonomy achieved in your jobs may be lost through the admission of loneliness. Sheila, a 33-year-old social worker from Chicago, put it this way:

"A lot of women who are working and building careers are seriously beginning to question what the work is about . . . We've
been funneling all of our energies and time into our jobs and we're
tired. But we're reluctant to talk about it because the loneliness in
our private lives doesn't fit the high-powered career woman image
. . . yet we desperately need something more . . ."

Sheila expressed what many women have either alluded to or secretly
fear. An admission of ambivalence or discontent might lead to a backlash
from those who oppose the changes the women's movement has wrought.
And yet, the fear of that admission leads to a massive denial of the need
for primary nourishments—love, affection, intimate ties with others,
maybe marriage, and perhaps a child. The denial creates a "stuck place,"
an inability to budge. To avoid a direct confrontation with the "crisis in
closeness," many women camouflage their distress by plunging themselves
deeper into their work and, of course, deeper into physical and emotional
burnout.

Paula, a 43-year-old single parent from San Francisco, went even further
by describing both the ambivalence associated with emotional need and
the frustration it engenders in her life:

"I've raised my daughter alone for eight years, and worked hard.
I'm what's called 'successful' by current standards. That means I've
achieved autonomy and am dependent on no one for myself or my
child. But, I'm damned alone, and I'm beginning to wonder what's
wrong with me . . . Is this something I have to learn to adjust to?
Is it some kind of maturation process that has no end? I need intimacy with a man for personal fulfillment, or, for lack of better
words, I need companionship, affection, and exchange. But how
much will I have to give up of myself to get it? I've fought too hard
to return to that dependent, deferring woman I used to be . . . So
what do I do? I'm absolutely worn out doing it all alone . . ."

Paula's statement poignantly highlights the irresolution and conflicted
desires of the aloneness and loneliness problems women like herself are
facing. "Doing it all alone" is a major setup for women's burnout. The
continual and unceasing exercise of emotional control and restraint breeds
inflexible attitudes, rigid responses, impaired judgment, and, ultimately, a
burned-out spirit. That stance is emblematic of the survivor—the woman

who meets life with clenched teeth to ward off the tyranny of her needs. But the other side which asks, ". . . how much will I have to give up of myself to get it?" speaks of a guardedness, a desire to protect herself against the loss of that hard-won autonomy. Paula is in another sort of "stuck place." Unlike Sheila, she is unafraid to boldly declare her dilemma. She knows what she needs, but she fears it. As she sees it, dependency is a dreaded and certain component of intimate relationships with men. The autonomy/dependency controversy keeps her treading water in a familiar pond of doubt and ambivalence. But her frequent outbursts of unrestrained frustration should signal to her that she's heading toward a serious stage of burnout.

Lorrie addressed yet another version of the "crisis in closeness" issue. At 28, she has locked herself into an either/or equation regarding her future:

> "This is all very stressful to me . . . I'm at sea for what to do. I have huge shifts in attitude. One day I'll walk into work ready to tackle anything, and filled with invincibility. The next day I hate my job, hate working, want to be married, have my children, and spend my days baking bread. I wonder then if I'm only pretending to be a career woman. I worry about my choice. Is this a defensive career? I don't think so, but I'm so tired from overworking and then going home to nothing . . . Can you understand that I love my job? I love what I do and what it gives me . . . but I just don't want to be alone . . . especially when I'm older."

Lorrie has been toying with these roller-coaster perceptions about her life for some time and, as a result, has set up an either/or prison for herself which is clearly defeating. Her neglected needs have backed up on her and, in a fierce reaction, she chooses to see her life in terms of work or love —mutually exclusive options. Lorrie's judgments have calcified. Burning out on her anxiety, her future fear, and an impoverished personal life, she can neither conceive of a middle ground which would provide her with the balance she needs to incorporate both, nor can she appreciate how, ultimately, work *and* love complement each other and help to sustain the energy some women demonstrate who do not burn out and seem to "have it all."

CAN YOU "HAVE IT ALL" WITHOUT BURNOUT?

It goes without saying that the ideal situation for women, as well as men, is that perfect symmetry between a satisfactory work life and a fulfilling intimate relationship. But this is not a perfect world; it's filled with inconsistencies and contradictions. Women in corporate positions are suffering what writers Christine Doudna and Fern McBride call "Single Shock"*—the absence of eligible men for women at the top. Yet, one doesn't have to be a high-achiever to discern this absence. Numbers of women in varying jobs and levels of accomplishment are uncomfortably aware of what seems to be a lack of not only available men, but men who are willing to commit themselves to one woman and work through the problems. And even those women who do have satisfying work, a husband or mate, and perhaps children, often complain of a flatness in their lives, an intimacy gone stale.**

Yet there are those women who do manage to juggle both work and love —jobs, mates, family, friends—sometimes even without a committed mate, who infrequently suffer from severe burnout exhaustion. When they do, the symptoms are of the short-term variety, and the women themselves are usually seeking more "alone" time. You may have observed that many of the women who appear to "have it all" also seem to be workaholics, and you may question how they avoid becoming "drained" and "wasted." It's important for you to understand that *all hardworking, high-achieving women do not burn out.*

This is not as contradictory a statement as it seems. If you scrutinize the life of a woman who seems to "have it all," you'll note that she may only have "some of it all," or she may have "all of it all," but sequentially. The myth of the indomitable superwoman who neatly juggles everything has acted as a catalyst for rampant anxiety, excessive drivenness, and severe burnout exhaustion in many women's lives. The woman who has "some of it all," however, usually offsets her expenditures of energy and intensity by a return somewhere in tenderness, affection, companionship, and play. Love, work, friends, family, and pleasurable activities are all aspects of her life. She's able to volley pieces of them all—perhaps two, three, or even

* *Savvy,* February 1980, p. 17.
** See Chapter VII, "Relationship Burnout."

four or more worlds—because she doesn't seek to merge with others and become as one with them, but to participate in their lives while enjoying her own. Often she has developed a sense of humor which provides her with perspective and allows her to laugh off the frequent idiosyncratic annoyances of others without absorbing the stings. She knows when to back off, when to detach, and when to say "no."

This doesn't mean that a balanced woman is impervious to hurt, insult, rejection, or, on the other side, to transcendent feelings of love, and it doesn't mean she is never overtired or cranky. But it does imply that she can distinguish between "I" and "you," and refrain from "fusing up" with either work or love, yet enjoy a satisfying collaboration with both without burning out. These women have *ego boundaries* which are intact. They're able to maintain a sense of self which is, in the main, constant and reliable.

YOUR EGO BOUNDARIES AND THE TYRANNY OF CLOSENESS

Inconstant or "fluid" ego boundaries are frequently the root culprits of loneliness, aloneness, relationship, and job burnout. Women with inconstant ego boundaries tend to "lose" themselves in other people or in situations. The strong identification with work or love allows you to merge with an object outside of yourself and obtain a symbolic anchor to which you are then "attached." A galaxy of dependency needs which have been suppressed, denied, neglected, or of which you were brutally deprived, perhaps since childhood, emerge and, like homing pigeons, fly to that desired object for nourishment and gratification. At that point, the boundaries of the self become blurred, and aspects of them collapse. As a consequence, it's difficult to distinguish where you leave off and the other person or situation begins. And if that phenomenon extends across the work-love axis, job or relationship burnout isn't far away.

When those boundaries are constant, or intact, there's an elasticity about them—you're able to stretch out beyond their familiar limits but are equally able to judge the extent of your limits, snap back and regain your own identity. Experiences are enlarging but not engulfing. When those boundaries are weak, your hungry dependency needs seek to devour the person or situation on which you have focused.

Behind those boundaries is your ego, or self, which operates as a mediator between external stimuli and your internal reactions or responses. As an infant, before your sense of self—your separateness—was established, there were no distinctions between you and the larger world. But as you developed and discovered that your needs would not be responded to with the immediacy of your demands, the limits on your sense of omnipotence were established. Your reactions and responses to the "otherness" of people allowed you to form viewpoints, preferences, tastes, and opinions about the world as separate from your own self, and fledgling ego boundaries were erected.

Those fledgling boundaries were strengthened in proportion to the degree of approval and security you felt with that new and separate identity. However, if your separation process was not treated lovingly, if your mother or father was disapproving of your developing individuality, yet smiled upon you for clinging to her or to him, the construction of healthy ego boundaries was infringed upon and arrested. In some homes, one parent may serve to offset the demands of the other and reinforce healthy boundaries. Your father, for instance, may have been the validating figure in your family, or your mother may have been the mainstay of psychic support and growth. Those two fundamental relationships are crucial to the way in which your ego developed. However, if either parent discouraged independent thinking and the movement away from them, if they simultaneously maintained an unresponsiveness to your dependency needs, or if their demands were inconsistent, then the message you received was confusing and painful.

As a daughter, you were probably taught the lessons mothers handed down through their training—to nurture others and to either put your own needs last or deny them.* But when your needs are systematically neglected, although you may attempt to bury them, they swell with a painfully felt hunger. When a mother is unresponsive to her daughter's needs, yet attentive to those of her husband, sons, relatives, or family friends, a young girl will ultimately see her needs as "wrong" or unimportant and attempt to flee from them. You may have learned to cope with the cries of your unmet needs by submerging and denying them—by presenting yourself as self-sufficient and self-reliant. This posture is acceptable to the world at large but alienating for you as a young girl. Instead of

* See Chapter II, "Why Women Burn Out."

your sense of self becoming stronger and more grounded, your image
assumes the top priority. Gradually and subtly you develop a superstruc-
ture of seeming competence, but without a securely defined foundation.
That starved self craves feeding; it increasingly experiences pangs of a
qualitative aloneness and will seek relief through others. Separateness then
is equated with aloneness, which may culminate in feelings of anxiety or
even panic. The ego boundaries you've erected to distinguish yourself
from the rest of the world are insubstantial, the self you project displays a
false infallibility, and the self which is authentic and human either never
fully and reliably functions or is abandoned.

That abandoned self is by no means quieted. It longs to reunite with a
"mothering," to return to a nurtured time of remembered beauty, and to
merge with that primal state of unconditional love and security. For this
reason, your ego boundaries tend to weaken or dissolve when the self is
provided with either a human alliance or a situation where it can "lose"
itself, "flow" into, "merge" with, or "fuse" together with an object, person, or situation outside of its boundaries. That wish for reunion is a
phenomenon which never completely disappears. Its power is witnessed in
those sexual experiences which women and men alike often refer to as
"transcendent." Those who have constant and reliable ego boundaries are
able to snap back and resume a mellowed sense of separateness. Those
whose ego boundaries are inconstant and unreliable long to remain in that
state of transcendent symbiosis, for when they snap back, their separateness is experienced as unacceptable, if not grievous.

For women whose needs have been neglected and then denied, that
feeling of fusion is irresistible. Loneliness is obliterated by throwing themselves into a relationship or work. But in time, reality emerges and they
fall into the old familiar pain. For this reason, many women who have
experienced these feelings have either resisted or retreated from forming
lover relationships. Their needs are so great, their fear of being "consumed" so apparent, that they avoid intimacy for fear of losing control
and independence. They frequently view themselves as stuck between a
rock and a hard place. To move forward means you risk experiencing those
feelings of caring too much, but to remain standing still means you risk
less and less and become increasingly tied to achievement and accomplishment as the mainstays of life.

Do you identify with the inconstancy and unreliability of your sense of

self and ego boundaries? If you do, you may be familiar with the language
of suspicion which accompanies the notion of a close relationship:

—"I don't want to meet anyone I'm too attracted to: I can't afford that
kind of *affliction.*"
—"Every time I've fallen in love, I get the *'fever'* and lose my connec-
tion to my work and my friends."
—"I get completely *possessed* and lose my center."
—"Please! No more attachments—that impassioned state is my *ruin.*"

The words which garnish the descriptions are all associated with illness
and destruction. Yet the potency of the expression is clearly intended.
When ego boundaries are weak, the sense of self is endangered. In a
symbiotic relationship, you may experience yourself as either being "swallowed up" by the felt intensity, or as continually resisting the desire to
"swallow up" the object yourself in order to deny the extent of your need.

THE SEVERED RELATIONSHIP AND BURNOUT

On the other side of the desire to "merge" is the terror of rejection and
psychic pain. One woman bluntly stated:

"I don't want to live with the waiting, the quashed hopes, the
terrible feelings of betrayal and loss I associate with relationships. I
invest too much in them and have been hurt too often. Whether
I'm falling in love, am in love, or recuperating from love, I'm a
wreck. I'm distracted from my work, my interests, my friends, my
life—I can't seem to hang on to what I value about myself, and if
that's a type of burnout, I've been there."

That is a "type of burnout." In the aftermath of a consuming or all-
enveloping relationship, those "terrible feelings of betrayal and loss" can
sap you of strength and leave you with both an inner flatness and a revived
fear of closeness which affect your motivation and your vision. Sometimes,
the anger which breaks through that "flatness" can act as a useful tool. It's
an authentic response to insult or injury and assists in redeeming the
"separateness" which was lost. But more often, the benefits of anger are
short-lived—the woman with weak ego boundaries experiences herself as
"wrong" and her self-esteem will take an agonizing dive.

In describing the emotional burnout she experienced after breaking up with a man she'd lived with for a little over a year, another woman said:

"I cried a lot then . . . I'd swing from tears to anger, to self-hatred, to fantasies of revenge, then back to tears. My self-esteem was shattered—I felt undesirable, unlovable . . . not enough . . . all wrong. I had opened myself up to this man and revealed all my sensitivities . . . It was a lousy time. There was no 'me' left—only the ghost of 'him' who had taken over. I would try to change the hurt to anger because anger was the only feeling that got me around the room. I was so obsessed with the loss, I couldn't focus on anything else. My concentration span was about sixteen seconds, and my work suffered immeasurably."

When the desire for "fusion" with another takes control, it's accompanied by a blind trust. The intensity of the connection obscures judgment, and that sense of "separateness" is lost. Those needs which were never attended to as a child rise to the surface and are exposed. Skepticism takes a holiday and is replaced by expectation. But when that relationship is severed, the "self" experiences a sharp cut, and the needs of the self relive the original sense of abandonment.

To ensure that those feelings will never again be experienced and to avoid the burnout devastation associated with such a profoundly felt loss, many women maintain an illusion of invulnerability and distance themselves from what's construed as danger. For some, it's a temporary distancing, "until I can find myself again," which is healthy and sound. Time off provides a private interval in which to reclaim and restore the ailing self. It's a time for healing wounds, for reassessing the dynamics of that washed-up relationship—the joy and the pain—and for renovating unrealistic expectations. Equally critical is the time that interval provides for revitalizing charred and burned-out emotions, as well as for reevaluating who you are—your strengths and your weaknesses, and what you need.

For other women, however, restoration is often delayed. You may decide to permanently remove yourself from the rigors of those inconstant ego boundaries. The joy of the relationship is remembered, but sealed away—the pleasures of closeness are now equated with pain. After experiencing a heavy dose of disillusionment, the equation seems reasonable—but only in theory. The repercussions of such decisions can, and often do, lead to what's called a "reaction formation"—an excessive devotion to an object completely unrelated to that which is needed.

REACTION FORMATIONS AND
THE LOSS OF CLOSENESS

A "reaction formation" is another type of denial and, in turn, a serious breeder of burnout. The suppression of a need and the subsequent displacement of your energy and focus onto something or someone else are the twofold dynamics. It may come about as the result—as has been discussed—of a painful experience, it could emerge as the by-product of a fierce dedication to a particular conviction, or it might develop out of an adherence to, or rebellion against, old family principles and philosophies.

The mechanism isn't usually easy to spot. It often takes the passing of time and the depletion of energies to perceive the changes in your attitudes and behavior. In this case, what *isn't* being addressed is the main clue. Outwardly, there's an avoidance of the usual banter concerning topics of closeness, affection, love, marriage, or the desire for a child. When other women discuss loneliness, the absence of intimacy, the baby decisions to come, or the juggling of work and love, if you are acting out a reaction formation, you'll either change the subject, become silent, or attempt to discredit those aspects of life experience. You may withdraw and become remote, declaring: "I don't have time for all that game playing . . ." "It's not one of my burning concerns . . ." "The whole topic neither appeals nor interests me . . ." "There are far more important aspects to living . . ." "I'm interested in success, financial security, and total independence . . ." or "My work is far more rewarding than any of those issues."

These verbal expressions are confusing because there's usually a degree of truth to what you're saying. Not everyone is dealing with the work-love controversy, the "crisis in closeness," finding a lover, planning a pregnancy, or coping with neglected needs. Yet for the woman burning out, issues concerning both work and love deserve equal emphasis, and a blanket denial of one side or the other requires serious attention.

If you're behaving out of a reaction formation, you may be pouring all of your time, energy, focus, intensity, and desire to "merge" into your job. Just as women will burn out from the excessive intensity of a "fusion" relationship, you can burn out on the excessive devotion to work, to family, to socializing, sex, weight-loss regimes, and the pursuit of perfect beauty and body images. And, once again, if your ego boundaries are unreliable, you'll be inclined to "fuse up" with one or several people or activities, find it difficult to maintain your separate identity with your own distinct values, and even twice as hard to detach.

JOB AS LOVER

As a consequence of a reaction formation, loneliness and aloneness anxiety, the fear of losing professional gains, or the exhilaration and reliability of the work itself, the "crisis in closeness" is sometimes seemingly rectified by symbolically "marrying" the job. Maureen, a divorced woman of 37 who works as a video production assistant, said:

> "When you have no support system after hours, it's easy to fall into a pattern of using your job as a love affair. The job really takes you over . . . You dress for it, socialize around it, talk about it, plan your future around it, and nurture the hell out of it . . . It's kind of insidious because I'm surrounded by people all day, the pace is very hectic, and I forget that I'm totally alone at night, or that I sleep my weekends away, sometimes with a report next to me on the bed . . . That reality hits me the hardest when I'm with couples—that's when my 'singleness' is palpable. When we say good night, I know they're going to chat about the evening together, and maybe snuggle up in bed . . . Then I remember . . . and I have to cope with a very real loneliness panic . . ."

The panic Maureen refers to is frequently talked about by women who have merged with their work to the exclusion of personal goals in their lives. Job burnout may become a real concern for you, but very often it's symptomatic of an underlying neglect. Aloneness or loneliness panic is a state of uncontrollable anxiety which perpetuates burnout momentum. It's a feeling of intense distress which, in order to continue on with the life-style you've established, by necessity must be suppressed, then denied. But those suppressed needs and longings often intrude upon the love affair with work in unexpected places and with stinging clarity. Maureen "remembers" the reality of her aloneness when she's confronted with couples. Other women feel jolted, then disoriented, when they hear a piece of music which triggers a sense memory of a connectedness to another, when they see a film or watch a television drama which disturbs anesthetized needs, when they attend a wedding, a baby shower, a nephew's birthday, a niece's high school graduation, school reunions, or when they find themselves alone on the year-end holidays. Maureen went on:

> "It's very difficult. Those terrible feelings of loss and aloneness are painful competitors with my independence. When they come up, there's a sense of threat, like witnessing a rival who's touching your lover's knee . . . and he's responding. You wish you hadn't seen that moment because you know you won't be able to erase it from your memory . . . You know it's going to haunt you . . ."

Maureen admits to being threatened by her need for an intimate life separate from her work. She interprets that need as a threatening "rival" to be held at bay. Marriage attracts and repels her.

> "My parents divorced when I was ten, and I divorced at 32. My dad was a vigorous man who drank too much, and I married someone very much like him—strong on the outside and weak inside. I've only been able to establish my own identity in the past five years— and I don't trust myself enough yet to juggle my career and those overpowering male needs for attention which I've experienced firsthand. And yet . . . I want to have that family . . . the family I missed two times around. I want babies, and a home—and my work. With the pace of my job, I don't think I could manage to fit it all in . . . I'm beginning to feel an exhaustion which I can't really explain, an irritability and an intolerance . . . Something's all wrong here . . ."

As Maureen struggles to flee from those feelings of personal longing, she weds herself more intensely to her work. She's gradually begun to associate her increasing feelings of burnout with the activity she most enjoys—her work. Paradoxically, by displacing those symptoms—"exhaustion . . . irritability . . . intolerance"—she continues to avoid the sustenance that could come from her work and ultimately give her "some of it all." This would help her to redeem her energies and, perhaps, fulfill the yearning for closeness.

The job marriage often grows static for the same reasons the "human" marriage falls apart. The concentrated focus diminishes a larger worldview and becomes insular and suffocating. As Maureen said: "The job really takes you over . . . You dress for it, socialize around it, talk about it, plan your future around it, and nurture the hell out of it . . ." Other women have made similar statements. They speak of attending to their job marriage with the same arduous intensity and attention to detail as they do to an impassioned relationship. One woman said:

> "I think that above and beyond the work itself, dress and appearance on the job are a major part of women's burnout for all of us. It's all so stressful. The company becomes the 'beloved' whom you desperately want to please. Everything else is secondary with me . . . my professional life *is* my personal life! I worry about the image I'm presenting, the fear of looking 'wrong.' Clothes are a constant concern. Is this the 'right' suit? Is this dress too sexy? Is red too bold or racy for that client? What should I wear to the tennis match? What are the appropriate clothes for the company weekend at my boss's country home? Then there are the conventions and hotel pools. Am I too fat for a bathing suit? For shorts? Will I embarrass anyone if I take a swim? And then there's the hair problem. How can I find time to have it done? When? And nails, and makeup. Is this too much or too little? It all boils down to wanting to look beautiful for the company, but not threatening. I want to be seen as an asset . . . as a woman with a future there . . ."

A woman in finance said:

> "My social life and my personal life are all work-related. Last week I was in Washington, out to dinners, at two receptions, then home and off to a celebration party for a colleague. Tonight I'm having dinner with a client, and next week I have to entertain a group of eight in my home—all principals of the firm. It sounds glamorous . . . and it used to be . . . but I'm so tired. I have no real sustenance, no intimate support or just plain comfort in my life. My leisure time is all connected to my work, and it's not meeting my needs. I'm continually 'digging up' the appropriate date to help me co-host, or escort me to various functions . . . It's exhausting. I've slept with hundreds of men, but I haven't got the time to develop a relationship . . ."

And a married woman who teaches ninth grade said:

"The kids wear me down tremendously—they need a great deal of support . . . It's a terrifically nurturing role, and even though they're draining, they give me a meaningful feeling about myself . . . I feel affirmed, needed . . . attached. My husband is very different from me . . . I need to have direct contact, that one-to-one intimacy to make me feel whole. He's very quiet, preoccupied with his own things . . . We have this kind of sustained noninvolvement . . . I know I avoid squaring off with what's happening to us by attaching myself to school, to the kids. I'm too tired, and at times too scared, to deal with my personal life. I used to attribute my burnout to my job, but I'm beginning to understand my romance with the kids is keeping me safe, but kind of lonely . . ."

Separating the professional from the personal isn't an easy proposition for most of us. There frequently are no finite lines or rules of conduct to use as a yardstick. Sometimes there are only suppressed longings, overtones of something amiss, to inform you of the need to detach and reassess the quality of your life. However, if you stop for a moment and size up your attitude toward your home, you might be provided with a clearer perspective.

How do you feel about returning from work in the evenings? Many, many women allude to a separation anxiety—the felt loss of attachment—which manifests in a dread of going home. You may spend less and less time there, using it as a hotel convenience, often with only a molding yogurt, a half tub of diet margarine, or a half picked-over chicken in the refrigerator to welcome you back. To assuage that feeling of dread and to avoid the aloneness anxiety associated with the rooms of your house, you might be working later and later into the night, or exhausting yourself in the local bars and discos, drinking to relax or perhaps using cocaine to give you a lift. Methods for avoiding home are inexhaustible.

Weekend fear or the privately perceived distress of separating from work for three-day holiday weekends or long vacations are also symptomatic of the need for an intimacy with yourself or with others. Sunday anxiety is especially grueling for those "married" to jobs. The emptiness of Sunday triggers separation pangs which often threaten to expose suppressed needs for closeness. Deprived of connectedness to the work affair, the yearnings for attachment to something or someone meaningful can manifest in hurtful feelings of aloneness. To avoid the alienation of Sunday, and perhaps to make up for the energy depletions from the previous week, you may sleep the day away, if not the entire weekend.

Total dependency on work for structure, definition, and emotional support creates a feeling of intimidation toward leisure time. When those "off hours" are upon you, life is no longer scheduled and controllable. As the job anchor lifts, you may feel unmoored and at sea by its absence. The nurturing woman often gives out so much during the week to gain a semblance of intimacy that she may feel disappointed by the gap in returns in her personal life and fill herself up by further overextending to friends or family on weekends. A woman who is divorced may be struggling with a state of transition, miss the communication with someone when she comes home—the absence of someone with whom to share the joys and tribulations of her day—and experience greater stress symptoms at home than at work. The single parent may be "running on empty" from merging with work all week, then coping with the responsibilities of her child's or children's needs in the evenings and begin to burnout from personal neglect. And a woman in a flattened marriage may prefer the demanding standards of perfection on the job to the frustration she is experiencing at home. She may begin to identify her home as "work" and her job as "love"—mutually exclusive options.

The telephone and appliances frequently act as the main connection for women who find themselves with scant personal contact away from the job. "The phone is my lifeline," one woman stated. "Sometimes, just as I get into bed, I'll call a friend so he or she can 'talk me to sleep.'" "I talk on the phone a lot," another woman said, "but after a while I begin to understand that it's a disembodied experience and something vital is still missing." A third woman succinctly declared: "Why do I use the phone so much? To stave off loneliness when work is over. I also turn on the radio, television, or a record the minute I get home . . . I need some voices or sounds that permeate my living space."

Do these experiences sound an alarm in you? If they do, it is critically important for you to take a few steps back and give a careful, thoughtful look at your life and its patterns.

SOME ALONENESS/LONELINESS
BURNOUT PREVENTION STEPS

When you've boxed yourself into a position or role to the exclusion of all others, burnout symptoms are certain to manifest. Satisfaction cannot be sustained when it's derived from a single aspiration. For this reason, it's imperative to listen to your suppressed longings, even though they may seem threatening.

Turn back to page 88 and take another look at the Burnout Symptom Cycle. When a burnout compulsiveness takes hold of you, by Stage 4 the main symptom is a dismissal of your conflicts and your needs. Coping mechanisms, often characterized by defensiveness, are erected to conceal self-neglect. By Stage 5, that compulsiveness and intensity of focus gradually distort your true values, and by Stage 6, denial is heightened. But by Stage 7 an actual disengagement from the self manifests. Disavowing emotional and physical needs breeds a detachment and distancing from the true self. Through the persistent denial of your needs, you create a lifestyle that becomes a habit and which is increasingly difficult to change. Remember, when you're fatigued or disillusioned from compulsively focusing on a single goal, feelings of alienation will ultimately interfere with your judgment, and your worldview will become somewhat distorted and cynical. At that point, there doesn't seem to be anything outside of your own immediate grasp which contains value or meaning. *This dynamic can be reversed.*

We all know that, ideally, the "crisis in closeness" would be solved by finding the perfect mate or by resolving intimacy complexities with present husbands or lovers. Unfortunately, that solution is not always easily obtained. Yet, in the meantime, there are methods of assuaging your aloneness and loneliness burnout symptoms, methods which might relax some of the growing fear about the future.

Have you excluded contact with others working in diverse fields, or with interests ostensibly unrelated to your own? Perhaps you could begin to develop relationships with people outside your immediate frame of reference. Burnout symptoms often diminish the value of opportunities that new people or interests can provide. Think about enlarging your perspective. The stress which manifests from "doing it all alone" feeds on itself. It doesn't just disappear, it accumulates and builds, creating ever deeper burnout wounds. If you're burning out on an absence of the personal, you may be unconsciously engaged in a battle to outwit your own needs. Women struggling with the loss of intimacy often try to toughen themselves up even more. Reaction formations then become trickier to identify and to break. As a result, new ideas, people, and opportunities are often dismissed as intrusions or boring obligations.

People with interests foreign to your own may have something enriching, if not lifesaving, to offer. They may not have the immediate answer to your neglected needs, but the fresh input and experience can open up new avenues of possibility for you. As people, women and men, move forward and upward in their lives, old friends whose lives have taken a different course are often dropped. Perhaps a reunion with friends from the past will create a new perspective. Current friends are also sometimes a source of overlooked closeness. You may want to encourage an intimacy with someone in your life whom you've previously only seen as a job "contact."

What are your interests? If you're of a political bent, you might attend local community board meetings and discover new people in your neighborhood or township. Perhaps you could begin to devote an evening to a class and reacquaint yourself with forgotten or buried enthusiasms for literature, music, art, national or international affairs, science, the environment, or psychology. In our fast-paced, electronic, and computerized society, the word "hobby" has gotten a bad name. Yet, by definition, a hobby is something one likes to do in their spare time. When there's no spare time, or when spare time is equated with alienation, it's easy to "forget" what you like to do—those activities that bring you a certain joy. Hobbies are important because they welcome one back to a healthy solitude and allow you to immerse yourself in creative and productive pleasures that are enriching to the self.

Self-nurturance is another method for gradually eliminating the sense of aloneness in your life. If you've always depended upon gaining a semblance of nurturance and self-value from a man, you may be consciously—and often unconsciously—waiting to make a comfortable home, to invest in a summer house, to take a trip to an island until he appears. As a result, all your energies are siphoned into your job while the waiting period extends itself into years.

Homes are basic and primal to women and men alike. If your home rings with emptiness, take some steps to change it into a space that invites and comforts. Even if you live in a one-room box, there are changes which can be made to revitalize your attitude toward home. Stock the cupboards and refrigerator with foods which are welcoming. If you're a serious dieter, make certain the foods you buy have variety. The sameness of cottage cheese and carrots will not act to beckon you back in the evenings. Many women have spoken of postponing buying or making something as simple as a new bedspread because "it's just me in the house." You may want to redecorate a bedroom or living room to accommodate a long-held vision of what home should be and what home means to you. One woman spoke of wandering through the china and crystal departments in stores for years but never investing in the "things" she loved because "you don't buy good dinnerware or glasses until you have someone to live with." When she was finally convinced she could make those purchases for herself, she began inviting people into her home and revived an old passion for cooking. Another woman only hung her prints and paintings when she began dating a man, and when they parted company said: "I don't know why I kept waiting to make this place into my own home . . ."

Other women have begun to nurture themselves by beginning to make what another woman called "strikes for independence." In this case she referred to relinquishing the waiting for a mate to give herself some of her postponed pleasures. Along with two other friends, she purchased a summer house which she had been putting off until she became a "couple." In time, her compulsive work intensity diminished and, although she maintained her job aspirations and her performance, her burnout symptoms leveled off.

Loneliness and aloneness burnout, however, have no fast remedies. They require small changes each day, a penchant for self-awareness, and a sense of what is needed. The waiting woman is usually a victim of not only her vulnerabilities, but also her own ambivalence. For this reason, it's a good idea to begin a Burnout Journal.

Journal writing has a threefold purpose. It allows you to safely explore your inner life, to discover your goals and ambitions, and to speak your innermost secrets without embarrassment. Denial is frequently unearthed and relieved through the writing. Rages, fears, jealousy, envy, sorrows, and longings can all be ventilated in the journal, as can aspirations, plans, and long-range goals.

At the outset, think about the following questions and, as you begin to record some of your thoughts and feelings, try to answer them as genuinely as possible. Remember, this is your journal and it's sacrosanct. You can write anything you wish, with any attitude which arises.

1. What do you have in your life which is concrete and stable?
2. What is missing from that picture?
3. Are any of your dependency needs being stifled? What are those needs?
4. Do you want a man or female mate in your life?
5. Have you created impossible standards for a mate?
6. Do you authentically want to live with someone, or do you wish you wanted intimacy but are beginning to suspect you're happier alone?
7. What do you usually "give up" for the sake of a relationship?
8. What makes you angry about the lovers you've been with?
9. Are you frightened of closeness because you tend to "fuse"?
10. Do feelings of jealousy, envy, anger, or competitiveness emerge when you're involved with someone?
11. What triggers those feelings?
12. Which conversations do you avoid in the company of people? Are there certain topics from which you "shrink" because of the longings they provoke?
13. Do you want a child? Are you denying that desire because a baby would interfere with your career? Or are you suppressing that desire because there's no one in your life?
14. Do you avoid sex? Do you indulge yourself often, but feel empty afterward?
15. Are you using your job to avoid closeness?
16. Are you postponing the attempt to meet a possible mate until you've lost enough weight?
17. Are you too tired of the whole dating scene to make the effort?
18. Are you frightened or put off by the men you've met?
19. Do you have male friends with whom you speak regularly and intimately?
20. Are your friends acquaintances or intimates?
21. Do you dislike going home because of the loneliness your rooms trigger? How could you change the environment for yourself?
22. Have you closed off people and ideas which are different from your own immediate focus?
23. Have you let others know of your interest in meeting a mate?

24. Is your job as satisfying as you believe it to be, or do you fantasize about another type of work which would be more compatible?
25. Are you making enough money to satisfy your needs?
26. Are you drinking more now? Why? When? And are you suffering hangovers which interfere with energy?
27. Are you using drugs—uppers, downers, coke, grass—to modulate your moods? Why? When?
28. Are you becoming more of a "loner"?
29. Are you taking care of your physical health?
30. What could you do to arrange your life so that you could ultimately have "some of it all"?

Over a period of days or weeks, as you write the answers to these questions, bear in mind that the Burnout Journal is private and exclusively yours. Through the writing, you may discover some interesting and valuable aspects about yourself which were previously buried, or lurking in the job shadows. If you're burning out on concerns and issues which are ultimately in conflict with your own values and needs, remember the most important question of all: "Whose life is this anyway?"

COCAINE AND ALCOHOL AS BEST FRIENDS

One of the most vivid characteristics of burnout is the phenomenon of tunnel vision. When one becomes compulsively attached to an ideal, a situation, or a person, that which intrudes upon the compulsion is regarded as dangerous, swiftly dismissed, suppressed, and then denied. As you begin to feel you're burning out, whether it be on work, loneliness, or love, your external vision of the world gradually narrows. The symptoms of fatigue, sluggish attitudes toward life, jaded suspicions of others, and feelings of inadequacy toward yourself tend to emerge and become engulfing. The sense of lost vitality and enthusiasm becomes a paramount concern. To ward off the distress of those symptoms, and to keep the compulsion going strong, many women have turned to cocaine as a "false cure" for burnout.

Marcia is one of many women who have come into the office with symptoms of depression which, after some exploration, proved to be the result of burnout exhaustion. On her first appointment, she spoke of cocaine as "the one thing that keeps me going." For several years Marcia frequently had been exposed to the coke experience but had only begun using it, "for a lift," the past six months. She said:

> "I was around people all the time who were doing coke, and I wasn't all that interested. Then I decided to experiment and felt my depression lifting. As the evening progressed, I slowly began to feel powerful, confident, in control, and filled with energy. My enthusiasm and joy were back . . . that zest for life was inside me again. I was talkative and involved . . . I guess my main recollection is that of being tremendously hopeful . . ."

Marcia's initial experiences with coke echo numbers of others who have turned to cocaine to defeat the feelings of futility and hopelessness so characteristic of the late stages of burnout. The drug was available, popular, and held no social stigma. But when the effects wore off, she was again saddled with the same burned-out attitudes and emotions. To regain her energy, she began to repeat the cocaine experience until it became not only habitual but also her solution.

At the outset, Marcia found it was fairly easy to obtain coke and never had to purchase it herself. "Somebody always had some and would offer it —like offering a cup of coffee to a neighbor . . . Or someone I was dating would bring some . . . instead of flowers. It's become an acceptable form of socializing," she said. Gradually, however, she came to depend on the "up" it provided and began buying small quantities herself. She continued:

> "When you know you can feel euphoric and at the same time think you're functioning beautifully, it's very tempting. It would take a lot of my anxiety away at business lunches, at meetings—and then at the end of the day it would give me the boost of energy to go out partying. It also helped me get through alone evenings and those lonely weekends. I didn't have to make an effort to get involved . . . Except for the times I'd become too frenetic and speedy, when I was on coke, I simply didn't have to deal with anything else . . . so I started budgeting it into my salary . . . as a necessity, like rent and car payments . . ."

For women who are trying to hold multiple roles together, cocaine initially appears as a boon. The cumulative exhaustion and stress caused by juggling many activities can be temporarily abated and replaced with a laundered sense of well-being. And for women who are struggling through aloneness or loneliness burnout, the deep feelings of alienation are temporarily obliterated by the high. In the course of her treatment, Marcia spoke of feeling empty—of "only coming alive" when she was faced with a work crisis or a family emergency. The intensity of the pace kept her from thinking about her future, her goals, or her genuine needs. She said:

> "For a long time I used sex to keep me from dealing with all those complex life issues, but then I burned out on sex and began to feel depressed and empty . . . When I started heavily indulging in coke, my interest in sex revived, which meant I could start all over again . . ."

As was discussed earlier in Chapter I, women suffering from burnout depression rarely turn to drugs to retreat from the world. To the contrary, drugs are used to temporarily regain and reclaim their initial vigor, which then allows them to jump back into life with the same compulsive head of steam. Marcia's story typifies this syndrome. In order to save face with herself, her friends, and her family, she felt compelled to camouflage her burnout symptoms. She said, sketching out her history:

> "I was always the one who 'had it down.' All A's in college and people telling me, 'You're going to go far.' My friends look at me with a kind of esteem that doesn't offer me the opportunity to say, 'I'm miserable in my job' or 'in my life,' or that I'm scared. They think I'm in control and 'going places.' That kind of thinking doesn't allow you to be taken seriously. If I tell the truth, they don't believe me—or don't want to believe me . . . it takes away their illusions and their hope. It's quite a responsibility . . . In order to avoid letting anyone down, I have to appear strong. When I'm using coke I don't have to worry about it . . ."

Marcia's "crisis in closeness" was doubly reflected in her life. To avoid intimacy with men, she had used sex; to avoid a critically needed closeness with friends, she turned to cocaine. The spiraling effects of her inner isolation prompted further symptoms of burnout. Cocaine quite literally became a substitute for her best friends, and she saw it as reliable, constant, and perfectly suited to mask her real needs.

Other women speak of cocaine with the same ambivalence. They describe the effects of the high with adoration, and the effects of habituation and dependency with repulsion. Another woman said:

"The high is just wonderful, but I'm often so frantic I can't sleep, and need to take downers which give me a drug hangover in the morning. That means I need another 'hit' to get up and get to work. Then I'm so wired from the loss of sleep and the coke, I get very talky and impatient . . . I decided I had to do something—my personality was totally changed. I didn't know the person inside me . . . and I was drowning in debt to friends . . ."

One of the most difficult addictions to deal with is a cocaine habit. Since the drug has achieved celebrity status, the social onus has been removed, and you can easily achieve a vicarious sense of elitism through both its use and the paraphernalia that accompanies it. For burnouts, coke is a most seductive drug. By cloaking the symptoms and the underlying conflicts, it perpetuates the compulsion to achieve, to race past yourself, and to maintain that desired intensity.

If you're using cocaine and perceive that you might be addicted, it's imperative to admit you've become dependent on it and, like Marcia, make a firm commitment to stop. Through the course of Marcia's treatment, she began to understand that her cocaine habit was covering burnout and depression symptoms that she found to be overwhelming. Her resistance to quitting cocaine was in direct proportion to her resistance to facing some of her long-held ideas about being a source of pride to her family and a role model for her friends. She was referred to a physician for medication and simultaneously continued therapy as well as attended AA groups. The pivotal point in her treatment arrived when she authentically began to understand that she did have other options.

Women who are burned out cannot see choices for themselves. The symptoms impair your worldview, judgment, and your ability to project a future other than your current routine. When the causes of your burnout are coupled with a cocaine camouflage, resistance to trusting something or someone other than the drug itself is often fierce. As Marcia began to receive and acknowledge glimpses of another quality to life, of other possibilities for friendships, and of other options for work and love, she was able to confront her need to get off coke.

However, a cocaine addiction is frequently not resolved through insight. In fact, a serious addiction initially can be as much of a medical-pharmacological problem as it is a psychological problem, and must be treated as such. Yet, ultimately, your own commitment to quitting is most critical to kicking cocaine. Professional help, specifically geared toward cocaine abuse, is now available in most cities. If you're stuck for an outlet, and are too embarrassed to talk to your doctor or friends, you can call the Cocaine Hotline (1-800)-COCAINE, a twenty-four-hour hotline service, or contact an Alcoholics Anonymous or a Narcotics Anonymous chapter, and receive information concerning counseling services, hospitals, and treatment programs in your area.

The use of alcohol as a "false cure" for burnout is also a frequently addressed problem among women. Unlike cocaine, however, there are social stigmas placed on the behavior of women who drink which are not placed on men. Because of the lingering sexist attitudes toward women and alcohol, it may be difficult to admit you have a drinking problem. You may be quite guarded about revealing an alcohol dependency, for with all of the changes our society has undergone, including the exposure to more and more social drinking through jobs and life-styles, as one woman put it, "too many drinks aren't considered feminine."

For this reason, burned-out women who have turned to alcohol to quiet anxieties are hard-put to admit the extent of their drinking problems and are often very secretive about its use. Carla, a copywriter for a national pictorial magazine, addressed her own alcohol problem, which, as she suggested, crept up on her several years ago when she was anxiously trying to cope with both her loneliness and her "private feelings of insecurity and distress."

> "I'd never had a drink alone before," she stated. "Then my husband and I separated . . . or, I should say, he left, and I couldn't bear the terrible abandonment pangs. I was in such turmoil and pain that I started drinking alone to kill off those nightmarish feelings. But I didn't want anyone to *see* me drinking or to know how often I'd have a drink to face the world. That would have made me look kind of . . . seedy. There are acceptable times and places a woman can drink and there are definite social taboos on others."

For women like Carla, it's socially acceptable to have drinks at lunch, after work, and before and after dinner, "but not before noon and not when you're alone," she added.

"If someone rang my bell and a glass was on the coffee table, I'd lie and say, 'Someone just left . . .' Sometimes I'd pour my drink down the drain, then offer a drink to whoever walked in and pretend it was my first. At other times I'd be afraid someone would smell it on my breath, or that I'd be slightly, but tellingly, slurred. Then I'd say I had just met a friend for some sort of minor celebration . . . anything to hide how much I needed the alcohol to get me through the pain I was feeling . . ."

When emotions become burned out, alcohol can act as an instrument of denial for dependency longings. Carla's separation and subsequent divorce triggered many of her fears of sole responsibility for herself.

"I still had to go to work, conduct business, complete assignments, be creative, have lunches . . . I was overwhelmed with the responsibility and the feelings of utter desolation . . . I'd drink until I felt that 'ping'—that's when I'd feel transformed . . . emotionally together. When the 'ping' hit, I'd feel pretty, sexy, like I belonged . . . not so alone, or so much of an outsider to events . . ."

The use of alcohol as an antidote to burnout ultimately turns into an abuse and an abandonment of the feeling self. As with cocaine, as long as there's a constant lid on those feelings, the underlying symptoms of stress, anguish, or aloneness cannot be located and treated. In this sense, what you think you want may be a drink, but what you know you need is someone to talk to, to share a closeness, to connect, and perhaps to touch. Confusion over the alcohol problem has been propagated by the idea that if you're malnourished in fun, or if there is a pleasure deficiency in your life, you will redeem excitement and sensuality through drinking. As Carla said, "It's easier to be sexual when I'm drinking." Another woman stated: "I don't even have to like the guy to sleep with him—as long as I can have a couple of drinks . . . I just don't like waking up with virtual strangers in the morning . . ."

If you have an alcohol problem, you might not be willing to admit to it, or you might not understand what is and isn't considered a problem. Think about the reasons behind each drink you take. You'll gain a deeper insight into what alcohol has come to mean in your life, and perhaps then be able to piece together why you've been drinking for so long, and how it got to be too much.

When a group of women interviewed for this book were queried about their reasons for drinking, they offered the following responses:

—"I drink when I'm bored with the people around me. When I've got a buzz on, I don't notice my restlessness or annoyance."

—"It helps me be more assertive."

—"Drinking helps me think."

—"It helps me speak."

—"I drink when I'm angry and need to hide it."

—"It takes the edge off and gives me the look of control."

—"I drink to quiet down my anxiety, my depression, and my impatience."

—"I drink to loosen up and gain courage."

—"It allows me to be more sexual . . . and free."

—"It takes the pressure off."

—"It takes away pain."

—"I drink to sleep."

—"It's like having someone to talk to at night."

—"It kills off loneliness."

—"It just helps me cope."

Again, burnouts are especially prone to alcohol abuse, as with cocaine. The immediacy of the release from fatigue, pressure, aloneness or loneliness provides what one woman called "a magical relief from the anxiety and stress of my existence." But there's no sorcery involved—only a perpetuation of the authentic conflicts, and usually some very nasty hangovers. If you're drinking more at lunch and in the evenings, the following mornings you've probably heard yourself swear off the bottle more than once. But if you begin drinking again that same evening, it's safe to say you're involved in severe denial and are probably not allowing yourself to "remember" the feelings of abuse you experienced just some twelve hours earlier.

When you're riding out a particularly trying period in your life and experiencing burnout symptoms of depersonalization, emptiness, or depression, you won't hasten the recovery process by overindulging in alcohol. To the contrary, alcohol is a depressant which often tends to aggravate grief, sorrow, and anger. When the difficult period ends, you may have a worse problem with which to contend. As another woman stated:

"I began drinking to cover up my insecurities . . . I was incredibly dependent on the man I was with and would drink to be more congenial, you know, not so anxious around him. But I'd get rather maudlin and teary . . . my emotional life was just hanging out all over the place. Over a year or so I put on about fifteen extra pounds and hated myself for that . . . Then I'd drink to forget the way I looked. When I made the decision to stop, I realized I was stuck with another dependency and had resolved nothing with all that constant drinking. I'm still not sure why I stopped—sometimes I think it was a question of vanity . . ."

A "drinking problem" is usually loosely interpreted by the individual woman according to her own knowledge of herself and her patterns. Each woman is triggered by something in her life which exposes the extent of the problem. Sometimes it's vanity. But if alcohol is interfering with your work, your personal life, your family, children, sexuality, relationships, or your health, and you continue to drink, you may have begun to unconsciously or consciously view it as a best friend and are probably engaged in denial. It would be wise to begin to examine the underlying causes for drinking. If you've begun to suspect the problem is serious, you can get help by calling Alcoholics Anonymous directly, or by writing for information to Alcoholics Anonymous World Services, Inc., Box 459, Grand Central Station, New York, N.Y. 10017. AA also puts out pamphlets specifically geared toward women and alcoholism. But whether you contact AA or seek professional counseling through local hospitals, task forces, or private practices, the main point is to reach out. Isolation will enlarge your alcohol dependency and guide you further into burnout depression.

SOLE RESPONSIBILITY AND BURNOUT

There is a stress factor unique to women divorced, widowed, or over-35 and single which has, over the past few years, created widespread anxiety and propelled numbers of women, in varying degrees, into the Burnout Cycle.

What happens when your firmly entrenched desire to share life with a husband and child has not been forthcoming? What fears are alerted when you, perhaps as the daughter of traditional parents, begin to understand you may not realize the home values endemic to your training? What disappointments and sorrows are incurred when a marriage is dissolved through divorce or death after years of companionship? In short, what happens when the shock of "sole responsibility" becomes an issue you never thought would touch your life?

These are grim thoughts. For many women, however, they are jolting realities. From the displaced homemaker—the widow or divorced single parent of young children or teenagers—to the woman who cannot find a mate to fill the marriage and family bill, the issue of sole responsibility for oneself, and perhaps one's children, was probably never an idea to be willingly embraced. Frequently, a woman who is attempting to grapple with all that "sole responsibility" implies, both real and imagined, initially tends to dissipate her energies in panic, and her psychic life will eventually respond to burnout exhaustion. "It's really hard," Leigh, a 40-year-old, divorced, single parent said. "I just push and push and push . . . How do you find a middle ground for yourself when you realize you may have to do it all alone the rest of your life?"

Leigh is mother to two preteen-aged children, and her experience typifies the pendulum swings feelings and attitudes take when confronted with this conflict. She said:

"I feel very angry about having sole responsibility. If I had known my marriage was going to turn out this way, I don't know if I would have had two kids, bought a house, gotten all the animals . . . I don't want all this responsibility. Just owning a home means when something breaks, it's me who has to call the appropriate people, arrange for time away from work to meet the repair people, negotiate prices, and make a dozen decisions which usually involve a lot of money. Like when the roof was leaking, or the garage door broke, or the refrigerator fizzled out—I didn't want this! As it is, I support the children, make the house payments, car payments, insurance payments, buy the kids' clothes, attend their activities, call and pay for doctors, feed everyone, get them to school, make sure they've done their homework, chauffeur them around, find out who their friends are and where they go. It just makes me very angry. If I dwell on it, I get into an absolute rage, so I try not to . . . I don't want it to build into something so monumental that I can't deal with it. If I let it overwhelm me, I'll get into burnout again . . ."

When Leigh's fourteen-year marriage dissolved, her husband moved away and subsequently remarried. For the first year, the shock of the aloneness frightened and disoriented her. She said:

> "I was off the wall. I couldn't stop running. There was no way I could be alone with myself . . . I had to be where things were alive —I had to go places or have an endless stream of people over . . . I was so frantic then: I couldn't sit still—I felt I had to keep moving to survive. That lasted six months, then I came to realize I was utterly depleted, really burned out. But I branched out during the next six months, and then, during the next six, felt myself changing again. By the rate I'm going, when I'm about 206 years old, I might have a whole new life . . . or I might have accepted myself as a solo act . . ."

Leigh's first ordeal with burnout exhaustion came about as the result of the race against her own feelings of loss and desolation. She never denied the feelings—she found them overwhelming. Desperate to maintain the illusion of attachment, she did what many women in her position do. She flailed about, overbooking her time, overplanning her activities, creating a wall of frenetic intensity behind which her anxieties and future fears would be sealed. She continued:

> "But, you can only race for just so long. When you've got children staring at you and they *need*, you can't keep ushering them off to McDonald's because you're hurting. There comes a point where no matter how burned out or crazy you feel, you've got to take hold of the responsibility and deal with the facts. You've got to understand that, like it or not, you are now both the benefactress and villain in their lives."

During the subsequent six months, Leigh switched her intense focus from racing "to survive" to her home and became "a tyrant for orderliness and precision." At this point she had the two children and herself on time schedules, had mapped out distinct chores for each. She said:

> "I had to. I didn't know any other way of managing it all. I needed a structure . . . I learned how to be a tough disciplinarian.

I felt so done in, so tricked by the divorce and the exhaustion of it all, I began to see myself as a machine—and the kids got the brunt of those feelings."

As she recalls, that period of tyranny gradually ended, and with the help of therapy she was able to piece together her fragmented feelings and gain some valuable insight into the history of her emotional wreckage. She went on:

"What was most important was the realization that I had been burned out *before* we divorced . . . but the symptoms were different. There wasn't any drama . . . there was deadness. It was dreary . . . no one ever changed . . . I was holding on as tight as I could to protect myself from those phobic aloneness feelings, but I wasn't enjoying any of it—not him, me, or us. I had become 'Mrs. Homemaker' who has a set of proscribed notions about what one does and doesn't think and do. There was a split in me. When I was at the office, I took the work seriously, but not myself. I didn't view myself as competent, strong-minded, or particularly talented—I never owned that part of myself. And I rarely talked about my work life at home—that wasn't part of the perfect wife role."

Armed with insights concerning the nature of her past marriage, Leigh went on to explore her present life. She discovered that she held many notions that kept her rigidly fixed and frightened. "I had a lot of internal edicts about what a 'good' mother never does, what a 'nice' wife won't say, and what a 'good little girl' won't get if she isn't polite." All of those notions were ingrained in her as part of her family dynamics. As Leigh said, "I was conditioned to be either a child or a mother—I never learned how to be a woman."

The anger Leigh demonstrated as she spoke about the sole responsibility issue is a recent twist in her life. Previously she had experienced herself as a victim of male domination and fickleness which prompted her feelings of powerlessness and inadequacy to the surface. She said:

"I think the anger is healthy, and I think it's fair. I don't linger as long in self-pity now, but that's because I've opened myself up to the idea of change. Sometimes I panic at the thought of being alone, but I've been going out with a few men and have been trying to see them as friends, not husbands. I do miss the emotional connection with a man, but I now know that's only a part of what I need—albeit, a vital part . . . It's when I lose hope that I fall into the burnout ruts. I become very brittle, pessimistic, and resentful—there's no sense of balance . . ."

Leigh's sentiments about the future are echoed in numbers by women who are divorced single parents coping with sole responsibility conflicts. If you were never trained to live on your own, to make use of your resources, to experiment, to branch out, to depend on yourself, or to reach out to friends for nurturance and intimacy, the prospect of living without a mate can achieve crisis proportions. Leigh's odyssey through divorce and its aftereffects reflect the various phases of that crisis, including the stress-producers and extenders which lead to burnout.

For many women, in the aftermath of estrangement and then divorce, renovating old self-images is the key to reversing the burnout process. The terror of sole responsibility should be a sign that during the marriage a part of you lived an underground existence, and that the powerlessness you feel now may be a corollary to an overdependent life-style. Often the desired change in emotional reactions to loss can be produced by employing some simple techniques.

When burnout is the result of panic, the accompanying stress often "orders" the body to shut down, almost as if it was "playing dead." Since physical, mental, and emotional aspects of the self are all interrelated, it follows that thoughts and feelings will also become deadened. This mode is quite characteristic of the burnout dynamic. However, you can help yourself to move beyond that panic by taking command of your body.

Start with your posture. You may have begun to slump, to hold yourself in an attitude of defeat. Try walking erect, and sitting as though in charge of the person in the chair. If you aren't already involved in some kind of exercise program, it might be helpful to begin with some stretches or aerobics at home or, if you can, at an outside class. Once you've got your body moving, your thoughts, attitudes, and feelings will experience a lift. You also might learn or relearn how to express yourself directly and with clarity, perhaps by listening to yourself on a tape recorder. Burnout depression is often observable by the vague, wishy-washy ambivalence of voice sound and expression. You don't have to attend an assertiveness class to begin ventilating your anger. If the anger is submerged, and all you can summon up are feelings of guilt, try to remember that the underbelly of guilt is usually resentment, and if you're able to locate the seeds of that resentment you'll be able to release some of that pent-up energy.

When do you feel the loss the most? At what time of day and during what activities? If you can pinpoint the triggers for those awful feelings of aloneness, you can then find ways of changing the patterns for yourself. Have you stopped communicating with friends and colleagues? Have you become withdrawn and isolated? Have you become ill a lot lately? Are you "taking to bed" frequently to blot out the world? Those symptoms are indicative of blocked perceptions and tunnel vision. You may have to relearn the skill of pleasure fantasizing. Often the bleakest days promote frightening fantasies of suicide and destruction. If you are familiar with those thought flights, it is imperative that you remember: *Suicide is a permanent solution to a temporary situation.* What you actually want to kill off is the part of you that is hurting—not your whole being. Those fantasies can be reversed. When you feel yourself drifting into a destructive daydream, switch it. Replace it with constructive thoughts, a projection for the future which includes rich possibilities for a balanced and fulfilling life. Retrieving yourself from the slough of despair isn't accomplished overnight. It takes commitment and small steps daily which are then experienced cumulatively over a period of time. It also takes the ability to learn how to negotiate your worth with yourself and perhaps with your children, to learn how to compromise the darker moods with lighter perceptions, to learn how to enjoy and to laugh again, and to learn to validate your own deepest needs with yourself and with the external world.

As Leigh quite succinctly pointed out, repeated burnout experiences aren't always identical. In her case, there was the "deadening" burnout she lived in her marriage; the burnout produced from the shock of separation and the subsequent race from feeling; the burnout from juggling all of the roles and responsibilities connected to her home, children, job, and self; and the burnout she is now attempting to diminish which arose from the aloneness feelings of sole responsibility. Like many of you, Leigh viewed herself as weak and ignoble in the face of crisis, yet the reality proved different. She experimented with methods for coping, and grabbed on to what she felt would ground her. Although she maintains she'll "have a whole new life . . . when I'm about 206 years old," the humor and pathos behind her statement are reflective of her desire for change and of her courage to persist.

Beverly has been grappling with the same issue, but with a different set of underlying twists. At 37 she began to view herself personally as "edgy and restless . . . incomplete, as though I was this deficient person." It didn't matter that her achievements in her job as a free-lance journalist had awarded her an excellent reputation among her colleagues; the fact that she didn't have a husband and child, that her biological time clock was ticking louder each day, and that her finances were unstructured, altered her perception of herself as successful. She said:

> "Intellectually, I understood that being fulfilled personally had little to do with my professional accomplishments. I'm good at what I do . . . and I've always liked reporting, being in the middle of things. But I didn't feel motivated . . . I felt tired—depressed. I was carrying around this weight and it scared me. In my profession you must be continually pushing yourself and your ideas. Money is dependent on spotting stories and following through—getting assignments and writing every day. You don't get paid for sick days, for vacations, for lost 'mental health' days, or for burnout days . . ."

For Beverly, the issue of sole responsibility had come to mean an absence of a home base and a set of deeply ingrained values turned upside down. She said:

> "I come from a traditional background. My mother never worked outside our home. Even when money was tight, there was never a question of her taking a job . . . It only clicked with me when I was in college that I not only wanted to work, I wanted a writing career. It was just understood that sometime later I'd get married and have babies, but not immediately. But, 'sometime later' was right here, in the present, and it wasn't working out . . ."

The agitation Beverly experienced was interpreted by her as depression, and, in fact, it was a form of burnout exhaustion. Future fear created an inner anxiety that often accelerated into panic. The frazzled feelings of panic manifested in an "edgy and restless" inner life which consumed her energy and drained her of creativity. She went on:

> "I'd begun to worry about small events. I strained a muscle playing tennis one day. The next morning I had a terrible pain in my

mid-back. I needed to rub some Ben-Gay into the muscle but couldn't reach it . . . That's when I panicked. It was a little problem, but it enlarged in my mind as a symbol of impotency and aloneness. Later in the day a friend stopped by and helped me out, but I couldn't stop obsessing about the 'what ifs.' What if I'm seriously ill? What if I can't work? What if I can't get to the phone? All of those questions kept nagging me . . . I felt so vulnerable at times. It became very depressing . . ."

Most people who live alone experience those moments of vulnerability. Yet Beverly's were compounded by her vision of herself as "deficient," a concept which promotes helplessness in the face of the unpredictable. Her sole-responsibility burnout had begun to manifest in symptoms observable to herself, as well as to others, in her wide swings in mood and intensity.

"There were—and still are—those days when I just want to be alone . . . I can't summon up the energy to indulge in polite conversations or even think . . . I sleep a lot and overeat junky food. The next few days I'm crazed with activity, in top form, and pushing like mad to sustain the creative energy. For a while I was obsessively running—six miles every day and no excuses. I felt as if I was accomplishing something and that I was only in control when I was moving. After a few months, I burned out on running. Sometimes I wished I wasn't secretly hopeful this would all change—then I would make the necessary adjustments—whatever they were—to the very real possibility that I wouldn't marry and wouldn't have a child. I kept thinking there was something I could change to make it happen, and if I couldn't, that there was something wrong with me."

Like many women in Beverly's position, she toyed with the notion of changing professions, reasoning that she might meet a man in a different job setting or city. In the meantime, to obtain a semblance of connectiveness, she had a series of affairs with men who were married, unable to commit themselves, or below her standards for a mate. She continued:

"At that point, I guess I could safely say I was experiencing date burnout, too. I'd gotten tired of the dating protocols and had begun looking at men with an eye toward having their child without marriage. I still don't believe I have the stuff to do this, but I think about it . . . What stops me is the anxiety about money."

The over-35 and single crunch has similarly affected many women. They experience an inner fatigue born of disappointment or disillusionment with the absence of a work/love balance in their lives. Not every woman feels this crisis. There are those of you who have found and maintained a sense of community and self through jobs, friends, and extended family systems. Some of you have taken the plunge and had babies without marriage, some have made the decision to adopt, while others have not felt compelled to have a child. Each woman is propelled by her own unique set of needs. But those of you deeply disturbed by the idea of sole responsibility sometimes speak of suffering from a sense of meaninglessness—a powerlessness to achieve domestic goals. For many of you, burnout symptoms frequently grow in direct proportion to either decreasing childbearing years, or the degree of financial insecurity. Sole responsibility acts as an umbrella theme for three main fears: the absence of a mate with whom to share your life, the unfulfilled yearning for a child, and chaotic bouts of anxiety concerning money.

Not all women respond to those three subthemes with equal intensity. Although a mate and child may have been scripted into your life but not as yet realized, your anxieties may be concentrated on money. However, the absence of a family often further accelerates financial insecurities. Beverly said:

"I'm in a financially unstable profession, but it wasn't until I hit 35 that I began to worry seriously about money. Prior to that, in the back of my head I just assumed that eventually I'd be part of a two-paycheck family and that during the tough times we'd be able to lean on each other. I wasn't paying attention to saving or investing for the future. Like most free-lancers, my income was too capricious . . . a big check one month, then nothing for the next two. I have a lot of insomniac litanies about money—health insurance, taxes, rent increases, debts, medical and dental bills . . . even getting my hair cut . . . When you're not making enough, you can't take vacations, go away for the weekend, take a class—all those activities which are needed to cool out. I've been very panicked about money. I feel I must secure myself. If it turns out that I will be living alone, I don't want to be impoverished as well . . ."

Salaried women are not exempt from Beverly's comment on the role money plays in facing sole responsibility. Although, unlike Beverly's, their income may be predictable, it still may not be enough. And once again, denial plays a critical part in whether you will or will not accurately perceive and project your own financial needs. Beverly said:

> "I think, in my twenties, I was living out a fairy-tale existence. I was ambitious without worry. I wanted recognition first. If I did think about real money, it was connected to my immediate needs . . . It was all of a piece with getting married and having children. Sometime later it would all fall into place."

The messages you received from your parents concerning financial responsibility usually act as an inner guide. Their attitudes are subtly grafted onto your own worldview. In the old traditional family setup, daughters were not always groomed or conditioned to live out financially independent lives. If the idea of sole responsibility is an unwieldy emotional stress, although you may have behaved as though you had grabbed on to the concept of self-support and fully accepted it, there may have been hidden expectations which prove to be quite different. When that breakthrough perception occurs—if, like Beverly, you're suddenly confronted with the reality of sole responsibility for yourself—a period of awkward and uneasy adjustment will usually follow. It's during this period that you may feel yourself burning out on anxiety, anger, disillusionment, or an obsessive drive to compensate for what is perceived as lost time. The way in which that reality is perceived, however, often makes the difference between viewing yourself as powerless or powerful.

Landmark perceptions concerning age, status, financial security, and connectedness to others can act as surprising catalysts for growth and change. That sense of aloneness and hopelessness wants to be recognized; it doesn't want to remain static. Beverly becomes a useful example of a woman who is using that fear—the "edgy and restless" feelings—to alter the contours of her life. She's beginning to understand that the feeling of dependency is the product of a long-term thinking habit. She said:

> "I've had to make some serious alterations in the way I've been approaching my life. I try not to depend upon the kindness of future strangers to make it right for me. Professionally, I've been revamping my options . . . upgrading the kinds of assignments I'll take,

and refusing those which don't pay enough. That, in itself, has given me a new sense of authority and control. There comes that moment when you must stop belittling your talents and understand that insecurity is part of the whole professional terrain . . . You have to stop looking at what you don't have and reassess what you do . . ."

Along with taking the reins of her professional life, Beverly has sought out a financial adviser, an act which forced her to begin projecting a solid future. Subsequently, she had a will drawn up which had some surprising emotional ramifications for her. She said:

"I approached the will with some morbidity, but, over a period of a few weeks, as I thought through the people in my life—family, relatives, friends—and what I had that I wanted to give to them, I began to get another take on myself. Simple items like books, records, tapes, pieces of manuscripts, journals, an antique desk, a family ring . . . things I value . . . found a place with people I love, am involved with, but tend to forget . . . When I had completed it, I had a sense of deeper relationship to people. Since then, I've felt much less alone . . ."

By providing herself with a sturdy base from which to operate, Beverly has gradually found herself less apt to descend into panic and depression. She is one of the many women for whom the sole responsibility issue has acted as a positive, growth-producing perception. By the process of unlearning denial, Beverly was able to gain the control she had previously been seeking through escape tactics. As a result, her bouts with burnout have been diminished and she admits to feeling in a better emotional position to look for a relationship with a man.

DATE BURNOUT

Not surprisingly, the search for a mate—man or woman—can also become a stressful burnout proposition. With the passing of time, you may feel an ongoing pressure to connect. "I don't know what I'll do if I don't meet someone soon" is a frequently heard lament, one that legitimately speaks to a primal need for emotional fulfillment. When that need is not met, and when your attempts to click with someone new continually prove disappointing, your response to the dating situation may become joyless. One woman stated:

> "Why bother going out? It's all become so predictable . . . I'm beginning to believe there's no one out there for me. I see this whole line of wasted evenings that go nowhere, and I'm worn out running around with high hopes that are ultimately squashed."

That heaviness of spirit which characterizes burnout often emanates in this situation from both the exhaustion of incessantly placing yourself "out there" to search for a mate and the dread of experiencing yet another date which will "go nowhere."

Rita, a woman in her early thirties, described her flattened attitude about dating this way:

> "There's an old Mary Tyler Moore show that says it all. Mary had gone out to dinner with a new man. When they returned to her apartment, she went into the kitchen to make coffee . . . When she came back into the living room, her date was taking off his clothes. Outraged, she demanded, 'What are you doing? Just STOP RIGHT THERE!' The man looked up at her and rather patronizingly said, 'Well, you certainly haven't been out there for too long.' Mary narrowed her eyes. 'I'm *thirty-seven years old*,' she said. 'I've been dating for about twenty years—approximately two times a week. That's two thousand dates! DON'T TELL ME I HAVEN'T BEEN OUT THERE!'

> "That's how I feel," Rita continued. "I've been in every conceivable date situation . . . I know all the stories, the protocols, the sexual tensions, the exhaustion when I get back home and can finally stop smiling, and the subsequent waiting for the telephone to ring. I'm no longer excited, or at times even interested, at the prospect of meeting yet another 'new' man. The ritual is too enervating. If I'm not burned out by it all yet, I'm getting there . . ."

Rita's complaint is repeated again and again by other women who offer variations on her theme:

> —"It's just too much work. I'm tired of worrying about how I look, cleaning my apartment, changing sheets, being pleasant, 'up,' funny, interesting, and bolstering to the male ego, when I just basically

want to cut to: 'Do you like me?' and 'Do I like you?' and if that chemistry exists, let's see what else we've got . . . don't run away."

—"I hate telling my 'story' over and over again . . . or feeling as if I'm conducting an interview. Drawing the person out, and keeping the illusion of camaraderie going for a whole evening with someone you barely know, takes a lot of energy. I've been on so many 'first dates' that fizzled out—they're a lot of hard work. I'm tired and I'm angry. I've begun to believe when a man tells me how 'interesting' I am, or how wonderfully 'independent,' that's a definite sign he'll never call me again."

—"I've always wanted to meet a man and, right off, say to him: 'Let's pretend we're each other's oldest and dearest friend.' That way we could get past those tedious 'where-did-you-go-to-school' stories that no one really cares about. I long for intimacy with a man, but I don't think it works that way. And now I've become almost phobic about rejection . . . I don't know if I should be cool and self-contained, or if I should be 'myself.' It's all very confusing to me . . ."

If these statements reflect your own dating experience, you're probably in a quandary as to how to proceed, and questioning whether the situation can be changed. Much of your disillusionment may be based on the effort spent animating what you fear will be a mechanical event, and much of it may be fostered by what one woman called "the mystery of male behavior." There is no quickie remedy for the current conflicts between women and men; however, some of the ongoing dating dynamics can be explored with an eye toward maximizing your pleasure in the situation and minimizing the drain.

SELF-IMPOSED EXPECTATIONS: PREVENTIVE STEPS TO DATE BURNOUT

While there is no method for predicting or controlling the feelings or behavior of the people you date, there are those conflicts you can try to resolve for yourself.

Date burnout commonly emerges as a consequence of outsized expectations that are basically self-imposed. Women tend to work very hard at relationships—many of you work too hard. When the criteria for a successful evening are based on "being pleasant, 'up,' funny, interesting," on maintaining "the illusion of camaraderie," or on presenting a "cool and self-contained" front, your enthusiasm for the ritual is bound to collapse.

As with other types of burnout, you might unconsciously shift responsibility for the success or failure of each situation onto your side of the court. The date becomes "work," a repetitive, predictable, ungratifying event, and the results are usually measured against the positive or negative responses of a virtual stranger.

Overnurturers are especially prone to self-imposed expectations and the subsequent drain of emotional energies. If you're predisposed to nurturing, you probably feel compelled to "take care of" the man, to ensure he's well entertained, and to prove your value by presupposing his likes and dislikes. In short, overnurturers are often short on self-confidence and conceal their anxieties by giving out much more than the situation actually warrants.

A good method for stopping the nurturing momentum is to make a conscious effort at restraining the impulse to anticipate what will or will not happen, or to intuit his undisclosed needs. Try to stay on top of your own needs. You might begin by attempting to untangle your own motives for accepting the date. Before your next date, ask yourself this question: "What do *I* require from this particular evening?" If your motive is to impress him with your value as a potential care-giving anticipator, you may not be defining yourself accurately. You may be catering to him to conceal your own dependency needs. Since it's commonly believed that men will flee at the mere whiff of a female demand, you might assume you must manipulate the situation by overextending your energies.

It is more important to ascertain his value to you. Do you genuinely "like" this man? Are you attracted to him? Is he interesting, and does he strike you as someone with whom you'd be comfortable? Once you understand your basic motives, you'll be in a better position to shift some of the responsibility for the evening onto him. Remember, as long as you're prepared to assume all of the "work," he's off the hook, leaving you with the job of two.

Many women and men attempt to diminish their dating tensions by jumping into a premature intimacy with each other. The longing for intimacy is a normal, human response. However, the need for immediate intimacy gratification on a first date is usually the consequence of backed-up and neglected needs. Deprivations deep within you may be crying out for satisfaction, but they're rarely replenished in one evening. Instant intimacy could ultimately boomerang. It's often a shallow cover for a deeper anxiety and frequently proves to be a flash-in-the-pan experience. If you're attempting to avoid more disappointments, you might want to begin distinguishing between those people who are "easy to talk to" from those who are instantly "intimate." The difference is significant.

Although you may want to move past the "tedious . . . stories" and polite mechanics of dating, you'd be wise to suspect a man, and yourself as well, when excesses of feeling are established too early. That dynamic can be thrilling but may prove deceptive. Frequently, when a woman glowingly reports the story of a first date and describes him as "totally *there*— no secrets, no boundaries," she is astonished when she doesn't hear from him again for several months. Instant intimacy can act to conceal multiple fears, ironically, not the least of which may be the fear of intimacy.

Learning another person is a process which must be digested slowly, over time. And it's a two-way process. If you require reciprocity and are not receiving it, back off. When you begin to perceive yourself as "working" too hard, or as jumping the intimacy gun, make a conscious attempt to halt that dynamic. Remember, it's not expected. You'll prevent much of the fatigue and disenchantment of date burnout if you follow your own rhythms, your own style, and stay connected to your own needs.

FEAR OF REJECTION: PREVENTIVE STEPS TO DATE BURNOUT

Quite often, those high, self-imposed expectations are rooted in the fear of experiencing another rejection—real or imagined. To circumvent that possibility, you may be neutralizing your true self and amplifying the false. When that experience is repeated over and over again, you may acquire an aversion to the whole notion of "going out." Anticipated rejections, in this case, carry more weight than anticipated pleasures. The struggle either to tone yourself down or rev yourself up in order to present the image of compatibility may leave you discouraged and spent.

Samantha, a woman in her mid-twenties, related an anecdote that captures the core of this problem:

"I went out with someone new last week. We went to a revival
theater and caught *Sophie's Choice*. Neither of us had seen it before. Later, walking out of the lobby, he asked me what I thought of
the film. I hated it. He loved it. That's when I began to hedge.
'Well, maybe it wasn't *that* bad,' I said. 'Maybe I feel that way
because I read the book . . .' It just went from bad to worse. I felt I
had to equalize our opinions to keep his interest. For the rest of the
night I became the person I thought he'd like me to be and totally
lost myself. Then I ended up sleeping with him, which made me
feel even worse . . . Sometimes when I'm out with a new man, I
feel like I'm in a 'freezer zone.' If I'm attracted to him, I lose myself
and 'freeze.' I'm so terrified of being rejected, I can't even remember what I like and don't like . . ."

The fear of rejection manifests in a number of other attitudes as well.
One woman concluded that "dating is too risky" because her "self-esteem
is on the line each and every moment." Another woman spoke of her high
anxiety: "I end up talking too much, filling in all the spaces, because I
don't know what he's thinking." Someone else said she expected rejection
because "I'm probably on a list of a hundred other women who are me-
thodically called for dinner and sex."

The fear of rejection is a potent stress-producer. It's frequently accelerated by the attempt to alter yourself for the occasion. There is, of course,
no surefire method for guaranteeing you will never experience rejection,
but you can take some steps to protect your feelings and to regain a livable
perspective.

Good male friends can often act as guides for demystifying the confusions and complexities of male behavior. Hilary, a divorced woman in her
early forties, maintains that she would have completely abandoned the
idea of searching for a new mate if it hadn't been for her male friends.

"After all that divorce torment, I couldn't handle any more rejection. I was too vulnerable. When you're my age and you've been
married, it's degrading to have to play this game and feel that your
self-worth is measured against all those glittering young women out
there. I talked about this with my men friends and they understood.
It was an interesting time. My friendships with two men in particular became closer and much more intimate. We came to know each
other's problems and were able to laugh off a lot of the nonsense.

We spent a lot of time together, and while we never crossed over the sexual border, I began to understand that what I had with them, I wanted in a mate. I began to make conscious efforts to approach new men as friends. I stopped behaving as though rejection was a life-or-death proposition. I had other men in my life to help me not only understand male terrors and narcissism, but also remind me of my value . . ."

Arlene is another woman who has found a method for coping with rejection. As a casting assistant for a major network, she is in touch with numbers of actors and actresses who handle rejection every day. She said:

"I've begun to mimic their attitudes toward rejection. When you're wrong for a part, you can't take it personally and survive. You may be too short, too tall, a brunette, not a blonde, remind someone of his ex-wife, or simply be in the right place at the wrong time . . . I don't mean to sound too cavalier about it, but that attitude has helped me, and I believe it's very real . . ."

Both Hilary and Arlene have been able to volley their rejection fears, yet neither of their methods may satisfy your need for physical and sexual affection. Like Samantha, you may find yourself sleeping with men prematurely to ward off the fear of rejection.

Noreen has discovered another solution to the fear of rejection on dates. She said:

"I've begun to assume what I call a 'male attitude.' I take care of my own personal, sexual needs first. It may sound cold to you, but I have a few men in my life whom I just sleep with . . . We enjoy each other and there are no illusions of a future. Then I have platonic male friends, and then, men I go out with, or date. I don't feel that desperation to impress anyone anymore—I'm not starving for affection. I don't feel emotionally satisfied either, but at least I'm in a position to get to know new men slowly . . . Since I've started to take care of myself, I find I'm more often the one in the rejecting position . . ."

The fear of rejection is basic to both women and men. It becomes a women's burnout issue when women begin to feel anxious, driven, and experience that disengagement from their authentic selves which

Samantha so vividly described. Perhaps you might take some time to think through the preventive steps and solutions other women have found and begin to relieve yourself of some of the stress you've come to associate with anticipated rejections.

And, while you're at it, you might gain further insight into the issue of date burnout by checking out your own standards for acceptability in a partner. You might want to make a list of all those features you expect in a mate. Are you willing to compromise any of those standards? Women often categorically reject any man who (1) doesn't make as much money, (2) isn't at least five years older, (3) isn't as successful in his field, (4) isn't as well versed in the same subjects, (5) isn't completely self-assured, (6) doesn't demonstrate overt sensitivity, and, (7) wears the wrong clothes, chews too loudly, laughs inappropriately, or doesn't play squash. The list for distancing oneself from new possibilities is inexhaustible. By refusing to resculpt the bottom line for your standards, you may be extending the search and exhausting your good energies unnecessarily.

The pressure to connect with an acceptable partner and the subsequent weariness attached to the search is a major contributor to women's burnout. If the search has become the main focus of your life, you may have developed a compulsion from which you'll need to detach in order to regain your vision and to restore a balance. This can only be achieved by refusing to believe your satisfaction is based on a single aspiration.

If you can begin to engage yourself in activities external to the search for a mate, you might, paradoxically, place yourself in a more advantageous position to find one. Compulsions are self-limiting; they tend to eclipse the unusual source of enjoyment. Since it may take some time before you do connect with a partner, you would be wise to find other outlets that are satisfying. Otherwise, as one woman put it, "there's just too much time and space to fill." Pacing yourself, day to day, will ultimately help you to avoid the stress of loneliness and provide you with the opportunity to create a harmony between work and love.

CHAPTER VII

Relationship Burnout

"I couldn't summon up any feeling toward him . . . Sex became a chore. I only slept with him to keep him happy, but I wasn't involved . . . I was burned out on the routines, the mechanical quality of sex, the sameness of it all . . . That wonderful *intensity* disappeared . . ."

Virginia L.

"His lethargy finally got to me . . . I could see he was just dulling me out. The only area where he showed any emotion was sex, but in every other way, we just fell out of rhythm . . . I couldn't take that deadness anymore—his burnout was becoming *infectious* . . . I was just sinking . . ."

Celia C.

"When I was burning out . . . I was so worn down by my job, the classes I was taking, my son, fixing meals, shopping . . . I was too worn out to deal with being a hot, sexual partner, too. My burnout just kept *spiraling* . . . Our marriage went flat and I was too tired to care . . ."

Lynn S.

Relationship burnout has a unique character with its own peculiar wrinkles and twists. It's one of the few types of burnout in which, once the symptoms are felt, the response is typically one of immediate and massive denial or a knee-jerk reaction of jumping ship. The flattened feelings can occur in you toward anyone to whom you are close—your husband, lover, friends, and sometimes your children. And it's a tricky form of burnout. It's not always you who is afflicted. Quite often, there may be a mutual dissolution of feelings, or your partner may be afflicted first and, like the flu, you might "pick it up."

There are three major types of relationship burnout: intensity burnout, infectious burnout, and spiraling burnout.

Relationships that burn out on intensity can usually be distinguished by a sense of disappointment in the reality of your partner's actual potential, perhaps in the reality of his or her ability to sustain high emotion, or, often, in the reality of that unspoken promise to make your life right for you. In the cool light of objectivity, when the intensity has burned off, outsized expectations assume normal proportions, and, often, differences too disappointing to sustain make themselves known. The relationship burns out on its own invented intensity. *This style of burnout can be reversed.*

Infectious relationship burnout relates directly to the contagious aspect of your partner's symptoms. The deadening effect of your mate's burnout often tends to rob you of your own vitality. Typically, when confronted with a lifeless, depressed person for a period of time, your own resources become numbed. If you don't respond to your desire to flee, you may succumb to the lethargy surrounding you and find yourself equally burned out. *This type of burnout can be prevented.*

Spiraling burnout is a phenomenon that has become quite common. When too many activities and crises are sapping your emotional and physical strength, or when isolation and boredom are draining your spirit, often, irritability and subsequent feelings of disengagement will be transferred onto your mate. The burnout symptoms spring forth and spiral out onto your personal life. Your mate may be the most convenient person on whom to focus your disenchantment. Rubbed raw by what appear to be insurmountable demands, you may consciously or unconsciously blame him or her for your joylessness and the relationship may begin to burn itself out. *This mode of burnout can be stopped.*

Whether you're afflicted by intensity, infectious, or spiraling burnout, the symptoms of these relationship burnout modes are similarly experienced. However, although you may be familiar with the attitudes attached to each, nonetheless, you may not understand what they mean, or why the leaden feelings seem such an insuperable proposition. When a relationship is fraught with stress and pressure, intimacy between partners is frequently put to the test. The wearing down and wearing out of energy challenges the best of relationships, and, sadly, all too frequently, burnout symptoms are confused with an irreversible emotional death. One of you may rush to "throw in the towel" before exploring the underlying causes for the lost closeness.

It's not too difficult to understand why rash and premature measures are often undertaken as a cure for relationship burnout—be it intensity, infectious, or spiraling. The feelings are not pleasant. As burnout progresses, there's an absence of enthusiasm, excitement, devotion, or interest in the other's fate. But, most critical, there is often a loss of sexual energy. The relationship turns humdrum and colorless. What was once experienced as stimulating is now perceived as commonplace and predictable. Interest and involvement in your partner's life subtly change to indifference. Intense feelings turn apathetic. Those private jokes and shared exchanges of humor are now experienced as annoyances. Efforts at intimacy are felt as intrusions, and demonstrations of sexual desire are experienced as tedious "traps." Even the desire to "fight it out" is missing. The relationship acquires a lackluster. Quite often your feelings become cluttered with guilt and resentment. Virginia, a woman who had been living with her lover for a little over two years, stated:

> "The fire went out. I couldn't summon up any feeling toward him. Our relationship became automatic, pleasureless. I knew that certain responses would be elicited if I said this, or did that . . . Everything was pretty predictable . . . and boring. Sex became a chore. I only slept with him to keep him happy, but I wasn't involved. I felt guilty about not feeling anything—then I'd feel resentful and angry. I was burned out on the routines, the mechanical quality of sex, the sameness of it all. I became very critical—mean sometimes—then, just tired. I slept a lot at home. Nothing made me feel good anymore. That wonderful intensity disappeared. I became kind of tone-deaf to what my lover was saying. At that point, I knew my relationship was burning out . . ."

The symptoms she speaks of began with the doused "fire" of sexual feeling, then gradually spread across the board into a sense of restlessness and dissatisfaction. She said:

> "Sex and resentment don't mix with me, especially if your partner isn't on the same wavelength anymore. I wasn't even fantasizing about another person . . . I was wondering how fast we could get this over with so I could go back to my private thoughts, or just have some privacy. Sometimes I used to wish he'd go off and have an affair, but that would frighten me, and I'd start pretending I was involved. It's a terrible jam . . . More and more we became hidden and distanced from each other."

Other women initially become sensitive to the possibility of burnout by the lack of interest in their partner's conversations. (Sexual disinterest lags behind.) In this case, you may feel dulled-out by a lack of mutuality in energy or interests and frequently become disengaged from what's being said. Although you may act "as if" you're listening and involved, in reality, at times, you're mentally drifting to another image, or thinking nothing at all. You may "forget" that tonight was the night you promised to go to the movies, or eat at the new Szechuan restaurant. Your relationship may be increasingly riddled with angry reminders: "Don't you remember this is the day I told you I was going to Boston?" "I told you about the party three days ago—it's right here on the calendar!" "You knew I invited them for dinner tonight—why did you accept those tickets?" If statements like these have become a repetitive part of your home sound systems, they indicate that one of you isn't listening anymore, that one of you has tuned out, and that the relationship may have swung onto a burnout path.

THE SYMPTOM CYCLE AND RELATIONSHIP BURNOUT

If you suspect your relationship may be in burnout trouble, you might want to check your feelings, or your partner's observable behavior changes, against the Symptom Cycle that was mapped out in Chapter IV, "The Symptoms of Women's Burnout." The feelings, behavior, and attitudes identified with intensity, infectious, or spiraling relationship burnout are

loosely reflected in the stages on that cycle. Let's take a look at the cycle
again. (See illustration on page 196.)

If either you or your partner is burning out, think back to the beginning
of that relationship. Did it kick itself off with an impassioned fervor,
perhaps bordering on a compulsive desire to "merge" with each other? In
the heat of that Compulsion to Prove (Stage 1), the mutual passion and
promise usually gain an Intensity (Stage 2) which is characterized by urgency and tenaciousness. Many women fear this stage. It's often described
as "that period of affliction," when those unreliable ego boundaries fold
up and there is little separation between "I" and "You."* In intensity
relationship burnout, this is a critical stage. It often triggers the momentum for subsequent and expanding symptoms.

It's important for you to understand that *all relationships beginning
with these feelings and symptoms do not burn out!* However, if either you
or your partner tend to feel helpless in the face of strong emotion, you
could become victimized by the vulnerabilities that emerge in Stages 1
and 2. Typically, as the relationship progresses, either of you could lose
sight of the complete picture of your life and focus solely on the strong
desire to "merge." It's here, through denial and the force of the compulsion, that you will probably begin to subtly deprive yourself (Stage 3) of
self-sustaining nurturance outside of the relationship. Those deprivations
may not be construed as self-neglect, but perhaps as desirable escapes from
ordinary reality. Your work may suffer, your friends may be put on "hold,"
there may be a waning attention to your home, your health, and even your
children. Important aspects of everyday self-care might be construed as
intrusive conflicts (Stage 4), and although you may be fully cognizant that
the compulsion "to make this relationship work" has taken you over, those
thoughts are quickly dismissed. The unconscious "wish for reunion" with
another often eclipses more practical matters, and it frequently blinds you
to the reality of your partner and his or her capability for meeting your
needs.

The feelings, behavior, and attitudes in these stages are not at all unlike
those experienced in job burnout. As the compulsion to achieve in your
work obtains a firm foothold, so here does the compulsion to make the
relationship successful. And, as with job burnout, at this juncture, a sense
of "drivenness" often overpowers the values you've incorporated and es-

* For a detailed discussion of ego boundaries, see Chapter VI, "So Little Time, So Little
Love."

THE BURNOUT SYMPTOM CYCLE

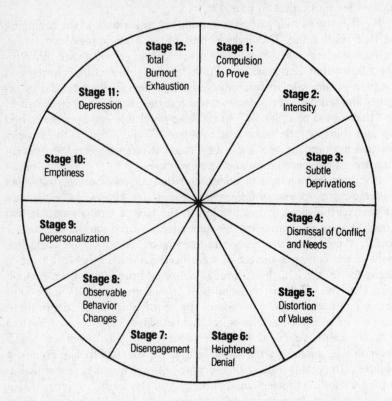

Stage 12:
Total
Burnout
Exhaustion

Stage 1:
Compulsion
to Prove

Stage 11:
Depression

Stage 2:
Intensity

Stage 10:
Emptiness

Stage 3:
Subtle
Deprivations

Stage 9:
Depersonalization

Stage 4:
Dismissal of Conflict
and Needs

Stage 8:
Observable
Behavior
Changes

Stage 5:
Distortion
of Values

Stage 7:
Disengagement

Stage 6:
Heightened
Denial

poused, and those values can become distorted or denied (Stage 5). Once again, either partner may experience this phenomenon. You may be unaware of each other's hidden or unspoken agendas, or even of your own. Either of you may view the demands of the relationship as healthy compromises one must make, yet be trading off critical aspects of your own values and many of your genuine needs for the sake of a shaky security.

Conversely, you and/or your partner could be experiencing job burnout and subtly begin to deprive each other of personal attention. In this case, one of you may be carrying burnout from another source back into your home and the relationship may begin to suffer from infectious or spiraling burnout. The demands of work or school drain your energies, and you or your mate could begin to feel deprived of intimacy.

Stage 5, Distortion of Values, is pivotal to the burnout process. In some relationships, the differences in values are immediately recognized as formidable roadblocks to the long haul and are confronted and explored with an eye toward livable compromise. Often, if the differences are too great or too unwieldy to manage, as in religious views, political perspectives, or ambition, the relationship is severed. The less obvious differences, however, are not as easily identified, and are frequently swallowed up, stuffed away, and denied, sometimes for years. When they flare up, you or your partner may secretly or verbally accuse and blame the other for dominating your true self for too long, and may look to get out. It sometimes takes a long time for your consciousness to catch up or catch onto either the denial you have imposed upon yourself, or the denial of your partner's behavior. This becomes a "long haul" problem. One woman described her denial and subsequent burnout depression:

> "For five years I've been avoiding this outburst inside of me. It's so hard to change things when you've let them go for so long . . . They sound so petty when I verbalize them, but they've been eating away at me . . . I've always loved living in the middle of activity—in the city. He wanted to live in the country. So I gave in and gave up what I value to complement his need. I like to have lots of people around; he likes the quiet, contemplative life. I need to talk things out—he maintains my need is 'anxious energy.' He's always felt that my pace is too fast and that we're out of sync. I toned myself down because I heard a threat there . . . Now I'm angry, exhausted, and feel like a stranger to myself . . . I didn't make myself known at the outset—and now I just don't care anymore . . . I've lost it."

Another woman told the story in reverse:

> "We've been together for close to twelve years and I've always been content, independent, and happy with my life. The power has, in the main, been on my side of the relationship . . . but then it switched. He started telling me he's not happy, he's not excited sexually, and that he's depressed. I never knew he was suffering until he told me; he always seemed as satisfied with our arrangement as me. He's burning out and I don't know what to do . . . He says

our values are not the same and that I always assumed, without asking, that they were. There's a lot of anger in him . . . It's all very difficult . . ."

Both of these women are dealing with the consequences of Stage 5 on the cycle, but from two different directions. Their stories are illustrative of the burnout momentum triggered at this critical juncture and felt some years later, over the long haul. The extent and degree of value distortion differs with each burnout case, but the underlying causes can often be traced back to that phase of the relationship when one or both mates began to distort and deny their authentic values and needs. Both examples highlight the consequences of denial.

Stage 6 on the cycle is referred to as Heightened Denial because it clearly illuminates the desire to press harder, dig in deeper, and cast off those aspects of yourself or your mate which might intrude upon or interfere with the smooth course of the relationship. You may deny your own fatigue or even illness, if your partner doesn't deal with sickness well. Conversely, you may have trouble with your partner's bad moods, ill temper, or fatigue and deny the symptoms that he or she demonstrates. If either of you throws a wrench into what is construed as a very fragile development between you, instead of sorting it out, you may increase your denial and pretend everything is fine. If, when asked how you're doing, you respond with "We're fine," you might use that as a signal that *you* are not fine, and that you're no longer perceiving yourself as an individual but as a symbiotic aspect of someone else. You're probably denying your individuality to cover a glaring threat.

Women frequently speak of pressing their mates to "talk out" the problems between them and open up more honest dialogues. But frequently, even after a "good conversation," the issues at hand may not have been resolved satisfactorily, out of a fear of pushing too hard or too much. Eventually a pattern is established in which one of you ostensibly has the power in the relationship and the other becomes deceptively submissive. As the denial of these internal intricacies heightens, you may begin to feel increasingly disengaged from yourself, yet nonetheless continue to perpetuate the established myths in the relationship through silent collusion.

Disengagement (Stage 7) is characterized by a desire to remain in tune with your partner, but an inability to sustain your involvement. You may not feel quite as sexual as you previously did, and you may not be quite as attentive to his or her needs. You may be behaving appropriately to avoid suspicion, but struggling to keep up your energy or interest. One woman said: "I understood I was losing feeling, but became so alarmed at my own burned-out emotions that I doubled up on my attentions to fool myself . . . I didn't want to know that I was the one who was falling away. If I admitted it, I would have had to do something to change it, and that was too complex and frightening." When you become disengaged from yourself, you begin to feel you're on "automatic." The relationship has become a familiar way of life, and although you may be disillusioned or over-stressed by the dynamics, you may continue to act "as if" nothing is amiss.

By Stage 8, Observable Behavior Changes are usually brought to your attention by others. Friends may tell you they're concerned by your absence in their lives, by your visible exhaustion, by your lack of spontaneity and humor, or by your preoccupation with your mate. You may have plunged yourself into your work to avoid the disturbance at home, or have isolated yourself from people. Another woman said, describing her observable changes:

" 'You don't look like you're enjoying yourself, or that you're very happy these days,' my friends would tell me. 'You're so serious about everything' or 'I miss seeing you' was the kind of thing people were telling me. I was just too distraught to listen to stories about their lives. I was too obsessed with my own problems, and I was pissed off by anyone criticizing me. I was riding on a very delicate balance and could be thrown when pushed. My home life was oppressive, my partner and I were in a cold war of politeness, and I was in the bathroom with the door shut, crying. The last thing I wanted to hear was someone telling me I was wrong."

As with job burnout, when you're coping with relationship burnout, by Stage 8, concern is typically construed as criticism. Precisely what is needed—warmth, loving attention, intimacy—is shut out. There are variations on that theme. You may seek out friends but have established an inconsolable position which is impenetrable. You may invite friends to speak with you not for counsel and consolation, but for validation of your victimized stance. Either way, however, your friends are viewed as people who "don't understand" what you're going through, and they are dismissed as insufficient to the task. This is what's frequently referred to as a "stuck place."

Depersonalization (Stage 9) is unqualifiedly unpleasant and disorienting. Routines between you and your partner have become rigid and inflexible. Conversations are usually pared down to essential exchanges, and sex is experienced as a "chore." In order to provide an illusion of closeness, you may live out the appropriate formats while feeling as though someone else is inhabiting your body. Depersonalization is sometimes characterized by a split between feeling and action. Feelings of anger, guilt, and resentment go underground and are replaced by lethargy, an uncommon lassitude that signals a drained, depleted spirit. You may sleep much more now, or be plagued by insomnia. Your concentration will most probably be easily broken, and you may not "hear" what people are saying. At this stage, many women are unable to achieve orgasm, and many men become temporarily impotent. Sometimes there is the desire to go off and have an affair with someone else, but usually infidelity is not the prime issue. The sex drive is either missing, or it's used as a narcotic, a false cure to revitalize burned-out emotions. Quite often, in relationships where one person is burning out, the other will "pick it up" and increasingly experience the same leaden feelings. This is the essence of infectious burnout.

A sense of Emptiness (Stage 10) follows closely behind depersonalization. The partner who is burning out may look to other areas to fill up the emptiness, and not necessarily other people. In this stage both women and men often become television addicts. Many women adopt food addictions or turn to alcohol or drugs. Exercise addicts may increase their jogging mileage, or the time spent in aerobics and workout classes. Shopping sprees with overextended credit cards are another indication of emptiness. Any activity which will obliterate the awful feelings, help you to avoid the primary issues between you and your mate, and perhaps aid in your denial of the problems will be utilized. "I just want to distance myself from him," a woman in the throes of Stage 10 said. "I've been reading one junky novel after the other to blot out this crisis . . . I know I should be doing something constructive, but I don't have any more energy. I just want to go off alone . . ."

Those feelings are quick to turn into burnout Depression (Stage 11), a stage which is closely related to emptiness. At this point, there is no sense of future time, yet there is no impulse to change. You or your partner may view the other as a "fixture" in the house and have truly lost the ability to perceive other options. Perspective fails, and because your energies may be depleted by pushing so hard to accommodate the flaws in the relationship, you may feel you simply don't care anymore. Your self-esteem is probably at its lowest ebb, and you may feel hopeless and despairing, yet too worn-out to move. With your high expectations dashed, you might intermittently entertain suicidal notions which are closely associated with burnout depression.

However, burnout depression isn't always experienced as a mourning. It sometimes manifests in a high-pitched nervousness. It's not that you don't care anymore, but that your caring has created a dangerous anxiety reaction that might have been operating under pressure for far too long. Your depression, in this instance, isn't experienced as lethargy but as agitation. The burden of stress may have sapped your resources and you may have become overly sensitized to any disturbance. You may experience a nervous, emotional intolerance characterized by frequent crying jags, outbursts of temper, and perhaps a continual need to be in motion—finger tapping, leg wagging, picking on cuticles, biting lips—as if your internal motor has revved to overdrive and stuck.

Women who have experienced burnout depression recall how they had no patience for the most commonplace breakdowns of everyday life. One woman said she "freaked out when the washing machines in my apartment complex were all in use. I took my laundry bag and threw it into the back of the closet, where it stayed for two weeks . . ." Another woman stated she never deposited the checks because "there was a small line in the bank and I was outraged. I stuffed them into the glove compartment and took off in a fury. I couldn't calm down . . . I felt like a basket case . . ."

Burnout depression which manifests as agitation places emergency proportions on the most benign of events. However, whether the depression turns into lethargy or agitation, your immune system, at this stage, has worn itself down and your resistance against illness and disease may not be functioning optimally.

As was discussed in Chapter IV, "The Symptoms of Women's Burnout," Stage 12, Total Burnout Exhaustion, is a dangerous and health-threatening plateau. It must be considered a red-light emergency situation and should be treated immediately. Your relationship is no longer the issue here. Your physical, emotional, and mental health may be precariously balanced. You may require professional counsel and/or medical assistance.

Please note: Relationship burnout rarely reaches total burnout exhaustion. Because there are two people involved in this particular type of burnout, the momentum is usually stopped before reaching that stage. However, in some situations, years of excessive denial and burnout depression culminate in this serious stage. When those symptoms of emptiness and depression are not checked, they can squire you into total burnout exhaustion.

If you are experiencing relationship burnout, you may be stuck in one stage for some time and never escalate to the next. Or you may be experiencing several stages simultaneously. What's important here is to understand that relationship burnout does not have to escalate. Once you've identified your symptoms, you'll be in a better position to prevent further burnout momentum or to totally reverse the process. There are many solutions. Just because you're stuck doesn't mean you can't move.

THREE TYPES OF RELATIONSHIP BURNOUT

Before looking to solutions, however, it might be prudent to identify the type of relationship burnout you're experiencing. You now understand what the symptoms signal, but let's take a look at the dynamics behind the symptoms.

Again, there are three major types of relationship burnout:
1. Intensity burnout
2. Infectious burnout
3. Spiraling burnout

Each of these types have specific causes and dynamics. The results are similar. Try to identify your problem.

1. *Intensity Burnout*

The loss of feeling toward a significant person in your life most frequently occurs in the aftermath of high, intense attraction and enthusiasm. The relationship was probably launched with "hot and heavy" feelings, and both of you were probably "at your best." After that phase, the relationship began to burn out. When feelings reach a fever pitch of excitement, they must, by necessity, take a dip, and, in the cool light of reality, subtle complaints and resentments indicative of burnout will frequently begin. This is a critical phase for couples—the image of the idealized savior vanishes—especially if the partnership is based exclusively on sexual attraction. Many short-lived marriages and affairs are products of intensity burnout. One or both partners go into the relationship with conscious or unconscious expectations of grandiose proportions and assume they'll remain in a sexually charged bliss and a tension-free Eden indefinitely.

Those expectations are not always understood but are, nonetheless, active elements in your psyche. In order to sort them out, you may have to make a distinction between what you say you want from a partner and what you feel you need to receive. The dichotomy between the two is frequently quite wide. For instance, you may state you want an equal partnership with little dependency, yet feel hurt and betrayed when your partner fails to behave protectively. Or you may consciously want a mate who is successful and powerful, yet resent him or her for not being as attentive as your needs require. Conversely, you might take the position that you want someone who is nurturing and sensitive, yet feel intruded upon when he or she seeks closeness, or when your own professional life is consuming your time, attention, and energy. This chasm between want and need is usually revealed when that initial high and magical sexuality levels off. It's then that disappointment gels, and often, one partner, unable to withstand either the absence of intensity or the abundance, will take the opportunity to flee. You may have found this particular dynamic to be a recurring pattern in your relationships, or you may view yourself as the unwilling victim of your partners' erratic flights.

Expectations also run high when you or your partner unconsciously dangle promises for the future which remain unfulfilled. Along with the sexual and romantic high, potential achievement is an inducement which feeds the intensity. There's the novel one of you is going to write, the business that will be started, the position that will be attained, the fame, fortune, or application of uncommon talent which will be heightened with you by his or her side. However, although ambition, skill, and promise may be present, the impulse to act may never be achieved. In this particular situation, each of you may perceive the other as larger, stronger, and perhaps more disciplined than the reality proves. In the throes of that initial intensity, lovers often "invent" each other and are genuinely astonished when they learn that the other is neither larger than life, nor the person who will "make everything right for me." The process of building the relationship by learning the other is either prematurely truncated, or the "inventions" are endured with disappointment and concealed acri-mony, and the stages of burnout are prolonged, sometimes for years.

In another version of intensity burnout, one partner believes that he or she can resculpt the sexual and/or emotional intensity patterns of the other, and sets out on a mission to create the perfect mate. In this case, the beloved becomes a "project person"—someone toward whom all of your creative energies are directed. Initially, as the recipient of all that energy, you might feel needed and protected, but eventually you'll begin to feel pressured—under the gun—to continually perform and react in accordance with your partner's dream. Increasingly the ability to respond authentically is lost. In time, the pressure to "be someone else" will wear you down. You'll begin to disengage and avoid, and the burnout of your affections will move into gear.

If, however, the burning intensity to alter your partner is on your side of the court, you may have a conscious or unconscious desire both to control and to become sexually and emotionally indispensable. Compulsive nur-turers are often caught in this trap. Insecurity runs high and is frequently concealed beneath what appears to be an abundant but unrelieved gener-osity. That "generosity" becomes stifling and intrusive, but, more impor-tant, the incessant "feeding"—the listening well, anticipating, entertain-ing, cooking, dressing to please, offering insight and advice—gradually depletes your energies and metamorphoses into a burden of stress. If you don't burn out, your partner could. The pressure on both of you is too exhaustive.

One woman in the throes of intensity burnout said:

> "I was doing the work of two. I felt responsible for maintaining the excitement between us . . . but it was all self-generated, and I was getting very little in return. I denied those facts because I didn't want to lose him . . . and because I never feel that I'm enough . . ."

As the relationship burns itself out, intensity is replaced by an emo-tional emptiness, and, often, bitter resentment emerges in the nurturer, who feels wronged.

Possessiveness is another component of intensity burnout. Once again, the power of possessiveness can be demonstrated by either partner. One of you will act the part of the "captive," and the other, the "captor."

A woman in the captive position stated:

"The quickest way for me to burn out in a relationship and then to leave it is when I begin to feel like a trapped rabbit. When he starts asking, 'Where did you go?' 'Who was that you were talking to?' 'Where were you when I called?' or 'How long did you talk to him?' I start feeling those trapped, smarmy feelings. It's like being under house arrest—as if my thoughts are being monitored and, unless I tow the line, I'll have to deal with all that repressed anger of his . . . I want to scream, "Hey, knock it off! Talk to me—don't interrogate me!' . . ."

Another woman spoke of the feelings associated with being the "captor":

"I'm a very intense person and I need to have that intensity met. I've never been able to use restraint in my relationships. I want to know what he's thinking, what he's feeling, and I need to hear words of reassurance. Unless we're in agreement, I don't feel secure. It takes a long time before I can feel relaxed, and then there's always something that happens to threaten me . . . I'm not filled with self-confidence . . ."

The experience of being suffocated by your partner and the converse experience of gripping anxiety in the absence of continual reassurance are equally debilitating. When you find yourself in either position, the feelings are laden with stress, often guilt, and, ultimately, exhaustion. Both of these women spoke of entering their relationships on a sexual high and referred to the "letdown" they experienced when the passions leveled off and they reclaimed their "vision." The intensity of the first woman leads her right past the reality of the partners she chooses, and the intensity of the second woman blinds her to the weight of the demands she places on the partners she picks.

There are as many variations on the intensity burnout theme as there are couples, but if you are familiar with these dynamics, you may need to begin exploring your patterns with an eye toward clarifying your needs and moderating your expectations.

Preventing and Reversing Intensity Burnout

Burnout thrives on intensity. Once that idea is firmly rooted, you might want to assess the degree to which your own intensity factor rules your emotional life and begin to understand why you're experiencing relationship burnout.

In and of themselves, intense feelings are not hazardous. However, when they blind or distort reality, or when they are the result of anxiety, you might begin to suspect the validity of your perceptions about your mate. Unrelieved intensity is enervating. Once it has leveled off, you or your partner can easily fall from grace in the other's eyes. For this reason, one step you can take to prevent relationship burnout is to immediately admit to yourself that you are susceptible to unrelieved intensity and that many of those idealized notions about your partner may be "inventions."

Do you describe your partner too "glowingly"? This should signal an alarm. You're probably denying those fleeting wild thoughts, those flashes of insight that act as warnings and safeguards. Building a relationship is a process, not a happening. If you find you're whitewashing personality traits which could become problematical, you're caught up in the intensity and not the person. The process is perverted. The realities of your mate have not been integrated into your invention. What aspects of his or her personality and behavior do you find troublesome? This question is not geared to encourage critical, picky, distancing methods, but to clear away some of the invention debris and obtain an honest reading on your feelings. As one woman said of herself:

> "When that intensity hits me, I pretend I don't know anything which might interfere with my good time . . . I alter reality to suit my immediate desires. Later, when the relationship turns bad, I'm usually furious at myself for having refused to acknowledge my own intuitions . . ."

What she's describing is one form of denial—conscious suppression. Although the desire to make a relationship work may be enormous, to avoid a quick burnout, you might want to acknowledge those intuitions and begin to deal with them. Many women are afraid of probing too much or of pressing for dialogues with their mates "because he (or she) might construe it as a demand and back off." Yet there is a qualitative difference between flooding someone with demands and seeking information.

The other side of the coin is equally important. Does your partner describe you too "glowingly"? Does he or she view you as the idealized savior? Since both of you are usually demonstrating the best within you, your partner may have little idea of what you like, want, or expect over a long haul.

Take a long, hard look at your expectations. Is this person capable of fulfilling those expectations? If your demands are of outsized proportion, you might have to make some alterations. Often, both women and men are seeking partners who have the attributes they feel they are lacking. If you feel a powerlessness or an absence of authority in your dealings with others, you may choose a partner who appears stronger than you. In essence, you "eat the heart of the lion" to become the lion. However, if that coveted strength fails, you could become disillusioned and feel betrayed. A struggling actress offered this account of her now-severed two-year marriage:

> "When he and I met, we were both up for parts in two different films. I got my part, but he didn't, and he began to view me with a new respect. After we were married, I had one rejection after the other. Neither of us were making it, and our marriage was getting very rocky. Then he just left. He told me later he thought I was going to become famous . . . I was hurt and enraged at this . . . but I understand now he thought my ambition and success would rub off on him and I'd make everything right in his life."

That dynamic is repeated over and over among couples whose expectations of the other are based on "making it right for me." To avoid this burnout path, it is essential that you catch that expectation before it escalates.

Are you able to tolerate each other's differences? In the throes of intensity, women frequently take on their partners' tastes and preferences. Another woman said:

> "I don't enjoy chamber music, but because my partner did, I pretended I did too. I didn't want her to know my tastes were not as 'highbrow,' that I'm crazy about country music, rock, and jazz. But you can't sustain those deceptions; you become fatigued and resentful, always on edge. Eventually your differences begin to leak out and your lover feels shortchanged . . ."

Differences are not always easily deciphered. Often they're blanketed in vague dissatisfactions or understated irritations. To avoid burnout, clarifying who you are, what you enjoy, and what you prefer is critical.

Can you laugh together? A mutual sense of humor often alleviates much of the drama and intensity between partners and allows both to sustain their intimacy. When differences in opinion, style, or behavior intrude upon your feelings, the ability to "have fun" with those skirmishes can reduce the tensions. It's hard to burn out when you're having fun.

Are you overnurturing your partner? If so, this is a good time to learn how to detach. The energy you're pouring into the relationship could easily prove to be unrewarding and debilitating. You may be making yourself indispensable, but the cost to your own needs may be exhaustive. Nurturers inevitably deny their own needs for "the sake of the relationship" and ultimately experience bitter and resentful feelings. If you are a nurturer, you might begin to stop yourself before unnecessarily giving more. When you catch yourself anticipating your partner's moods, appetite, need for rest, desire for company, or any number of unstated possibilities—stop! When you catch yourself continually rearranging your priorities to match his or hers—stop! The ceaseless mental and physical activity will not "help" the relationship. You might even have to make a list of those activities and concerns which were present before you became a couple and refer to it from time to time as a reminder that you, too, exist. One woman who was interviewed spoke of a technique she used to halt the overnurturing impulse:

> "I have a friend who has the exact same tendency. We instituted what we refer to as 'restraint calls.' When either of us feels anxious about the need to overdo, or if either is premenstrual and especially needy, we phone each other for counsel. We've seen each other through a few relationships and both know we get caught up in becoming the perfect mates . . . real superwomen. It's been extremely helpful. Sometimes I don't even have to make the call—I can hear her advice in my head."

This is not to imply that your sensitive care-giving attributes are undesirable, but it does mean that when they become compulsions and are goaded by anxiety, the art of graceful detachment can halt burnout momentum.

Are you attempting to "resculpt" your partner's emotional or sexual intensity patterns? If you have it in mind that through your own brave and perhaps virtuous attempts you're going to "change" your partner's ostensible unwillingness to express strong emotion, to equal your desire for dialogues, to reflect your need for "space," to match your rhythms and style, or to mirror your sensitivities, either you or your partner could be ripe for burnout. Many women believe that their influence and impact is large enough to alter years of conditioned responses in their lovers. This also applies to men, but women tend to demonstrate this dynamic in many more obvious no-win situations. Hooking up with an alcoholic or a drug abuser are extreme examples; however, they highlight the mechanism at its most exaggerated. You might involve yourself with someone whom you believe to have hidden potential and whom you feel you can change by making him or her believe in themselves. When you have too many "changes" in mind for your partner on your hidden agenda, he or she is no longer being regarded as a separate person, but as a "project" or an "issue." At this point, whoever is doing the resculpting is, perhaps, not after a relationship, but after a resolution of their own tensions. The tensions will not be resolved. They will deepen and extend into symptoms of stress, fatigue, and resentment. To prevent burnout in this situation, you must realistically assess your own expectations, and perhaps those of your partner, and begin to either appreciate the differences or back off. You may be using your partner's alleged weaknesses as a method for camouflaging your own.

Is too much possessiveness the intensity factor in your relationship burnout? If the possessiveness is emanating from you, you might try to ascertain if the feelings belong in the present with your partner, or if they are transference reactions from the past which are inappropriate to the new situation. Those hidden stress-extenders—backed-up anger, guilt, denied hostility, neglected needs, and low self-esteem—are often churning from within and help to promote apprehension and suspicion between partners. Much good energy is siphoned off by the strain of the concealed stress leaving you with frayed and depleted emotions and judgments.

The need for continual reassurance cannot be derived solely from one person. However, this type of "tunnel vision" is often a product of intensity burnout. You may believe the only true and satisfactory source of reassurance resides with your partner. This is a critical mistake, and numbers of women suffer intensity burnout for just this reason. "If I can't get it from him, I won't be able to get it, or won't try to get it from anyone else," is the typical response to the felt deprivation. If your need for reassurance seems to be greater than your partner's, you may need to obtain it from friends, through your work, and from your own resourcefulness. If your self-image and confidence are dangerously low, you may need to seek professional counseling. Either way, the possessiveness is a symptom of a need far more extensive than your partner's inability to satisfy the demand. Frequently, multiple anxieties are percolating beneath the possessiveness. Those are the issues that must be addressed to reverse the burnout momentum.

"The bottom-line fear," another woman stated, "is that I'll be thrown away . . . That's why I need him to tell me so often how he's feeling about us." "Thrown away" is a potent phrase which should signal that the problem is older than the current relationship. If you relate to that phrase, with a little investigation into the past, you might rediscover the memory of a parent who either threatened to abandon you or, in fact, psychically or physically left. That trauma has been carried into your adult life and now is transferred onto your partner. You may feel surrounded by imagined threats—from the woman he speaks to at the party a minute too long, to the check-in call that he didn't make today, to his preoccupation with something or someone other than you, to his desire to "go to bed early"—to sleep. If this is the inner environment in which you live, it's imperative for you to begin to separate the real from the imagined in your life. In this way, you'll perhaps be able to salvage the relationship from intensity burnout and perhaps save yourself from the ongoing, agonizing threat of rejection.

If, however, you're on the other side of the possessiveness, you may be experiencing those "trapped rabbit" feelings and find yourself beginning to describe your relationship in less than glowing terms. Since your partner is probably suffering from the above description, and assuming you'd like to save the relationship, you might want to make it a point not only to offer the reassurance he or she needs, but also to describe how the incessant demand for attention acts to alienate you. You might want to offer suggestions that will satisfy both your needs.

Encourage your partner to reestablish relationships with his or her friends, to attend activities without you, to resume that part of his or her life which has been abandoned for the relationship. You could explain that it's not a question of overcommitment, but of an intensity that will eventually deaden enthusiasm in both of you. There's no absolute method for circumventing your partner's pain. If he or she is being led by anxiety, feelings will be hurt. However, it could circumvent the more grisly effects of a lost, burned-out relationship.

There are also no sure cures for intensity burnout. But self-awareness and the willingness to halt your denial and reclaim your intuitions, feelings, and needs could give you both a fresh start.

2. Infectious Burnout

Is burnout "catching"? In some instances, yes. This will depend upon the state of your emotional immune system and the strength of your physical resistance to illness. Either you or your partner may be contagious —it depends upon how the other's burnout is handled.

Living with a burnout isn't pleasurable. When your partner's feelings, attitudes, and behavior are affected by burnout, and when the symptoms escalate and are prolonged, after a period of time you too can become contaminated and begin to mimic the same mood.

Consider this scenario: You've been running all day on the job, handling problems, going to meetings, arranging appointments. You're revved up from the pace, and when you enter your home you're looking forward to chitchatting about the day, having dinner together, maybe sharing a bottle of wine, exchanging stories, laughing a little, and maybe making love. What you're confronted with, however, is an energyless person, with a thin, tight smile, mechanical responses, too much politeness, sitting on the couch with the television blaring, daring you to maintain your high spirits in the face of grimness. The conversation goes something like this: "How are you feeling?" "Fine." "Did you have an okay day?" "Yes." "Are you hungry?" "No." "Do you want to talk about it?" "Get off my back!"

Now replay that scenario over a week, a month, a half year, and imagine your reactions. Will you be able to maintain your own spirit in the face of your partner's attitude? Chances are, coupled with your own feelings of rejection, it will be a matter of a few weeks before you'll begin to feel drained, impotent, irritable, and angry, and after that, disengaged, depersonalized, empty, and then depressed. You will have "picked up" your partner's burnout.

Now, reverse the scenario: You're coping with relationship burnout, you've been home all day with the kids, you're suffering from too many unrewarding tasks, too much guilt over your desire to get away from your children, too many pesky demands, and your youngest child comes down with a cold. You're bored but agitated, overstressed, overburdened, and your husband walks in the house with what you perceive as a claim on your attention. He wants you to listen to an update on the office politics, and he's littering the living room you've just cleaned with his newspapers, briefcase, and jacket, which he just tossed on a chair. He appears to want something from you and you just want to be left alone. The conversation goes something like this: "How was your day?" "What do you think?" "Are the kids okay?" "Jeffrey's got a cold." "Did you call a doctor?" "He doesn't need a doctor." "Look, why don't we go out for dinner?" "Because I don't feel like getting dressed." "Come on . . ." "Get off my back!"

Again, replay that scenario over and over for a week, a month, a half year, and imagine your partner's reactions. In time, he, too, could succumb to your symptoms and begin to demonstrate a similar attitude, and feelings of disengagement, depersonalization, emptiness, and depression. He will have "caught" your burnout.

When you or your mate are suffering from burnout, the apathetic attitudes and unwillingness to communicate tend to provide the other with feelings of rejection, or even abandonment. Reciprocity within the relationship is seriously impaired and the balance of affections and energy takes a dangerous tilt.

As with intensity burnout, overnurturers are especially prone to infectious burnout. The unresponsiveness of your partner may act as a bellows to your care-giving impulse. You may not understand what is happening or what is required, yet believe it's your responsibility to make it right. No matter what you do to alleviate your partner's distress, nothing works. The situation often becomes explosive. Celia, a homemaker, said:

> "I tried talking to him, but his lethargy finally got to me. I'd summon up the strength to initiate discussions that might offer me a clue, but he'd insist nothing was wrong, or blow up and leave the room, or bury himself in newspapers or the television. My feelings would be hurt, so I'd leave him alone, and he'd accuse me of being insensitive. I began tiptoeing around him, keeping the kids away, trying to cheer him up . . . I even bought him surprises—a book he expressed an interest in, a cassette, his favorite foods . . . There'd be a few moments of polite gratitude, then he'd sink again.

I could see he was just dulling me out. The only area where he showed any emotion was sex, but in every other way we just fell out of rhythm. After a few months of this, I began to get very tired. I dreaded the evenings, and usually fell asleep early. I began to see him as another child in the house. I couldn't take that deadness anymore—his burnout was becoming infectious. Then I started getting headaches, unusually painful menstrual cramps, colds . . . you name it. But the worst were the extreme bouts of fatigue . . . It was ridiculous, but I was just sinking into my own burnout . . ."

Like Celia's husband, your partner may not know what's happening or be unwilling to express it and distance himself or herself further every day. He or she may blame work, the kids, lack of money, politics, the country, the world, the weather, or you, but not be specific enough to provide you with a handle. This kind of "umbrella" blame is unsatisfactory and creates frustration and impatience in you. "Umbrella" blame is usually a red herring burnouts use to throw both of you off the scent of the authentic underlying cause. As an overnurturer, however, you may pick up false clues from these red herrings and begin to flood your partner with attentions which are not appropriate, wanted, or needed. Over a period of time, your overly ambitious gestures will whittle away your energies. Without rewards or reciprocity, you'll begin to feel angry, used, depleted, and in time your home will be occupied by two burnouts.

Even those women who are not given to abundant nurturing can "catch" their partner's burnout. Martha, another woman diagnosed as the recipient of infectious burnout, began to tire in the face of his depressing attitude.

"I'd step in the door in the evenings and instantly know it was another of *those* nights . . . the peck on the cheek without looking up, no emotion, no excitement, just *deadness!* We'd spent a lot of time discussing the problem, but it was difficult—he was drinking too much and would twist my words to make it appear that I was responsible for all his bad feeling. It was very alarming . . . I felt he had lost interest in me—we hadn't made love in weeks, and my confidence was very shaky. I needed something for myself from him, but nothing was coming back. I began to actively dislike him and was fantasizing about other men. I had the impulse to bolt. Then I started 'taking to bed' a lot. At first I thought it was to avoid his depressing demeanor. Then I realized I had exhausted myself by worrying, with the endless talks, and with my own sense of impotence. I had picked up his disease . . ."

Many women have alluded to the "taking to bed" aspect of infectious burnout. Sometimes, as Martha suggested, it's done "to avoid his depressing demeanor," but at other times it may be a bid for the attention you're not receiving—a way of demonstrating the effect of your partner's attitude. Either way, the gesture should signal an alarm in you. In the absence of joy, energy, or life-force, and in the presence of listlessness, remoteness, and anger, there is no emotional replenishment and no motivational charge to keep the dynamic alive. It's not unusual, either, for hypochondriacal symptoms to emerge in the face of your partner's burnout. Sometimes illness appears to be the only method for reestablishing a communication both of you can accept, cope with, or understand—but it will perpetuate the symptoms in both of you.

Martha's bout with infectious burnout has a rather unusual but not surprising finale:

"I was walking around in a daze at home. Then I tripped on the step to the backyard and broke a bone in my foot. It hurt like hell, but the emergency seemed to activate his concern. The accident temporarily jolted him out of himself, but it didn't last . . . Nothing had been worked through . . ."

Martha's husband finally did agree to get some professional counseling, but not before their relationship had taken a critical dip.

If your partner is burning out, you don't need to break a leg or even become a victim of repetitive headaches, back pains, colds, or any number of hypochondriacal symptoms in an attempt to diminish your anxiety or in an effort to reconnect. And you don't have to slip away into burnout in the face of your partner's. There are some steps you can take to prevent a double burnout in your house.

Preventing and Reversing Infectious Burnout

It must be remembered at the outset that burnout is defined as ". . . a wearing down and wearing out of energies. It's an exhaustion born of excessive demands which may be self-imposed or externally imposed by families, jobs, friends or lovers, which deplete one's energy, coping mechanisms, and internal resources. It is a feeling state that is accompanied by an overload of stress, and which eventually impacts on one's motivation, attitudes, and behavior."

In infectious relationship burnout, coping mechanisms and internal resources become depleted by the absence of emotional supplies coming back to you from the primary person in your life. This type of burnout poses an additional conflict, and therefore a new question:

Can you maintain your own mental, physical, and emotional health when your main source of support—your partner—is burning out?

Right off, it's imperative for you to be in a position to take preventive steps against infecting yourself. Perhaps you can use some of these suggestions as guides:

(1) When your husband or lover has grown distant, critical, and perhaps deadened out, the immediate tendency of many women is to become frightened and experience his or her withdrawal as a very personal rejection. While this period of time may be hurtful and angering, you must nonetheless guard your own well-being. Therefore, it is critical for you to get the proper rest, eat well, and stay alert to your own physical needs. It is equally critical that you protect your emotional energies by being extra-attentive to yourself and by maintaining a firm grip on your life outside of the relationship.

(2) You must make it a point to get some outside stimulation and support. This is not the time to withdraw from friends or to continue telling them, "Everything's fine." On the contrary, it is vitally important that you stay in touch with confidantes—you need emotional nourishment. When your mate is burning out, the stress can be managed and the subsequent energy drain refueled by connecting with other people. You need affiliation, closeness, and intimacy with friends. You may be misconstruing the situation with your partner, missing a much-needed objective view, and mentally escalating the doom factor of the relationship.

Old friends are often in a good position to remember your history and to steer you away from destructive thinking. They may be able to shed light on aspects of your mate's behavior that you have overlooked. An astute and loving friend will, perhaps, also be able to alert you to your own condition, help you to keep your needs balanced, and aid you in avoiding a similar burnout.

(3) To keep yourself intact, try to separate your partner's needs from

your own. While in the same burned-out and distraught condition you may require a lot of attention, caring, and warmth. Your partner may feel smothered by too much attention and feel unable to express his or her annoyance except by lashing out. This event could feed your stress index, enlarge your own sense of rejection, and push you further into burnout.

(4) With infectious burnout, a degree of detachment will help you to hold your own and protect yourself from "catching" the symptoms. This does *not* mean that you begin to behave in a cool and aloof fashion, abandoning him or her at this critical juncture. What it does mean, however, is that compassion is far more useful than pity or self-denigration. You can be sympathetic to your mate's feelings without fusing up with them. Compassion will allow you to do your best in a bad situation without either taking full responsibility for your mate's feelings or berating yourself for not being "enough."

Do remember, if you begin to "pity" him or her, you'll place yourself in a superior position. This dynamic is a defensive posturing—it could allow you to feel exaggeratedly needed, and provide a new reason for overextending, overattending to his or her needs, and further depleting your own energy and resources.

(5) When your partner is burning out, the psychological drain on your own emotional life may seem insurmountable. Therefore, it's critical that you distinguish between the blame that may be heaped on you, and the other troubled aspects of your partner's life. He or she may be on a fault-finding mission and direct the cynical feelings toward you. Once again, a degree of detachment is necessary at this point. You must try to unravel the pieces of your partner's burnout problems and separate those that relate to you from those that belong elsewhere. (See "Spiraling Burnout," page 218.)

Quite often, immediately after completing a master's or doctoral thesis, finishing up a long-term project, returning from a vacation or a vital and exciting business trip, a postpartum burnout depression may flare up. Your mate might be unconsciously seeking rewards, or a continuity of that project intensity from you. When the rewards or the intensity are not forthcoming, he or she could blame you for the gap in feeling, for the frustration, and for the loss of intense focus. You must not take responsibility for this dynamic. Try to find out what has promoted the burnout *without joining in.* (For further discussion, see Chapter VIII, "How to Handle a Burned-out Person.")

(6) Try to avoid stressful conversations that continue late into the night, that are circular in their content, and are directed toward "analyzing" each other. Don't "psychologize" or "diagnose" his or her behavior. These conversations tend to promote defensiveness. You cannot talk anyone out of burnout, but you can save your own strength by disengaging from draining repetitions, from tears, anguish, and the emotional pressure endemic to these "talks." Women suffering from infectious burnout often speak of the long, drawn-out discussions that tend to further aggravate the situation and push their own burnout proclivities to the edge. Exhaustion will distort your judgment and force you deeper into the burnout stages.

(7) Conversely, if your mate is withdrawn, overly polite, uninvolved, and distant, the constant search for a point of contact with him or her will likewise burn you out. Your mate may be unavailable not only to you, but to himself. By incessantly pressing for reassurance and answers, you may be polluting your own reserves and feeding your own burnout momentum.

(8) Do not try to match your partner's mood. While false cheerfulness will exhaust you, so will mock cynicism. In order to diminish the chasm between the two of you, and in order to form a common bridge, you may unconsciously begin to mimic his or her attitudes and behavior. This particular dynamic is an important aspect of the contagion burnout provides between partners and is based on the notion "If you can't beat 'em, join 'em." Ultimately, if you "join" him or her, you could actually begin to *feel* what your partner is feeling and have trouble distinguishing between what is real and what is invention. Try to keep your own values, your own feelings, your own sense of humor, and your own needs intact.

(9) Pace yourself with your mate. Remember that you have your own unique rhythms and resources. Your body will tell you when it's time to back off and when it's time to be helpful. You cannot let your own life wither away. It's crucial that you nourish yourself with friends, interests, activities—all of your warmer connections to the outside world. You may be giving out exactly what you need to receive and have little idea of how worn-down you've become. Try to ascertain if you have an investment in presenting yourself as a role model of strength and courage. If that idea rings true, you may believe you cannot demonstrate any weakness in the light of your partner's condition. By acting the sturdy soldier, you are guaranteeing your own burnout.

(10) If you've always looked to your partner for your total fulfillment, perhaps you should begin to reflect upon and reassess that focus. Please

remember, this is not the time to abandon your mate. However, if through his or her remoteness and irritability you've begun to realize that your personal comfort and stability begin and end with your partner's moods, you might use some of this time to reevaluate that total dependency. As your partner's burnout slowly reverses itself, you may want to expand your own focus.

(11) And, finally, it would be most prudent to admit you're confronted with real stress and begin to find methods for coping. If you're denying the situation, you're adding to the pressure. Infectious relationship burnout is unpleasant and often difficult to identify. However, it can be prevented. You can guard your own inner resources without feeling selfish and, ultimately, place yourself in a better position to avoid a double burnout in your house.

3. Spiraling Burnout

Relationship burnout can also occur as a result of an outside overload that is projected onto your partner. This is often a case of "mistaken" or "misplaced" burnout feelings and frequently affects women who are juggling too many functions and roles—burning out from "having it all"—as well as those women who are burning out from the isolation of homemaker and mother roles. In this situation, your mate becomes the "fall guy." The true source of the burnout is denied. The feelings of futility, cynicism, and intolerance spiral out and are shifted onto husbands or lovers. The misplaced blame for your negative feelings creates an atmosphere of remoteness and, in time, the relationship begins to disintegrate.

With spiraling burnout, your relationship may have been intact initially, but as other areas of your life begin to sap your energy and basic vitality, your mate may end up taking the brunt. If you're overstressed, overburdened, and/or have taken on the responsibility for too many people, situations, and tasks, if you're suffering from a financial setback, if you've incurred a bad punch to your self-esteem through a missed promotion, an absence of recognition, an inability to be as perfect as you believe you should be, or if you're unsatisfied and unfulfilled as a homemaker and mother and have become bogged down in too many depersonalized tasks, you may consciously or unconsciously make your mate the scapegoat.

Frequently either the external pressures to perform or the internal feelings of isolation are blamed on the person closest to you for not "making it right." Pinpointing the reasons behind the relationship problems goes askew. You may feel too exhausted from your daytime schedule to deal with your partner at night; you may be too dulled-out by thankless daytime tasks to give any more of yourself in the evenings. When you're coping with the stress of "having it all," you may begin to view your mate as just another burdensome demand. And, when you're suffering from boredom and loneliness, you may view your mate as the prime betrayer of your expectations and dreams.

In either case, your partner ends up the recipient of the agitation and negativity that accompanies burnout. Lynn, a 34-year-old news researcher, said:

> "When I was burning out, I'd steel myself before opening the door in the evenings to keep my husband at a distance. I was so worn-down by my job, the classes I was taking, my son, fixing meals, shopping, thinking ahead. I was too worn-out to deal with being a hot, sexual partner, too. My burnout just kept spiraling. I'd get sulky, removed, snappish, and blame the exhaustion in my life on my husband. If someone's need for attention had to go, it was his. Our marriage went flat and I was too tired to care . . ."

Lynn admitted that during that time she construed any sort of plea for closeness as a further demand on her energy, and that as her exhaustion increased, so did her resentment of her mate. She said:

> "I secretly accused him for everything wrong in my outside life. It was a very troubled time. I was overextended but never actually told him how drained I felt from the pace of my job, the pressure to get top grades for my advanced degree, or the worry over how much time I should be spending with the baby, and the million-and-one household chores I had to remember. I was under major stress, which I never showed to anyone—except my husband. I carried the burnout home with me and dumped it on him. We became unnaturally polite to each other . . . If I needed to communicate something important, I'd leave notes on the kitchen table and messages on the phone machine. He became an issue for me to deal with—not a person. Basically, I just iced him out . . ."

On weekends Lynn was too tired and too turned off to "deal" with her husband. Often she'd sleep both days away. When she wasn't dozing on the bed, she'd focus her attention on her young son, consciously avoiding the growing tension in the house. "When my husband would approach me to talk, I'd fly into a rage, or stiffen up with dread . . . I don't know what I expected of him. It's a miracle that we got through it . . ."

The "miracle" did not occur overnight. As Lynn's energies increasingly wore down, she began to experience severe burnout depression accompanied by erratic crying jags. In her particular case, the crying proved to be cathartic. The release of tension through tears broke through the wall of denial she had erected. Slowly she began to realize that she couldn't handle the excessive and exhaustive demands on her life, and that she could no longer live with the emotional deprivations she had imposed on herself. As she and her husband began to talk, she said:

> "I'd feel these swells of love for him that would make me cry even harder. I just wanted him to hold me . . . I felt like I was unleashing a dam, that I'd been living in this steel-and-concrete cage, and that I was human again. I also realized that he had little to do with my burnout—I loved him, but I had brought it home with me and made him the culprit."

Like many other women, Lynn felt compelled to keep her fears—the stress and pressure of her many roles—to herself. She believed not only that she had to be perfect in her work and in her classes, but also that she had to continue being perfect as a mother and wife. She felt it was expected of her, that in order to legitimize her elected roles, she couldn't demonstrate any weakness. The more stress she experienced, the more silent she became. When communication in her home broke down, a solid source of support was tossed away. Fortunately, she had a husband who weathered her burnout without joining in or running out.

Erica, a homemaker and mother of two, is another woman who experienced spiraling burnout and focused it on her mate. In her case, however, the burnout emanated from the boredom and loneliness she felt compelled to endure in order to guarantee a seal of approval for her excellence and perfection as a wife and mother. She said:

> "When I'd wake up in the mornings, all I could envision for myself was work and more work. I've never enjoyed the housework —cleaning and cooking—it's a thankless job. There's no accomplishment in having your toilet bowl shine. It's all a waste of time. I

remember that my biggest decision for the day was what to cook for dinner . . . It wasn't enough. Then one kid would have to be at religious instruction on time, and the other one needed to be carted to the library, there were sneakers to buy, ovens to clean, dishes to wash . . . When I did get some time for myself, I was either too tired to enjoy it, or I'd stare into space wondering what to do with it . . . I felt guilty if I wasn't busy.

"My husband is not a talker—I guess you could describe him as laid-back. I used to pressure him to talk to me to cut the boredom, but I got tired of struggling. I began to resent him for everything wrong in my life. I never wanted to be one of those couples in restaurants who eat in silence, and there it was, happening to me. When we'd go out alone, we'd talk about the kids, and then nothing. I'd sit and fantasize about being with someone new. Both of us would sigh and yawn. I really couldn't stand my life . . . I imagined it would be different with a different man, that somehow maybe an affair would brighten my existence. I just got worse and worse. I was drowsy all the time and had no energy for anything . . ."

To assuage her listlessness and inner loneliness, Erica began taking stimulants—nonprescriptive diet pills—and then started drinking during the day. Unfortunately the combination tended to send her feeling state up and down, masking many of her true needs. Increasingly she would flare up around her husband and in time began to feel nothing but annoyance, irritation, and anger in his presence.

"I didn't like the way he chewed his food, I hated the way he spoke, I was angry at the way his shirt puffed out around his belt . . . I mean, I just didn't like him and wanted to lash out just to get a response. Everything about him set my teeth on edge—my feelings for him had totally burned out. I wanted that fantasy man who did everything perfectly and made my life right for me . . ."

Erica's relationship burnout momentum had, at this point, become seriously unwieldy. Then her sister suggested she seek professional counseling and, shortly, the causes for the dissolution of her feelings for her husband began to be made clear. In the course of her treatment, she began to understand that the humdrum quality of her daily life, coupled with a noncommunicative husband, had led her into burnout depression. Yet Erica still felt powerless to change her traditional script. Her conditioning dictated that her feelings of dissatisfaction and nonfulfillment as a wife and mother were wrong, that it was imperative she continue grafting a false set of values onto her true feelings.

As she began to gain some insight into the source of her spiraling relationship burnout, she also began to understand that she had placed the burden of making her life interesting, exciting, and fulfilling totally on her husband's back. In time, she was able to solve the authentic burnout problem by slowly extending herself into the larger world and creating a life for herself which was challenging and satisfying.

At this date, Erica's relationship with her husband is still up in the air. However, her ambivalence about the marriage is no longer based on blame, false accusations, or fantasy figures. She's beginning to question her motives for marrying a distant, nonexpressive man and is coming up with some interesting, but unresolved answers. She said:

> "I think there was a part of me that wanted to be kept in check. I think I was afraid to seek out men who were more spontaneous, more alive . . . maybe they would have expected more from me. I don't know . . . but I'm working on it. Right now I'm going to continue finding out what my husband and I have together . . . It takes some time."

Preventing and Reversing Spiraling Burnout

As you can see, spiraling burnout is difficult to distinguish and therefore not always easy to immediately identify. When it lands on your mate, it's hard to admit that your focus is misplaced. When too many arguments have flared up and feelings are raw from too much anguish, pride and anger frequently act as barriers to insight. However, in spite of the rigidities that have invaded the atmosphere, there are steps you can take to explore the genesis of your burned-out emotions and perhaps clear away some of the debris that is threatening the relationship.

(1) At the outset, try to pinpoint when and how your burnout began. At what point did you begin to feel stressed, pressured, lonely, or bored? By ferreting out the root cause of your symptoms, you'll be able to shift the blame off your partner and onto the appropriate situation.

(2) If, like Lynn, your daily responsibilities and activities are overwhelming, you might try to work out an equitable distribution of those chores that can be shared with your mate. If your schedule remains overburdened—if you hold a competitive, fast-paced job, perhaps attending classes for a degree, caring for a child, attending to social obligations—you may have to begin to detach from some of the high intensity you bring to each function and role. Learn to pace yourself. Back off from the excess perfectionism. Your burnout will begin to reverse itself, and at that point you can begin to establish some new priorities with your partner.

(3) You might want to make a list of your daily activities and responsibilities. How much time do you leave for simple enjoyments with your partner? If the romance has gone dead, the causes may be less complex than you think. You may feel sexually unavailable simply because you're too overextended and exhausted—and therefore preoccupied—for immersions in playfulness, affection, and lovemaking. That exhaustion may lead you to resent your partner for placing yet another demand on your energies. You may consciously or unconsciously use your deadened sexuality as evidence of relationship burnout. Perhaps you could take some time, today, to go over your list and discover what is authentically depleting you.

(4) It is imperative for you to keep the lines of communication open between you and your husband or lover. When you begin to experience yourself as withdrawn, withholding, and intractable in your position, you may be denying yourself the need for closeness and intimacy and, simultaneously, denying your partner the opportunity to lend support. Chances are you won't "lose face" by admitting your fatigues or confusions. Your partner will probably be relieved to learn that he or she is not being rejected.

(5) If you have a dual-career relationship, both you and your partner may have hectic schedules and both of you may be touched by spiraling burnout. To avoid a mutual dissolution of affections, before the spiraling burnout lands on either you or your partner, perhaps you both could agree to set aside one night a week as a "date" night. Arrange for a baby-sitter and decide on an activity—a film, theater, a concert, or a sporting event—that will prove pleasurable and maybe even rejuvenating for both of you. If your communication has diminished, dinner out alone together could provide the right atmosphere for talking through some of the knotty areas of your lives without being distracted. Learn to share your feelings once again without focusing on the usual day-to-day chores and responsibilities.

In this way, you'll have a better opportunity for remaining in touch with each other's feelings and possibly prevent burnout from touching the relationship.

(6) If, however, like Erica, your daily life is basically monotonous and unchallenging, you might list the chores and tasks for which you're responsible, then try to ascertain how much time you've provided for more stimulating activities—situations or people. You'll probably discover that your sources of joy are basically impoverished. Perhaps you could then write down those activities you need in your life to provide yourself with both some inspiration and aspirations external to your mate's attentions.

(7) Try to catch yourself when you begin to blame your boredom and anxieties solely on your mate. If you believe someone else can "make it right for you," and that he or she is not living up to the promised potential, you may be immersed in magical thinking. The best your partner can do is help you sort out the origins of the burnout and offer emotional support as you begin to alter your known script for living. He or she cannot live your life for you or become another type of personality. However, you do have the power within yourself to change your life. By taking some unexpected initiative, you could surprise yourself. You might find that as your sense of self is restored, the relationship could simultaneously grow stronger.

(8) Taking some initiative means taking steps to expand your world outside the home. For starters, you could go to the library and read up on jobs that are available, appropriate to your skills, and seemingly satisfying to your desire for challenge. A part-time job might fill the bill. But be certain to avoid those jobs that isolate you in a small office.

If there are small children at home, you could request catalogs from colleges in your city or community and enroll in a night class. This could provide you with stimulation, as well as other people with whom you would share a common interest.

If you're politically inclined, why not offer your services to your chosen party and spend some time working for a candidate or issue?

The point here is to enlarge your life, bolster your self-esteem, and help yourself discover some of your otherwise hidden talents and resources. By giving yourself the opportunity to luxuriate in new experiences, you could be lifting some of the pressure off your marriage.

(9) If your partner, like Erica's, is basically noncommunicative and tends to retreat in the face of conflict, perhaps you could tell him or her

directly how much you need some support. Your honesty could be helpful in securing his or her trust in you. If, however, he or she is unshakably laconic and feels unnatural with intimacy external to sex, like Erica, you may need to turn to a professional counselor or to supportive friends to help you defuse some of the irritability and sort out the conflict.

(10) Please be cautious. This is not the time to make any major decisions about your relationship. Spiraling burnout frequently leads to impulsive reactions. Avoid the tendency to make ultimatums or to jump ship before you've had the opportunity to plumb the real causes of your anger, feelings of powerlessness, or frustration. When your responses to your mate either become rigidly controlled or are characterized by slamming doors, you should begin to suspect that the causes of your irritation may have less to do with your mate than with issues external to the relationship.

(11) And, finally, it's important that you learn to separate the essential in your life from the unessential. With spiraling relationship burnout, your mate usually becomes the victim of your symptoms by virtue of his or her proximity and connection to you. The stress on your relationship can be relieved and the burnout momentum reversed, but only when the real conflicts dominating your internal landscape are accurately identified.

Relationship burnout, whether it be intensity, infectious, or spiraling, is often the result of denial—by either one partner or both. When denial tightens its grip, passions are dampened and antagonism is quick to emerge. As you begin to confront the true underlying causes for your burned-out emotions, the original allure of the relationship might not only be restored, but also eventually deepen. As Lynn said, "Once I understood what was really driving me away, I felt I'd been sprung from jail. As I've learned to pace myself better, our relationship has grown much more secure . . . Who knows, maybe it will even last . . ."

CHAPTER VIII

How to Handle
a Burned-out Person

Up to this point, the focus of *Women's Burnout* has been primarily directed toward the identification of your own specific symptoms and suggestions for self-treatment. Hopefully, the signs and signals of an incipient or severe burnout condition have been digested well enough to ensure prevention, reversal, and a lasting cure.

However, having become well-informed and better able to deal with burnout symptoms when they begin to emerge in your life, perhaps you'll need to know how to handle someone else who, you may suspect, is burning out.

Not surprisingly, in our fast-paced society, burnout has achieved epidemic proportions, and while numbers of people complain of its symptoms, few understand the seriousness of that complaint. Fewer still are trained in spotting symptoms, taking the appropriate preventive steps to stop the momentum, or in advising others when the telltale signs appear.

You're now in a good position to offer some support, guidance, or assistance to a friend, a family member, a husband or lover, a woman on your staff, or a colleague who is demonstrating the symptoms of stress and strain endemic to burnout.

Suppose, for a moment, you have a friend who has, over the past few weeks or months, grown rather distant and remote, unexpectedly bursts out in tears, frequently complains of colds, headaches, and fatigue, has taken on an earnestness which belies her characteristic sense of irony and humor, complains of sleepless nights, and perhaps is drinking far more than her usual limit. You've also noticed that she's become quite inflexible in her opinions and judgments, is deeply involved in "having things done the right way," and has begun to speak with a bitter cynicism about the ways of people and the world.

Before you were educated in the dynamics of burnout, you might have backed off until she was "herself again," or jumped in and tried to "save" her by jointly commiserating over the rotten deal life turned out to be. Now, however, since you've got a handle on the attitudes, behavior, feelings, and language of a burnout, both of those reactions can be rejected. You know what's happening to her, but does she? And how can you help her without pushing her further away?

Here are some suggestions for handling a burned-out person. But, before you begin to act on them, *please hear this note of caution:* If in offering some guidance to a friend you're putting an additional burden of stress and pressure on yourself and are overextending your limits, you may have to attend to your own needs first. These suggestions are not intended to place you in another nurturing role, nor are they designed to tug at the strings of your sense of virtue. However, if you are not burning out yourself, by all means do offer your support and intelligence to that other person.

1. Approach your friend with sincerity and compassion. You might want to open up the issue by suggesting she may be experiencing burnout and that you might be able to help. If you've been through the burnout experience yourself, you could describe some of the feelings and attitudes that reflect hers to both gain her trust and put her at ease.

2. It is imperative that you *listen* to what she's saying, and that your responses be noncritical and nonjudgmental. Urge her to ventilate her angers, frustrations, hurts, loneliness, feelings of powerlessness, dependencies, and fears. Allow her to repeat herself. She may be so backed up with exhaustion and irritability that she may need to be repetitive.

Along the way, you might encourage her to talk about positive aspects of herself—her accomplishments, her competence, her desirability as a friend, her personality, and even her personal charm—her looks, hair, clothes, body image, or manner of speaking. Although she's dealing with the confusion of burnout, she may still inwardly respond to the more flattering aspects of herself and be grateful for the reminders.

3. Be honest with her. Don't dismiss, deny, or diminish her feelings. Don't try to fool her with false cheerfulness or optimism. Burnouts are particularly sensitive to the false fronts of others. While she may be denying the neglect in her own life, she may be, nonetheless, unconsciously attuned to her need for sincerity and empathy. Initially, if you try to laugh it up with her, she might outwardly respond in like fashion, but inwardly back away and feel disappointed.

4. Try to help her to think through her maze of confusions. Avoid analyzing, "psychologizing," or using any expressions which could be construed as superior, patronizing, or condescending. She may be struggling with similar disparaging attitudes on the job or at home, and could either shrink from further discussion, or lash out unexpectedly. Her emotions are raw right now. While she may need to lean, she might also be fiercely attempting to keep her dignity intact.

5. Don't flood her with advice. She may be unable to hear what you're saying, or take it all in. Her concentration span may be limited. Too much advice may overwhelm and frighten her. She may act as if she's listening, but may be secretly regarding your overzealousness as yet another demand.

6. Encourage her to trace when and how she began to feel troubled—overstressed, frightened, and fatigued. Ask her to try to ascertain what events were taking place at that time, what person or people she was bent on pleasing and impressing to gain approval, what models she was trying to duplicate, what she felt necessary to prove, and then, how those factors promoted burnout within her. If it helps her to organize her thoughts, write down some of the main points of your conversation, or perhaps even tape it. It will help you both to reflect as your conversations occur.

7. Ask her if she perceives herself as changed—different from the ways in which she perceived herself in the past. Encourage her to talk about the changes she recognizes in her attitudes, her behavior, her feelings, and perhaps her appearance. Point out to her that others who have undergone burnout have experienced the same changes and that, because she's burning out, they're not unusual. This will help to diminish some of her anxiety.

8. Suggest that she begin to explore those situations, people, and events which cause her to overreact or underreact. Ask her to try and pinpoint what makes her angry, what disappoints her, bores her, frustrates her, and what promotes the sense of powerlessness in her. Help her to detect those same trouble spots on the job, socially, at home, and in her intimate

relationships. This will aid her in diminishing some of the jolts and uncomfortable surprises she may repeatedly experience in her life.

9. Open up the issue of the "musts" and "shoulds" women commonly fall prey to. Help her to speak about her early family conditioning and what was expected of her. You might point out how those older family dynamics have transferred themselves onto her adult life and are now acting as additional stress-extenders. *REMEMBER:* What you're opting for here is some guidance in self-awareness. It may take some time before she's willing or able to incorporate this information.

10. Encourage her to speak about her values. She may have grown too distant from her authentic values to distinguish between the real and essential and the unreal and unessential. In the talking, she'll be reminding herself of what is deeply precious to her and what has been superimposed upon her life. Urge her to reevaluate where she wants to go, where she needs to go, and where she's actually going. This might provide her with fresh insight and help to reground her.

11. Help her to organize some short-term and some long-term goals. Introduce the idea of pacing to her—how necessary it is to balance her life according to her own style and rhythms. Don't be afraid to express your concern if, in describing her goals, you understand she's set up excessive burdens, grandiose standards of perfection, and impossible achievements and accomplishments. She may not respond to your concern or take it in at that moment, but she'll think about your words later, at another time.

12. You might ask her to figure out what she authentically feels she can change in her life and what is impossible to change. By facing the realities head on, she may slowly begin to back off from struggling against those areas of her life which are indelibly set.

13. In discussing the areas she can change, help her to think through different coping skills. At this point, you might introduce the topic of denial, and suggest to her that by denying her stress, she's simultaneously perpetuating it. She may only know how to cope by denying. *Over a period of time,* you might want to explain how denial manifests, the conscious and unconscious techniques—from suppression to displacement. You might also suggest other approaches to her problems, but only if she appears ready to hear it.

14. It is critical that she understand the value of affiliation, closeness, and intimacy. It would be most helpful if she became aware of how much her anxiety diminishes when talking it out with you. She might not con-

nect that feeling with the larger world. Point out how sharing, communicating, and expressing her feelings help to defuse burnout tension. Suggest that she begin to develop a support system for herself at work and at home. Let her know just how valuable the help, support, and reinforcement of others can be in reversing burnout. And, while you're at it, you might underscore her need to avoid isolation.

15. Encourage her to trust her feelings, and not to back down because they're politically, socially, or traditionally incorrect. Propriety has little to do with feelings. Point out to her that she needs no permission to love, to hate, to be angry, sexual, or to laugh or cry. There is no right and wrong here. If she suggests that her feelings are holding her back from exploring new terrain, allow her to research those frightened feelings with an eye toward clearing up the emotional debris that promoted them.

16. Ask her to explore what she feels she wants right now, and what she feels she needs. If her "wants" are longer or greater than her "needs," you might point out how her needs have been eclipsed and neglected by the compulsion of her wants. Again, remind her of pacing and balance in her life. If her career is receiving most of the attention, ask her to discuss what she needs in her personal life. If her relationship has obliterated all other concerns, ask her what she needs outside of that relationship to defuse some of the intensity.

17. If she is a woman with her nose to the grindstone everyday, let her know that she might begin to take her work a little less seriously and, more important, a little less personally. Suggest methods she can employ to care more for herself, attend to her neglected needs, and begin to enjoy time spent unstructured. Make inquiries into the amount of sleep she's getting, ask if she's eating properly, and if she's had a medical checkup recently. As she begins to absorb the need she has for some of these self-caring functions, her focus might take a much needed shift.

18. Suggest that she read some of the literature on stress, anxiety, and burnout. She may only be ready to absorb and correlate the suggestions you've been encouraging after she's read the material and identified with her symptoms on the printed page.

19. If she's too deeply into the burnout stages to reflect upon these ideas, refer her to a professional for either counseling or therapy. Sit with her while she makes the call, and perhaps, if your schedule permits, offer her further support by accompanying her to her first appointment.

20. By all means, tell her to take heart. There are scores of other

women, like herself, who have unwittingly veered onto the Burnout Cycle, yet who have been able not only to reverse the process, but also to prevent its recurring under similar circumstances. By following some simple steps, she will regain her sense of joy, her humor, and her spirit.

When you're helping a burned-out person, it is crucial she be made aware that her condition is caused by stress, pressure, and subsequent exhaustion, and that she not assume all the blame for this occurrence. Too many women have come to believe that they are responsible for the feelings of others, for changing that which is unchangeable, and are therefore culpable for events beyond their control. It would be especially wise to aid her in relieving any additional guilt-provoking burdens. After all, you've been there, and will undoubtedly remember that the harshness with which you handled yourself was your biggest battle with burnout.

CONCLUSION

A Twelve-Point Checklist
for Burnout Prevention
and Recovery

If you feel you may be verging on burnout, or that you've already slipped into one or more of the critical stages, it will be helpful to refer to the checklist below. This list can be used as a reminder—a quick-study guide for reversing the symptoms and for maintaining an awareness of their causes.

Read the checklist carefully and, if necessary, memorize the information. The items which have the most impact on you are undoubtedly the areas in which you need to concentrate the bulk of your efforts. Remember: Burnout can be prevented and reversed—self-awareness is the key.

1. *Stop denying.* Listen to the wisdom of your body. Begin to freely admit the stresses and pressures which have manifested physically, mentally, or emotionally.

2. *Avoid isolation.* Don't do everything alone! Develop or renew intimacies with friends and loved ones. Closeness not only brings new insights, but also is anathema to agitation and depression.

3. *Change your circumstances.* If your job, your relationships, a situation, or person is dragging you under, try to alter the circumstances, or, if necessary, leave.

4. *Diminish intensity in your life.* Pinpoint those areas or aspects which summon up the most concentrated intensity and work toward alleviating that pressure.

5. *Stop overnurturing.* If you routinely take on other people's problems and responsibilities, learn to gracefully disengage. Try to get some nurturing for yourself.

6. *Learn to say "no."* You'll help diminish intensity by speaking up for yourself. This means refusing additional requests or demands on your time or emotions.

7. *Begin to back off and detach.* Learn to delegate, not only at work, but also at home and with friends. In this case, detachment means rescuing yourself for yourself.

8. *Reassess your values.* Try to sort out the meaningful values from the temporary and fleeting, the essential from the unessential. You'll conserve energy and time, and begin to feel more centered.

9. *Learn to pace yourself.* Try to take life in moderation. You only have so much energy available. Ascertain what is wanted and needed in your life, then begin to balance work with love, pleasure, and relaxation.

10. *Take care of your body.* Don't skip meals, abuse yourself with rigid diets, disregard your need for sleep, or break the doctor appointments. Take care of yourself nutritionally.

11. *Diminish worry and anxiety.* Try to keep superstitious worrying to a minimum—it changes nothing. You'll have a better grip on your situation if you spend less time worrying and more time taking care of your real needs.

12. *Keep your sense of humor!* Begin to bring joy and happy moments into your life. Very few people suffer burnout when they're having fun.

BIBLIOGRAPHY

BATTLE, C. "The Iatrogenic Disease Called Burnout, in Physicians," *Journal of the American Medical Women's Association*, 36(12), 1981, pp. 357–59.

BECK, C. L., and GARGIULO, R. M. "Burnout in Teachers of Retarded and Non-Retarded Children," *Journal of Educational Research*, 73(3), 1983, pp. 168–73.

BENSON, H., and ALLEN, R. L. "How Much Stress Is Too Much?" *Harvard Business Review*, 58, 1980, pp. 86–92.

BERNIKOW, L. *Among Women.* New York: Crown Publishers, 1980.

BLOCK, A. M. "The Battered Teacher," *Today's Education*, 66(2), 1977, pp. 58–63.

BORLAND, J. J. "Burnout Among Workers and Administrators," *Health and Social Work*, 6(1), 1981, pp. 73–78.

BRAMHALL, M., and EZELL, S. "How Burned Out Are You?" *American Public Welfare Association*, Winter 1981, pp. 23–27.

BRYAN, W. L. "Preventing Burnout in the Public Interest Community," *The Grantsmanship Center News*, March–April 1981, pp. 15–28.

CEDOLINE, A. J. *Job Burnout in Public Education.* New York: Teachers College Press, 1982.

CHERNISS, C. *Professional Burnout in Human Service Organizations.* New York: Praeger Publishers, 1980.

CHESSICK, R. D. "The Sad Soul of the Psychoanalyst," *Bulletin of the Menninger Clinic*, January 1978, pp. 1–9.

CLARK, C. C. "Burnout, Assessment and Intervention," *Journal of Nursing Administration*, 10(9), 1980, pp. 39–44.

DALEY, M. R. "Preventing Worker Burnout in Child Welfare," *Child Welfare*, LVIII(7), 1979, pp. 443–51.

DANIEL, S., and ROGER, M. "Burnout and the Pastorate: A Critical Review with Implications for Pastors," *Journal of Psychology and Theology*, 9(3), 1981, pp. 232–49.

DINNERSTEIN, D. *The Mermaid and the Minotaur: Sexual Arrangements and Human Malaise.* New York: Harper Colophon Books, 1976.

DOWLING, C. *The Cinderella Complex: Women's Hidden Fear of Independence.* New York: Summit Books, 1981.

DuBRIN, A. J. "Teacher Burnout: How to Cope When Your World Goes Black," *Instructor*, 88(6), 1979, pp. 55–62.

EDELWICH, J., and BRODSKY, A. *Burn-out: Stages of Disillusionment in the Helping Profession.* New York: Human Sciences Press, 1980.

EICHENBAUM, L., and ORBACH, S. *What Do Women Want: Exploding the Myth of Dependency.* New York: Coward-McCann, 1983.

EMENER, W. G. "Professional Burnout: Rehabilitation's Hidden Handicap," *Journal of Rehabilitation*, February–March 1979, pp. 55–58.

FARBER, B. A., ed. *Stress and Burnout in the Human Service Professions*, Elmsford, N.Y.: Pergamon Press, 1983.

FARBER, B., and HEIFEZ, L. J. "The Process and Dimensions of Burnout in Psychotherapists," *Professional Psychology*, 13(2), 1982, pp. 293–301.

FEINSTEIN, K. W., ed. *Working Women and Families.* Beverly Hills, Calif.: Sage Publications, 1979.

FREUDENBERGER, H. J. "Burnout and Job Dissatisfaction: Impact on the Family," in Hansen, T. C., ed., *Perspectives on Work and the Family*, Rockville, Md.: Aspen Systems Corp., 1984.

———. "Burnout; Contemporary Issues, Trends and Concerns," in Farber, B. A., ed., *Stress and Burnout in the Human Services Professions*, Elmsford, N.Y.: Pergamon Press, 1983.

———. "Burnout: Occupational Hazard of the Child Care Worker," *Child Care Quarterly*, 6(2), 1977, pp. 90–99.

———. "Burnout on the Job," IBIS Media Tapes, New York, 1982.

———. "Burnout Seen as a Problem for Alcohol Counselors," *National Institute of Alcohol Abuse, Information and Feature Service*, 96, 1982, pp. 3–5.

———. "Burnout: The Organizational Menace," *American Society for Training and Development*, July 1977, pp. 26–28.

———. "Coping with Job Burnout," *Law and Order*, 30(5), 1982, pp. 64–68.

———. "Counseling and Dynamics: Treating the End-Stage Burnout Person," in Paine, W. S., ed., *Job Stress and Burnout: Research, Theory, and Intervention Perspectives*, Beverly Hills, Calif.: Sage Publications, 1982.

———. "Executive Burnout," unpublished lecture, Harvard Business Club, New York, 1981, pp. 1–22.

————. "The Gay Addict in a Drug and Alcohol Abuse Therapeutic Community," *Homosexual Counseling Journal,* 3(1), 1976, pp. 34–45.

————. "Hazards of Psychotherapeutic Practice," *Psychotherapy in Private Practice,* 1(1), 1983, pp. 83–89.

————. "Impaired Clinicians: Coping with Burnout" in Keller, P. A., and Ritt, L. G., eds., *Innovations in Clinical Practice,* Florida Professional Resource Exchange, 1984.

————. "New Psychotherapy Approaches, with Teenagers in a New World," *Psychotherapy: Theory, Research and Practice,* 8(1), 1971, pp. 38–43.

————. "Organizational Stress and Staff Burnout," *Dialysis and Transplantation,* 13(2), 1984, pp. 104–6.

————. "A Patient in Need of Mothering," *The Psychoanalytic Review,* 60(17), 1973, pp. 8–13.

————. "The Professional and the Human Services Worker: Some Solutions to Burnout Problems They Face in Working Together," *Journal of Drug Issues,* 6(3), 1976, pp. 273–82.

————. "Rabbinic Burnout: Symptoms and Prevention," in Central Conference of American Rabbis, Yearbook, XCII, 1982, pp. 44–52.

————. "Staff Burnout and Crisis Intervention," in Freudenberger, H. J., ed., *The Free Clinic Handbook. Journal of Social Issues,* 30(1), 1974.

————. "The Staff Burnout Syndrome," Monograph, Drug Abuse Council, Washington, D.C., 1975, pp. 1–30.

————. "The Staff Burn-out Syndrome in Alternative Institutions," *Psychotherapy: Theory, Research and Practice,* 12(1), 1975, pp. 73–83.

————. "Substance Abuse in the Work Place," *Contemporary Drug Problems,* 11(2), 1982, pp. 243–50.

FREUDENBERGER, H. J., and NORTH, G. *Situational Anxiety.* Garden City, N.Y.: Anchor Press/Doubleday, 1982.

————. *Situational Anxiety.* New York: Carroll & Graf Publishers, 1982.

FREUDENBERGER, H. J., and RICHELSON, G. *Burn-out: The High Cost of High Achievement.* Garden City, N.Y.: Anchor Press/Doubleday, 1980.

————. *Burnout: How to Beat the High Cost of Success.* New York: Bantam Books, 1981.

FREUDENBERGER, H. J., and ROBBINS, A. "The Hazards of Being a Psychoanalyst," *The Psychoanalytic Review,* 66(2), 1976, pp. 275–96.

FRIEDAN, B. *The Second Stage.* New York: Summit Books, 1981.

GILBERT, L., and WEBSTER, P. *Bound by Love: the Sweet Trap of Daughterhood.* Boston: Beacon Press, 1982.

GILLIGAN, C. *In a Different Voice: Psychological Theory and Women's Development.* Cambridge, Mass.: Harvard University Press, 1982.

GORNICK, V. *Essays in Feminism.* New York: Harper & Row, 1978.

GROESBECK, J. C., and TAYLOR, R. "The Psychiatrist as a Wounded Physician," *The American Journal of Psychoanalysis*, 37, 1977, pp. 131–39.

HENNIG, M., and JARDIM, A. *The Managerial Woman*. New York: Pocket Books, 1978.

KAFRY, D., and PINES, A. "The Experience of Tedium in Life and Work," *Human Relations*, 33(7), 1980, pp. 477–503.

KELSEY, J. E., "The Stress of Relocating: Helping the Employees Ease the Pain," *Occupational Health and Safety*, January–February 1979, pp. 26–30.

LEVINSON, H. "When Executives Burn Out," *Harvard Business Review*, May–June 1981, pp. 73–81.

MCCONNELL, E. "How Close Are You to Burnout?" *RN*, 44(5), 1981, pp. 29–33.

MAHER, E. L. "Burnout and Commitment: A Theoretical Alternative," *The Personnel and Guidance Journal*, 61(7), 1983, pp. 390–95.

MARSHALL, M. *The Cost of Loving: Women and the New Fear of Intimacy*. New York: G. P. Putnam's Sons, 1984.

MARSHALL, R. E., and KASMAN, C. "Burnout in the Neonatal Intensive Care Unit," *Pediatrics*, 65(6), 1980, pp. 1161–65.

MARTINDALE, D. "Sweaty Palms in the Control Tower," *Psychology Today*, February 1977, pp. 71–75.

MASLACH, C. *Burnout: The Cost of Caring*, Englewood Cliffs, N.J.: Prentice-Hall, 1982.

————. "The Client Role in Staff Burnout," *Journal of Social Issues*, 34(4), 1978, pp. 111–24.

MILLER, J. B. *Toward a New Psychology of Women*. Boston: Beacon Press, 1977.

NIEHOUSE, O. L. "Burnout: A Real Threat to Human Resources Managers," *Personnel*, September 1981, pp. 25–32.

NOVAK, W. *The Great American Man Shortage*. New York: Rawson Associates, 1983.

PAINE, W. S., ed. *Job Stress and Burnout: Research, Theory, and Intervention Perspectives*, Beverly Hills, Calif.: Sage Publications, 1982.

PERLMAN, B., and HARTMAN, E. A. "Burnout: Summary and Future Research." *Human Relations*, 35(4), 1982, pp. 283–305.

PFIFFERLING, J. H., BLUM, J., and WOOD, W. "The Prevention of Physician Impairment," *Journal of Florida Medical Association*, 68, April 1981, pp. 268–73.

PINES, A. "The Influence of Goals on People's Perception of Competent Women," *Sex Roles*, 5(1), 1979, pp. 71–76.

PINES, A., ARONSON, E., and KAFRY, D. *Burnout: From Tedium to Personal Growth*, New York: The Free Press, 1981.

PROCACCINI, JOSEPH, and KIEFABER, MARK W. *Parent Burnout*. Garden City, N.Y.: Doubleday & Company, 1983.

RADDE, P. O. "Recognizing, Reversing, and Preventing Pharmacist Burnout," *American Journal of Hospital Pharmacy*, 39, July 1982, pp. 1161–66.

ROHRLICH, J. B. *Work and Love: The Crucial Balance*. New York: Summit Books, 1980.

ROLAND, A., and HARRIS, B. *Career and Motherhood: Struggles for a New Identity*. New York: Human Sciences Press, 1979.

SANDMAIER, M. *The Invisible Alcoholics: Women and Alcohol Abuse in America*. New York: McGraw-Hill, 1980.

SANGIULIANO, I. *In Her Time*. New York: William Morrow & Co., 1978.

SCARF, M. *Unfinished Business: Pressure Points in the Lives of Women*. Garden City, N.Y.: Doubleday & Company, 1980.

SHERIDAN, E. P., and SHERIDAN, K. "The Troubled Attorney," *Barrister*, 7(3), 1980, pp. 42–56.

SHUBIN, S. "Burnout: The Professional Hazard You Face in Nursing," *Nursing*, 8(7), 1978, pp. 31–38.

SKELEV, D. L., and KLEIN, R. M. "Mental Disability and Lawyer Discipline," *The John Marshall Journal of Practice and Procedure*, 12, 1979, pp. 227–252.

SURAN, B. G., "Psychological Disabilities Among Judges and other Professions," *Judicature*, 66(5), 1982, pp. 184–93.

TAVERNIER, G. "Decruitment: A Solution for Burned-out Executives, *International Management*, April 1978, pp. 44–47.

VENINGA, R. L., and SPRADLEY, J. P. *The Work/Stress Connection: How to Cope with Job Burnout*. Boston: Little, Brown & Co., 1981.

VICKERY, H. B. "What Happens When the Chief Executive Burns Out? *Association Management*, August 1982, pp. 69–73.

WATSON, K. W. "Social Work Stress and Personal Relief," *Child Welfare*, LVIII (1), 1979, pp. 3–12.

WHITE, W. "Incest in the Organizational Family: The Unspoken Issue in Staff and Program Burnout," Monograph, HCS, Rockville, Md., 1978.

WRIGHT, D., and THOMAS, J. "Role Strain Among School Psychologists in the Midwest," *Journal of School Psychology*, 20(2), 1982, pp. 96–102.

ZAHN, J. "Burnout in Adult Educations," *Lifelong Learning—The Adult Years*, IV(4), 1980, pp. 4–6.

INDEX